D1208477

the Complete Guide to

SHIRLEY TEMPLE DOLLS and COLLECTIBLES

identification & value guide

Tonya Bervaldi-Camaratta

COLLECTOR BOOKS

A Division of Schroeder Publishing Co., Inc.

Front cover:
Upper left, 27" composition **Little Colonel** Shirley Temple doll from the 1930s, $3,000.00 and up. Lower left, 15" vinyl Shirley Temple doll from the late 1950s, wearing a **Heidi** outfit. $300.00. Keith and Loretta McKenzie collection. Lower middle, Shirley Temple books by Saalfield from the 1930s. $20.00 – 30.00 each. Keith and Loretta McKenzie collection. Middle right, 18" composition Shirley Temple doll from the 1930s in the original doll trunk, with an assortment of original outfits. $2,000.00 and up.

Back cover:
Upper left, 11" composition Texas Centennial Shirley Temple doll, 1936. $1,200.00. Lower left, 17" vinyl Shirley Temple doll from 1958. $250.00. Middle right, 18" composition Shirley Temple doll wearing a Chinese outfit from **Stowaway**, with the Saalfield book **Shirley Temple in Stowaway**, both from 1936. Doll, $1,500.00; book, $20.00. Upper right, Shirley Temple handkerchiefs from the 1930s. $150.00. Keith and Loretta McKenzie collection.

Cover design by Beth Summers
Book design by Marty Turner

Collector Books
P.O. Box 3009
Paducah, Kentucky 42002-3009
www.collectorbooks.com

The current values of this book should be used only as a guide. They are not intended to set prices, which vary from one section of the country to another. Auction prices as well as dealer prices vary greatly and are affected by condition as well as demand. Neither the authors nor the publisher assumes any responsibility for any losses that might be incurred as a result of consulting this guide.

Searching for a Publisher?

We are always looking for knowledgeable people considered to be experts within their fields. If you feel that there is a real need for a book on your collectible subject and have a large comprehensive collection, contact Collector Books.

★☆Contents★☆

Acknowledgments 4

Introduction: A Few Words about Pricing 4

Chapter 1: The Beginning: Shirley Saves the Day (1934) 5

Chapter 2: The Star: Shirley Rules the Movies (1935 – 1936) 18

Chapter 3: The End of an Era: Shirley Temple Grows Up (1937 – 1940) . . . 58

Chapter 4: Foreign Shirley Temple Dolls: Shirley Temple around the World . 78

Chapter 5: Profiting from the Magic: Shirley Temple Look-alike Dolls 92

Chapter 6: Defining Condition and Fixing Up Composition Dolls 116

Chapter 7: Rediscovering Shirley: Dolls of the 1950s and 1960s 136

Chapter 8: The 1970s: Shirley Temple Dolls Live On 176

Chapter 9: Defining Condition and Fixing Up Vinyl Dolls 180

Chapter 10: Honoring a Legend: Shirley Temple Collector Dolls 186

Chapter 11: Shirley Temple Paper Products 205

Chapter 12: Shirley Temple Clothing and Accessories 273

Chapter 13: Miscellaneous Shirley Temple Items 311

Chapter 14: The Shirley Temple Autograph 349

Chapter 15: Shirley Stories Spanning the Generations 355

Chapter 16: Shirley Temple Inventory 364

Appendix 367

Bibliography 368

A Few Final Words 368

Acknowledgments

This book could not have been completed without the help of Marge and Earl Meisinger, Keith and Loretta McKenzie, Bob and Leslie Tannenbaum, Iva Mae Jones, Janet Mitchell, Loretta Beilstein, Suzi Reed, Rita Dubas, Rosemary Dent, Rachel Quigley, Lorna Erb, Mary Williams, and Dorothy Cassidy. Thank you so much for so generously sharing your time, collectibles, and Shirley knowledge with me. A special thank-you to Matt, for your patience and support, to Mom and Dad, for all those special Shirley Christmases, and to Jameka, because you're you.

Introduction: A Few Words about Pricing

The most valuable information in any book dealing with collectibles concerns value. Pricing is also the most difficult job to get right. Overall, the value of Shirley Temple items can vary greatly, for a number of different reasons.

Prices can vary significantly depending on where you buy an item. For the most part, eBay is the cheapest place to buy Shirley Temple items; however, you are not guaranteed to get exactly what you are looking for. The best way to take advantage of eBay is by becoming as informed as possible about the collectible that you want to purchase, and, of course, only buying items from members with a high percentage of positive feedback. The most reputable places to buy Shirley Temple items, doll shops and collector auction houses, can be the most expensive; however, you are guaranteed to get what you pay for. Nonetheless, it is hard to find a bargain anywhere on the rarest Shirley Temple items. Often, eBay is the most expensive place to buy the most hard-to-find items because of the bidding wars that can take place. A few years ago, a rare Shirley Temple doll snowsuit, which would have sold for about $1,500 at a top-price doll shop (though finding one at a doll shop might take decades), was run up to $3,000 on eBay because of a bidding war between two collectors.

The price of a Shirley Temple item can also vary with time of year. Usually prices are lowest during the summer months, when people are on vacation and the fewest people are buying. The collectibles are often most expensive during the winter months, the holiday season, when most people are interested in buying.

Finally, values can fluctuate with the amount of current Shirley Temple exposure in the media. In the late 1990s, Shirley Temple was in the news quite a bit. She was present at the 1998 Oscars, was featured two times in **People Magazine**, and hosted the TV program "100 Greatest Movie Stars of All Time." In May 2001, when **The Shirley Temple Story** was shown on TV, the prices for Shirley Temple items reached an all-time high; however, presently Shirley has not been in the news as much, and prices have fallen about 25% from those highs.

This book attempts to give reasonable estimates of current market values for the items pictured. However, prices will vary over time. Buying a Shirley Temple item is an investment. Always remember that the more informed you are, the better deal you will get. I hope that this book will help you become an informed collector and allow you to acquire the Shirley Temple collection that you've always wanted.

Chapter 1
The Beginning: Shirley Saves the Day (1934)

By 1934, the United States was in the midst of the Great Depression. More than a quarter of the working population was unemployed; people from every realm of society were affected. The impact of the Depression was felt on the movie industry in a number of ways. Because of the economic risks associated with making a movie, the movie star became a studio's most precious "possession." Having a bankable star could determine whether a movie was successful or not. When a studio signed a contract with an actor, the person was required to act exclusively in pictures for that studio. In many ways, the relationship between studio and actor was more than just business; the studio wanted to control every part of an actor's life in order to insure that he or she stayed perfect in the eyes of the public. Attracting the big-name stars was of the utmost importance. The most successful studio in that respect was MGM, with stars including Clark Gable, Greta Garbo, and Jean Harlow. The only big star contracted to the Fox Film Corporation at that time was Will Rogers. Reliance on one bankable star led to steadily decreasing box-office revenues for Fox. This, combined with the bankruptcy of William Fox (the namesake of the studio) during the 1929 stock market crash, left the Fox Film Corporation in a fight for its survival.

As legend has it, on January 29, 1934, a songwriter for the Fox studio, Jay Gorney, went to the theater to watch the movie **42nd Street**. A short film, shown before the main feature, co-starred an adorable little five-year-old named Shirley Temple. A veteran of the short film, Shirley was absolutely charming, with a dimpled smile and golden curls. Coincidentally, Shirley and her family were at the same theater at the same time to see her short film. When Gorney saw Shirley in person, he immediately started up a conversation with her parents. They spoke about placing her in the new movie he was writing songs for, tentatively called **Fox Movietone Follies** (it was eventually renamed **Stand Up and Cheer**). A small part was written into the film for Shirley; she sang and tap danced with James Dunn to the song "Baby Take a Bow."

Stand Up and Cheer was released during the week of April 19. Both audiences and critics fell in love with Shirley Temple. The boss at Fox Films, Winfield Sheenan, knew that he had something very special. He quickly signed her to an exclusive contract for $150 a week, cast her in small parts in two other Fox movies already in production, **Now I'll Tell** and **Change of Heart**, and loaned her to Paramount studios for a prized starring role in the film **Little Miss Marker**. Each of these movies was more successful than the last, in large part due to little Shirley. With the release of **Little Miss Marker**, Fox was sure that it had a very valuable new star.

Paramount also realized her potential. It offered to buy out Shirley's Fox contract and raise her salary to $1,000 a week. But Fox was not about to let her get away. Her contract was soon renegotiated to $1,250 a week. New storylines were written and developed just for her. By Christmas, Shirley was the star of three new films: **Baby Take a Bow** (a direct reference to the song she sang in **Stand Up and Cheer**), **Now and Forever** (a final loan-out to Paramount), and **Bright Eyes** (the movie in which she sang "On the Good Ship Lollipop").

In a Shirley Temple movie, no matter how bad things were, with a bright smile, a song, and a dance, little Shirley would overcome any hardship. Audiences loved Shirley. She was just what they needed to help them forget their troubles. In 1934, Shirley made five films for Fox and two for Paramount. The more Shirley appeared in a movie, the more successful it was. Shirley Temple was the top box-office star in the world. Many believe Shirley saved the Fox Film Corporation from bankruptcy during this year.

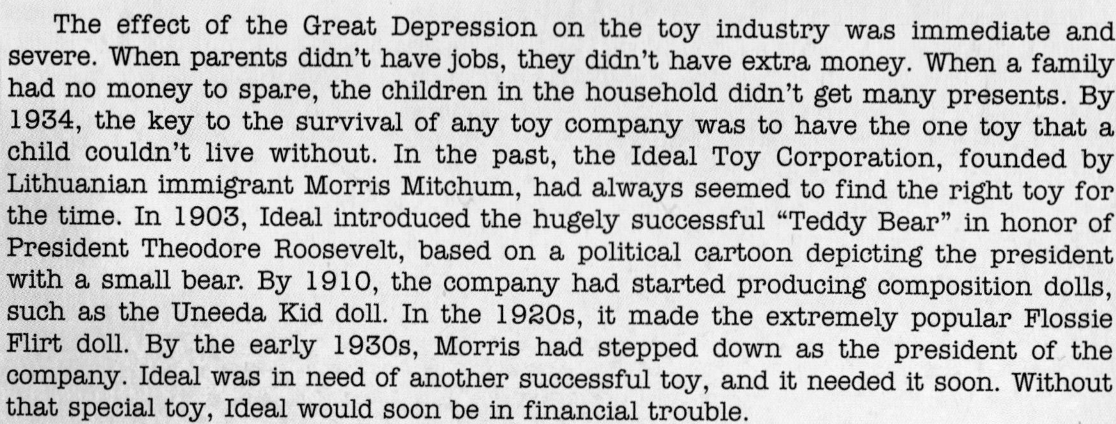

The effect of the Great Depression on the toy industry was immediate and severe. When parents didn't have jobs, they didn't have extra money. When a family had no money to spare, the children in the household didn't get many presents. By 1934, the key to the survival of any toy company was to have the one toy that a child couldn't live without. In the past, the Ideal Toy Corporation, founded by Lithuanian immigrant Morris Mitchum, had always seemed to find the right toy for the time. In 1903, Ideal introduced the hugely successful "Teddy Bear" in honor of President Theodore Roosevelt, based on a political cartoon depicting the president with a small bear. By 1910, the company had started producing composition dolls, such as the Uneeda Kid doll. In the 1920s, it made the extremely popular Flossie Flirt doll. By the early 1930s, Morris had stepped down as the president of the company. Ideal was in need of another successful toy, and it needed it soon. Without that special toy, Ideal would soon be in financial trouble.

In late 1933, a well-known doll dress designer, Mollye Goldman, employed by the Ideal Toy Company, saw the movie **Merrily Yours**, a short film costarring Shirley Temple. She saw something very special in Shirley. After the movie, Mollye immediately called her boss, Morris Mitchum (who was still on the board of directors at Ideal) to tell him about little Shirley. The first thing he asked her was, "What is a Shirley Temple?" He would soon find out.

By 1934, Ideal was in the process of negotiating with Shirley and her parents to obtain the exclusive rights to the Shirley Temple doll. One of its most talented sculptors, Bernard Lipfert, was commissioned to design the doll molds. Shirley's mother had final approval on the doll. It took more than 20 molds to fully satisfy Ideal's production team and Shirley's mother. The initial advertisement for the Shirley doll did not use Shirley's last name, and it offered the choice of three wig colors: brunette, blonde, or auburn. The reason for this may have been that Ideal had not finalized the contracts yet and was still perfecting the doll.

On October 24, 1934, Ideal filed for a patent on the Shirley Temple image. In the October edition of **Playthings**, the Shirley Temple doll was officially introduced to the public. The official Shirley Temple dolls were marked "COP IDEAL N&T Co." on the backs of the heads, and had no markings on the backs of the bodies. The coloring of the composition was peaches and cream. The eye color was hazel (a first for a doll). The mohair wig was strawberry blonde with loose curls all over the head, taken after Shirley's own style; it had bias tape around the edges. The first dolls wore coin-dotted organdy dresses modeled after Shirley's dancing dress in **Stand Up and Cheer**. The dresses came with a woven official Shirley Temple tag with the National Recovery Administration (NRA) eagle logo. They also had an official Shirley Temple celluloid button. These earliest dolls came in four sizes: 15", which sold for $3.00, 18", which sold for $5.00, 20", which sold for $6.00, and 22", which sold for $7.00. Compared to other dolls, the Shirley Temple dolls were very expensive. But with Shirley's growing popularity, the dolls made in her likeness proved to be even more successful than Ideal had imagined. To capitalize on the success of the Shirley Temple doll, Ideal commissioned Mollye Goldman to design outfits similar to many of the dresses Shirley wore in her movie roles and in her publicity stills. These outfits were sold either on the dolls or separately for $1.00 to $2.00 each. With seven Shirley Temple films released during 1934 alone, the dolls soon had a very large clothing selection.

By Christmas, Ideal marked dolls with "SHIRLEY TEMPLE" on the backs of the heads (accompanied by "COP IDEAL N&TCo.") and "SHIRLEY TEMPLE" on the backs of the torsos. The dolls quickly sold out, and Ideal employees worked overtime to fill as many orders as they possibly could. It is estimated that between October and December 1934, Ideal sold more than 50,000 Shirley Temple dolls. To a great extent, Shirley Temple was responsible for the success of Ideal as well as the success of Fox.

★ ★

It is remarkable to think of how many people benefited from the appeal of Shirley Temple. For many families during this time, Shirley really did save the day.

Registered Oct. 8, 1935

Trade-Mark 328,814

UNITED STATES PATENT OFFICE

Ideal Novelty & Toy Company, Brooklyn, N. Y.

Act of February 20, 1905

Application October 21, 1934, Serial No. 357,464

SHIRLEY TEMPLE

STATEMENT

To all whom it may concern:

Be it known that Ideal Novelty & Toy Company, a corporation duly organized under the laws of the State of New York, located and doing business at 273 Van Sinderen Avenue, in the county of Kings, Borough of Brooklyn, city and State of New York, has adopted for its use the trade-mark shown in the accompanying drawing.

The trade-mark has been continuously used in its business in interstate commerce since October 10, 1934. The portrait shown is that of Shirley Temple.

The particular description of goods to which the trade-mark is appropriated, is DOLLS, COSTUMES FOR DOLLS, PARTS OF COSTUMES FOR DOLLS, AND DOLLS' WIGS, comprised in [illegible] Games, toys, and sporting goods.

The trade-mark is usually displayed by printing the same on labels which are attached to packages containing the goods.

IDEAL NOVELTY & TOY COMPANY,
By MORRIS MICHTOM,
President.

The first Shirley Temple pin is marked "C IDEAL Novelty and Toy Co." around the edges. Two versions of the "overalls" pin were produced. The one pictured reads "Genuine Shirley Temple Doll" at the bottom; the other reads "Genuine Shirley Temple Doll — An Ideal Doll" at the bottom. $80.00.

Patent for the Shirley Temple trademark.
Marge Meisinger collection.

The first Shirley Temple doll, wearing a *Stand Up and Cheer* dress, is worth $650.00.

Details

- Mohair wig is strawberry blonde, with loosely styled curls similar to Shirley's own at the time. Bias tape around the edge and silk hair ribbon finish off the look.
- Peaches and cream complexion, rosy cheeks, hazel open-close "sleep" eyes with human hair upper lashes, hand-painted eyebrows and lower eyelashes, lip paint.
- Open mouth with six tiny plastic teeth, dimples appropriately placed at the lower corners of her mouth.
- Detailed dress was styled after Shirley's own movie outfit.
- In the very first production run, the underskirt was attached to the dress, with separate full underwear and a safety-pin closure. However, soon after, this was changed to a separate panties/slip combination.
- Celluloid button with a picture of Shirley in overalls.
- Rayon socks, usually with a colored band around the top that matched the color of the dress.
- White oilcloth shoes with center-snap closure and buckle at the front. A few of the earliest shoes could also be found with a buckle closure.

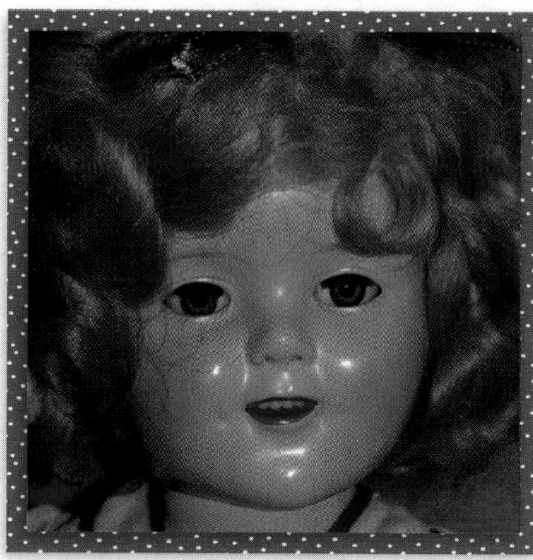

Close-up of the face mold of the Shirley Temple doll. Special attention was given to the placement of the dimples and the shape of the eyes. Note the unusual hazel eye color and detailed hand-painted features.

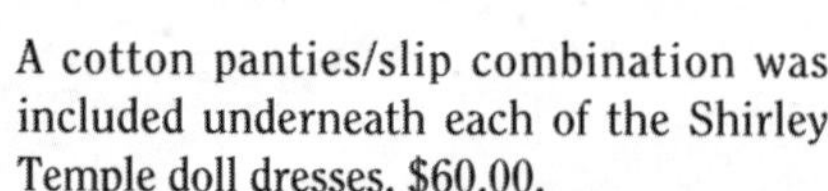

A cotton panties/slip combination was included underneath each of the Shirley Temple doll dresses. $60.00.

Close-up of label attached to the first Shirley Temple doll dresses. The words were embroidered on the tag. Has an NRA logo (only used until May 1935).

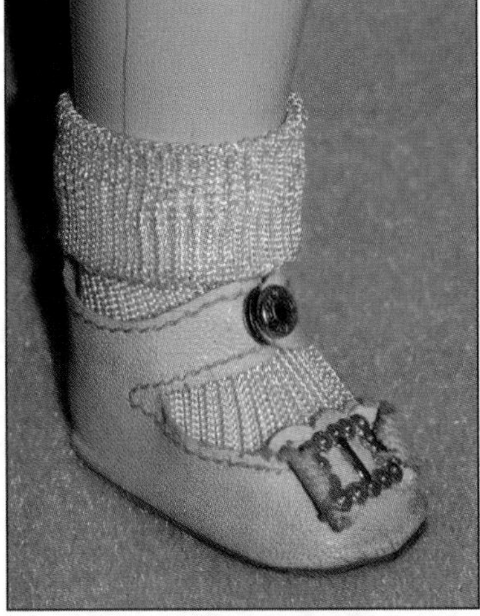

Close-up of the oilcloth shoe and rayon sock. Detail was extremely important; note the stitching around all edges and the unique buckle design. Shoe and sock set, $80.00.

Close-up of paper tag inside the head cavity of the unmarked "prototype" Shirley Temple dolls, the earliest Shirley dolls, released between October and early December 1934. (Sometimes the paper tag can fall off, but the prototype Shirley dolls have a very distinctive chubby look.)

Details

- The back of the mohair wig has loose curls at the ends.
- The back of the head of this Shirley Temple doll is marked "COP IDEAL N&T Co." She was a first-production-run doll.
- By December 1934, the dolls were marked "SHIRLEY TEMPLE COP IDEAL N&T Co." on the backs of the heads and "SHIRLEY TEMPLE" on the backs.
- A woven cloth tag was commonly attached to the dress. It is very common for these tags to be missing nowadays.

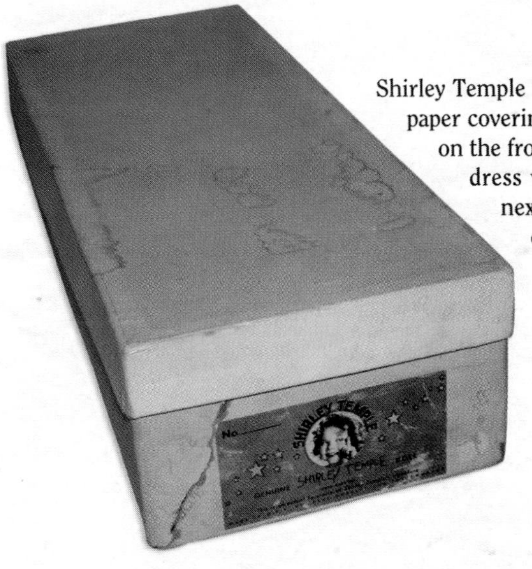

Shirley Temple box with texturized paper covering and Shirley label on the front. The color of the dress was often stamped next to the label. Box only, $100.00.

The first Shirley Temple doll, wearing the *Stand Up and Cheer* dress.

8" x 10" giveaway photos were also included with the Shirley Temple dolls. This was one of many used over the years.

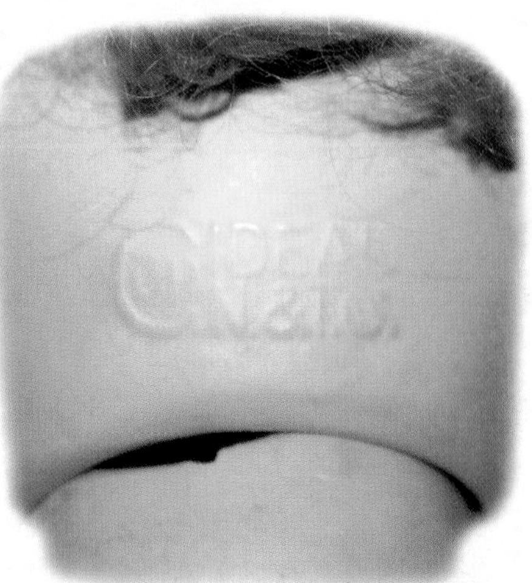

Markings on the back of the head of the first-production-run Shirley Temple doll, late 1934.

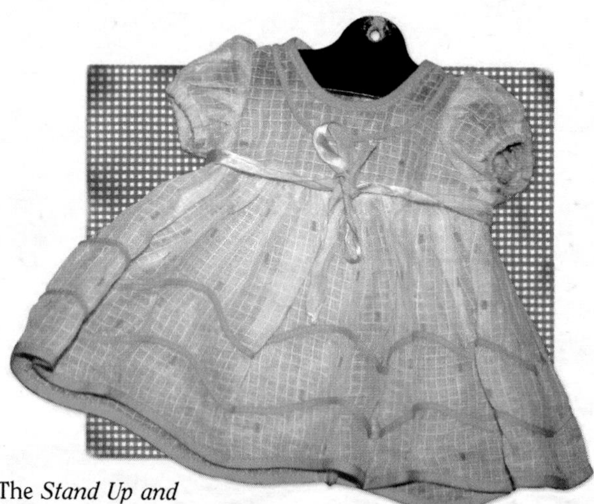

The *Stand Up and Cheer* dress was very popular; it was made in a number of different colors, fabrics, and fabric patterns during the Shirley production run. This unusual yellow variation has an NRA woven cloth tag from 1934. $300.00. A normal coin-dotted *Stand Up and Cheer* dress is valued at $150.00. Keith and Loretta McKenzie collection.

18" first-production-run Shirley in a woven cloth NRA-tagged very unusual swirling pattern variation of the *Stand Up and Cheer* dress with attached slip. $750.00. Dress alone, $300.00. Keith and Loretta McKenzie collection.

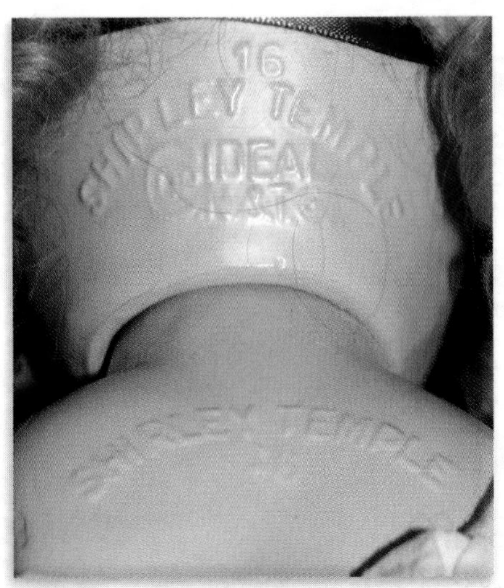

Markings on the backs of the dolls released in December 1934 and sold through 1935.

A later version of the *Stand Up and Cheer* dress with the rayon tag. $250.00. Keith and Loretta McKenzie collection.

One of the first ads for the Shirley Temple doll. From the Sears Roebuck catalog, November 1934. At the time, the doll mold was still being finalized, so a drawing was used to illustrate the doll. Marge Meisinger collection.

18" Shirley Temple doll is marked "SHIRLEY TEMPLE COP IDEAL N&T Co." on the back of her head and "SHIRLEY TEMPLE" on her back. Light coloring and hair of the earliest Shirley dolls. The dress can be found in early publicity photos, but Shirley does not wear this dress in a movie role. This dress is often referred to as the "waffle dress" because of the fabric that it was made with. A rare find. Woven cloth NRA tag. $900.00.

Often called the "Anchor dress." Made of dimity, with woven cloth NRA tag. This dress is based on one that Shirley wore in the movie *Now and Forever*. $350.00.

Rare early magazine advertisement showing Shirley Temple with the Shirley Temple doll. At the time that this picture was taken, the actual mold of the doll face had still not been finalized, so a picture of Shirley's actual face was superimposed on the doll body. Keith and Loretta McKenzie collection.

18" Shirley Temple doll marked "SHIRLEY TEMPLE COP IDEAL N&T Co." on back of head and "SHIRLEY TEMPLE 18" on back. Made in late 1934. Light blonde mohair wig in loose curls. Wearing a sailboat dress (which was not worn in any Shirley movies, but was commonly seen in early publicity stills). Very rare, with woven cloth NRA tag. Dress came with either red or blue sailboat. $800.00.

A different version of the sailboat dress, made of cotton, the "improved" version of the earlier one. Woven cloth NRA tag in back. $350.00.

Early 18" Shirley Temple doll from late 1934, wearing a rarer variation of the pleated dress; it is made of silk instead of organdy. Old silk is incredibly fragile, and frays easily, so this is hard to find in good condition. Further variation in the bib design also seen. Woven cloth NRA tag. $700.00. Dress alone is worth $250.00. Keith and Loretta McKenzie collection.

Beautiful advertisement for the Shirley Temple doll wearing a pleated organdy dress. Though often identified as the *Baby Take a Bow* dress, it was actually from Shirley's personal wardrobe, worn by Shirley in many early publicity stills and in the movie *Dora's Dunkin' Donuts*. This dress was one of the most popular ones made for the Shirley Temple doll and was sold throughout the doll production run with slight modifications of the dress design. Notice the detailed accessories that came with the doll. This beautiful ad was found in *The Larkin Premium Book*. Marge Meisinger collection.

Rare size 17" Shirley Temple doll, marked "SHIRLEY TEMPLE" on head and back. This is a later version of the Shirley doll, with a common version of the dancing dress with tighter pleats, brighter color, and a slightly different bib design then the ones made in 1934. Later rayon tag (no NRA logo). Dress came in many colors: pink, blue, yellow, green, and even purple. $1,200.00 (because of the doll's mint condition). A good-condition doll in this dress is worth around $500.00. Keith and Loretta McKenzie collection.

Box-pleated silk dancing dress with intricate embroidery on the collar. NRA woven cloth tag. Very rare version of this dress. $350.00.

One of Shirley's most famous publicity stills is often called the "Got Milk" pose. The original 8" x 10" photo is worth $30.00. There are many recent reproductions of this photo, and these are valued at $5.00. Keith and Loretta McKenzie collection.

18" Shirley Temple doll marked "SHIRLEY TEMPLE COP Ideal N&T Co." on the back of her head and "SHIRLEY TEMPLE" on her back, circa Dec. 1934. In near-mint condition, wearing what is often called the "Got Milk" dress. This dress did not appear in any of Shirley's movies, but was often seen in publicity stills. Very rare dress. Woven cloth NRA tag. $1,000.00. Dress alone, $500.00 (one sold for $700.00 recently on eBay). Keith and Loretta McKenzie collection.

Small green organdy dancing dress, early style from 1934 with NRA tag. $175.00. Keith and Loretta McKenzie collection.

Early-style light pink dancing dress with unusual embroidery on the bib collar. $150.00.

Another dress commonly seen in early promotional stills but not in a particular movie. Cloth NRA tag in back button. $350.00.

Very rare movie dress from *Now and Forever*. $500.00. Keith and Loretta McKenzie collection.

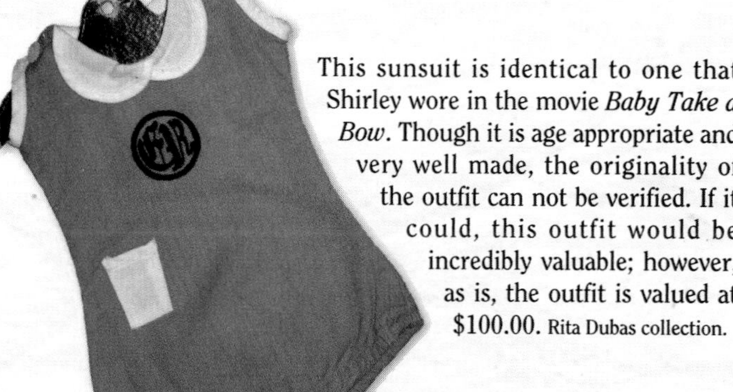

This sunsuit is identical to one that Shirley wore in the movie *Baby Take a Bow*. Though it is age appropriate and very well made, the originality of the outfit can not be verified. If it could, this outfit would be incredibly valuable; however, as is, the outfit is valued at $100.00. Rita Dubas collection.

16" prototype Shirley Temple doll, has slightly chubbier cheeks than the regular production-run dolls. No outward markings, but has a paper tag inside her head that states "Copyright 1934 Ideal Novelty & Toy Co." Doll has been restored (completely repainted), so she does not have the exact paint characteristics she originally had. Unique original dark blonde human hair wig is tagged on the inside of the wig cap with a Shirley Temple tag. A few of the earliest (prototype) dolls had human hair wigs; these dolls are very rare. Doll is wearing original dotted cotton dress that is exactly like one Shirley wore in publicity stills for the movie Baby Take a Bow. Woven cloth NRA tag in the buttonhole. $600.00 (the restoration, though well done, lowers the value of the doll). Dress only, $300.00.

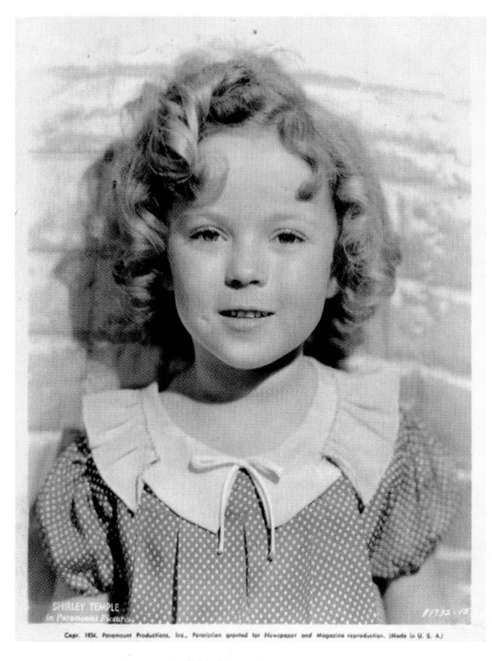

Publicity still of Shirley Temple from *Now and Forever* wearing a similar dress.

Movie dress from *Now and Forever*. Woven cloth NRA tag. Produced in many different fabric patterns and later released as a specialty dress in honor of Shirley's birthday (see next chapter). $300.00.

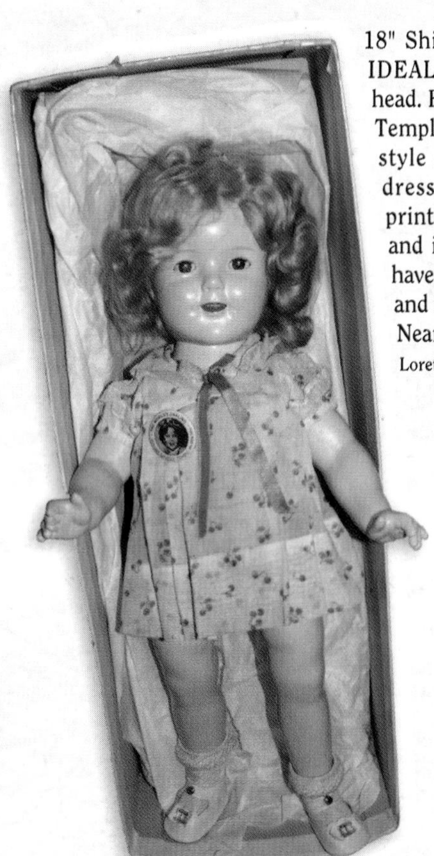

18" Shirley Temple doll, marked "COP IDEAL N&T Co." on the back of her head. First production run of the Shirley Temple doll. Note the distinctive hairstyle and facial expression. Original dress is organdy with blue cherries printed on it. This dress is very rare, and is the only known example that I have been able to find. It is untagged, and the origin of the style is unknown. Near mint in box. $1,800.00. Keith and Loretta McKenzie collection.

25" Shirley Temple doll wearing corduroy coat, attached scarf with foxtails, and matching corduroy hat made to resemble one that was worn in the final scene of the movie *Bright Eyes*. Very hard-to-find set, especially with the foxtails still attached (this one is missing a few of the foxtails). Woven cloth NRA tag. $1,500.00. Coat/hat set alone, $500.00. Iva Mae Jones collection.

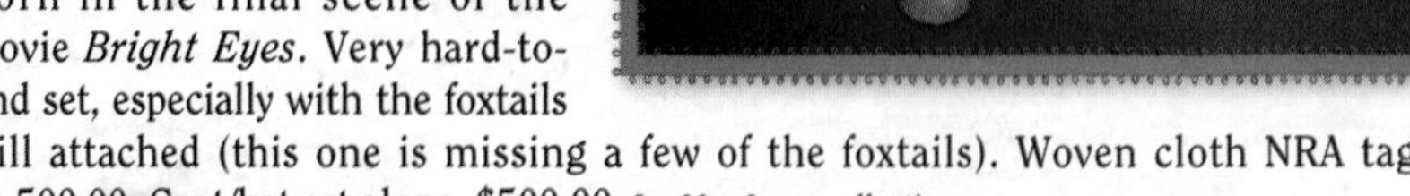

Aviator outfit, without the jacket and hat. $500.00. Shirley Temple hanger, $75.00, is from the trunk sets.

MY WEEKLY READER

The little girl is Shirley Temple.
She is in the movies.
These are Shirley Temple dolls.
Many people make dolls
for little girls.

Even *My Weekly Reader*, a children's magazine, advertised the Shirley Temple dolls. December 1934. Janet Mitchell collection.

This publicity still from 1934 shows Shirley wearing the aviator outfit from the movie *Bright Eyes*. Keith and Loretta McKenzie collection.

Mint-in-box *Bright Eyes* plaid schoolgirl dress. This outfit was sold separately, with a panties/slip and a pin. This is one of the more sought-after (and common) dresses, because it is the one in which Shirley sang "On the Good Ship Lollipop." $500.00 in the original dress box. Keith and Loretta McKenzie collection.

Shirley Temple doll in the aviator outfit from the movie *Bright Eyes*. First-production-run doll from fall 1934, marked "COP IDEAL N&T Co." on the back of her head. Wearing one of the rarest and most sought-after outfits (the most recognizable movie outfits are also the most valuable to collectors). Tagged in back seam with woven cloth NRA tag and complete with oilcloth hat and jacket. Jacket and hat are the hardest to find, because the fragile oilcloth deteriorates so quickly. $5,000.00 and up (a tattered jacket and hat alone has sold for more than $2,500.00 on eBay). Keith and Loretta McKenzie collection.

In the mid-1930s the Depression was still dragging on, and people were desperate for something to smile about. At the same time, the conditions in eastern Europe were becoming quite tense. In 1933, a young ruler named Adolph Hitler had come to power in Germany. He fed off of the anger that the German people still held toward the Treaty of Versailles and off the hopelessness that they were feeling due to the economic depression. By 1936, he had already begun rearmament, reoccupied Rhineland, and sent forces to fight in a Spanish civil war. The American people were not ready to acknowledge that something bad could be happening. World War I had been over for only 15 years, America was in its own economic depression, and the American people were looking for an escape.

In contrast, the bosses at Fox Films couldn't be happier. The success of Shirley Temple's films from 1934 had made her a star, and audiences couldn't get enough of her. Fox now had two major movie stars, Will Rogers and Shirley Temple. Financially, it was doing better than it had in years. Greater confidence in the studio allowed it to consider a big change.

A former chief of production at Warner Brothers, Darryl Zanuck, had created his own studio in 1933. He had named it Twentieth Century Pictures and worked out a deal with Joseph Schenck, head of United Artists, that allowed Zanuck to fund and distribute films. Though small, Zanuck's studio was well respected for creating very good movie story lines. The one thing it lacked was a star. Zanuck and Schenck partnered up and made a bid to merge their Twentieth Century Pictures with the larger Fox Films. The merger was approved in mid-1935, and Twentieth Century Fox was born. Soon, former Fox head Sheenan was out of a job and Darryl Zanuck was the new head of production. Zanuck was skilled at knowing what the public wanted. He noticed how audiences loved the "Shirley Temple formula," which usually consisted of Shirley being orphaned or abandoned, finding a father figure, singing and dancing, and then living happily ever after. He began hiring the best writers to write the best stories for her and for his cowboy star, Will Rogers. Tragically, within six weeks of the merger, Will Rogers was killed in a plane crash. The studio was now focused solely on little Shirley Temple. Zanuck wanted to take good care of his star, and her contract was renegotiated once again, to $4,000 a week, with yearly bonuses and raises. He also hired a bodyguard to keep her safe and gave her a private bungalow on the Fox lot.

During these years, the studio made sure that Shirley was a very busy little girl. In February 1935, Shirley starred in the American Civil War–era drama **The Little Colonel** with Lionel Barrymore. Though similar in storyline to her previous film roles, a little bit of magic happened in this film with the pairing of Shirley with skilled tap dancer Bill "Bojangles" Robinson. Two months later, her film **Our Little Girl** was released. Panned by critics, it was nonetheless a box-office success because Shirley was in it. In August, Shirley starred in **Curly Top**, her last film for Sheenan. This classic Shirley movie showcased all of her talents and was a huge success. With Christmas came Shirley's first film with Zanuck, **The Littlest Rebel**. In 1935, Shirley Temple was the number-one box-office star in the world.

Zanuck decided that Shirley's first picture in 1936 would be **Captain January**, a remake of a silent film that had featured child star Baby Peggy. In order to keep to the Shirley Temple formula, there were many changes made to the first drafts of the script. A Shirley movie always had to have a happy ending. Once an intricate tap-dancing number with Buddy Ebsen was added, **Captain January** was a guaranteed success. **Poor Little Rich Girl** was released a few months later and was also extremely successful at the box office. Shirley's next film, **Dimples**, didn't live up to expectations. Not only did it receive negative reviews, but it was also met with tepid box-office ticket sales. Even more significantly, critics started to comment that Shirley was growing up. Christmas week brought her next film, **Stowaway**, and to the relief Twentieth Century Fox, it was extremely successful. For the third consecutive year, Shirley was the top box office star in the world.

Between 1935 and 1936, Shirley's movies brought more than twelve million dollars in profit to Twentieth Century Fox. The success of the studio was primarily dependent on Shirley's appeal to audiences, though Zanuck knew that it couldn't last forever. "What a shame it is that she has to grow up," he would often say.

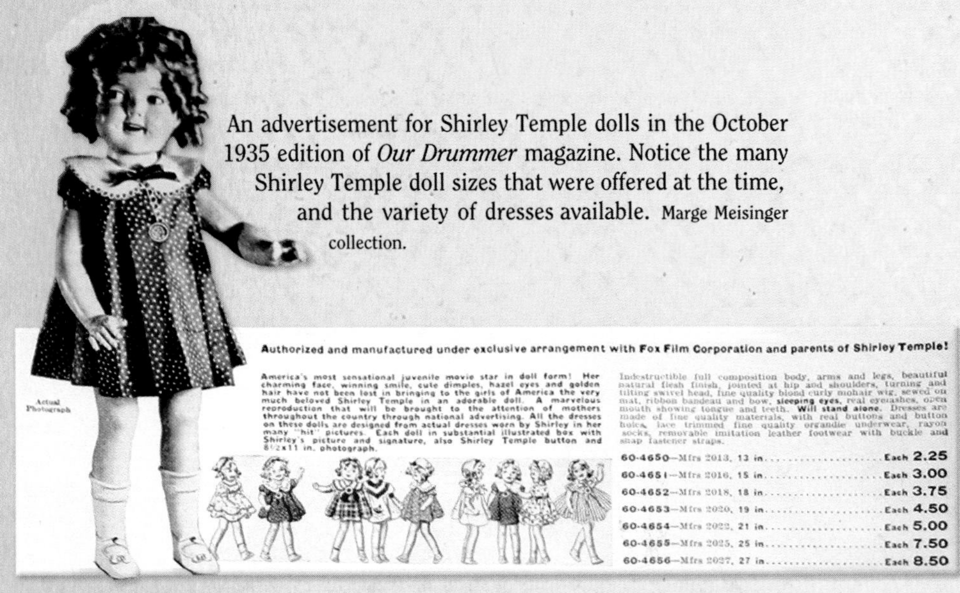

An advertisement for Shirley Temple dolls in the October 1935 edition of *Our Drummer* magazine. Notice the many Shirley Temple doll sizes that were offered at the time, and the variety of dresses available. Marge Meisinger collection.

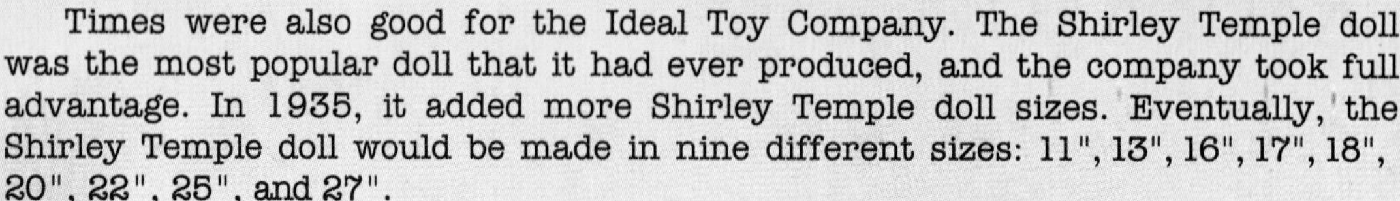

Times were also good for the Ideal Toy Company. The Shirley Temple doll was the most popular doll that it had ever produced, and the company took full advantage. In 1935, it added more Shirley Temple doll sizes. Eventually, the Shirley Temple doll would be made in nine different sizes: 11", 13", 16", 17", 18", 20", 22", 25", and 27".

The Shirley Temple doll changed as Shirley grew, and in 1935, slight modifications were made to the original 1934 molds. The doll's face mold was slimmed slightly, supposedly because Shirley's mother thought the original face mold made the Shirley doll look a bit chubby. The coloring was made rosier and the Shirley wig was changed to a more golden color and styled in more distinct curls going around the entire head. The dolls were marked "SHIRLEY TEMPLE" in raised letters on the back of the head and back, along with the size in inches of the doll. Other changes included a different picture on the celluloid button and a change to the dress tag.*

Mollye Goldman continued to faithfully reproduce Shirley's movie outfits for the dolls. She also made specialty costumes for them, one of the most popular being a cowboy outfit in honor of the Texas Centennial Celebration of 1936. The most popular outfits from 1934 continued to be produced with different fabrics and fabric designs.

In the fall of 1935, Ideal also released a Shirley Temple baby doll. Made in six sizes, 16", 18", 20", 22", 25", and 27", these dolls were meant to represent Shirley when she was two years old. They were sold with either molded painted hair or with curly blonde mohair wigs. This doll had a cloth kapok-stuffed body with compo arms, legs, chest plate, and head (in later dolls, rubber arms were used instead of ones made of compo). The Shirley Temple baby dolls were marked "SHIRLEY TEMPLE" on the backs of the heads.

Ideal also began to offer Shirley Temple wardrobe sets. These featured wooden trunks with stickers from Shirley's movies on the outsides. Each trunk opened up to reveal a Shirley Temple doll and a complete wardrobe, usually three dresses and a playsuit. These sets were offered for the 13", 16", and 18" dolls.

In 1936, Ideal used the same doll mold as it did in 1935 but made a few little changes to the dolls. The complexion was made even rosier, and the painted features were darkened slightly. The color of the mohair wig was also darkened slightly, and the curls were made even more distinct.

Ideal sold more than 100,000 dolls in the years 1935 and 1936 and made a multimillion dollar profit. By the end of 1936, Ideal began to design the new grown-up Shirley Temple doll. But would the public want it?

*The National Industrial Recovery Act (NIRA) was established in 1933 to help create jobs and establish good working conditions. Companies that abided by it marked their products with the National Recovery Administration (NRA) logo. On May 7, 1935, the NIRA was determined to be unconstitutional by the Supreme Court of the United States. At that time, the NRA logo was removed from the dress tags of the Shirley Temple doll dresses.

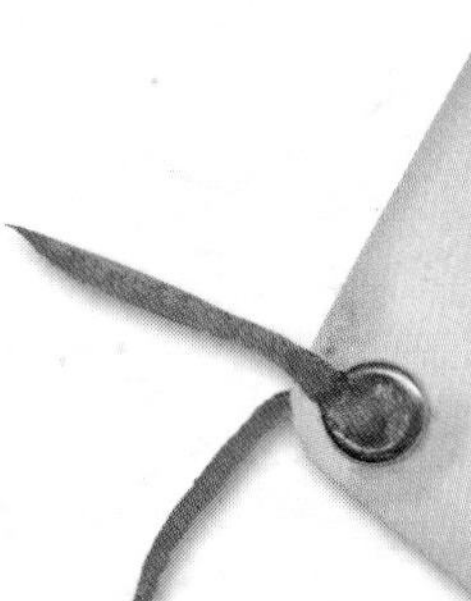

Polls showed that Shirley Temple was even more recognizable than the president of the United States. Box-office champion for three consecutive years, she ruled the movies during the mid-1930s.

Revised version of the Shirley Temple pin. "Marked Ideal Novelty & Toy Co." and "Reg. U.S. Pat. Off" around the edge. This version was released in mid-to-late 1935 and continued to be used through the rest of the doll production run. $80.00.

Giveaway photo often found with the dolls from 1935 and 1936.

This Shirley Temple doll (1935) wearing the "loop dress" is worth $700.00.

Close-up of the face mold of the doll made in 1935. Notice the darker facial paint, the blonder hair, and the thinner cheeks.

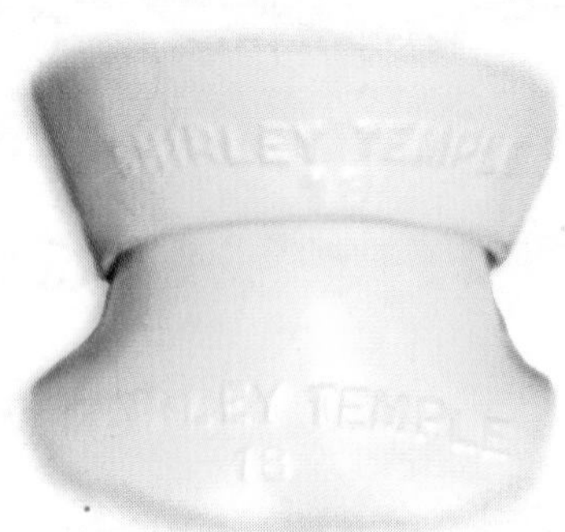

Markings on the back of an 18" tall Shirley Temple doll from 1935. Notice how the size is also labeled. The 22" doll sometimes included "IDEAL" in a diamond on the back as well.

Details

- Mohair wig is light golden blond with distinct curls going all the way around the head. This was an updated look, as Shirley's own curls became tighter and more distinct. Matching silk ribbon completes the look.
- Rosy coloring to the composition.
- Open mouth shows small teeth. In late 1935, some of the larger dolls were given new, larger teeth to reflect Shirley's new grown-up teeth.
- Movie outfits are identical to those that Shirley herself wore in the movies, down to the intricate details. Rayon socks with matching color stripes around the top, oilcloth shoes.
- Underneath her dress, Shirley wore organdy panties with an attached slip, decorated with lace going around the edges of the skirt and panties.

Shirley Temple box with texturized paper covering and new Shirley label on the front. Often the color of the dress, the size, and the price were also stamped on the front of the box.

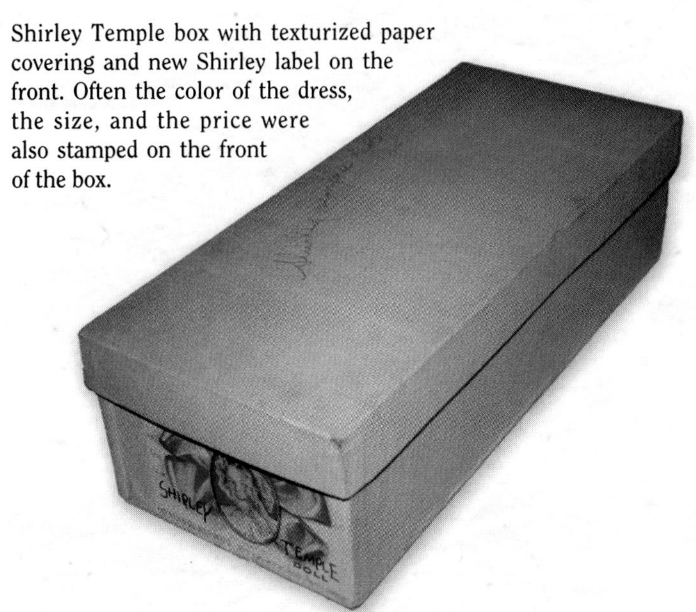

Shirley Temple doll (1935) wearing the loop dress.

Details

- Back of mohair wig was styled into distinct banana curls.
- By 1935, most Shirley Temple dolls were marked "SHIRLEY TEMPLE" on the backs of the heads and on the backs, and were often marked with the size in inches as well.
- A Shirley Temple tag was attached to the clothes. Up until May 1935, a cloth woven or rayon printed (see picture upper right) NRA tag was used. After May 1935, a rayon tag without the NRA logo (pictured right) was used to label the clothes.
- The label on the shoebox-style box was changed in mid-to-late 1935. This new label was used throughout the rest of the production of the Shirley Temple dolls.

This rayon tag was attached to the Shirley Temple dresses after May 1935, when the NRA logo was removed from the doll clothes.

Variation of the Little Colonel military outfit made for the smaller, 13" doll. It does not have the large dots on the skirt. Has been found in both red/white and blue/white and does not come with a matching hat. NRA woven cloth tag. $400.00.

Shirley Temple wearing the military outfit from the movie, *The Little Colonel*. Janet Mitchell collection.

20" tall Shirley Temple doll wearing the Little Colonel military outfit. This is an early doll, with the lighter hair and coloring characteristic of the dolls from early 1935. She is marked "SHIRLEY TEMPLE COP IDEAL N&T Co." on the back of her head and "SHIRLEY TEMPLE 20" on the back of her body. Her dress is styled after the military outfit that Shirley wore in the movie *The Little Colonel*. This outfit is unusual because it is not exactly like the style that was shown in the movie. There is no jacket, and the hat is quite different from the one shown in the movie. This dress can be found in yellow/brown, white/red, and white/blue and has an NRA woven cloth tag. Oftentimes, the most famous and recognized movie outfits are the most sought after by collectors. $1,800.00. Dress and hat alone, $700.00 and up. Keith and Loretta McKenzie collection.

Publicity still of Shirley in the fancy dress from *The Little Colonel*. $20.00. Iva Mae Jones collection.

27" *Little Colonel* Shirley Temple doll. Often considered to be the dream doll of a Shirley Temple collection, because it is the largest Shirley Temple doll made, wearing probably the prettiest and most ornate Shirley Temple dress there is. This doll was my own dream doll, and I received her as a birthday present from my husband many years ago (what a perfect present she was). The 27" dolls (and often the 25" dolls as well) have "flirty" eyes (they move back and forth) that the smaller dolls do not. This is the version of the *Little Colonel* dress that often came on the largest dolls. The dress is made of taffeta and came in pink or yellow. The cotton pantaloons and long skirt have lace edges and picoting. The matching taffeta hat has netting around the edge, silk ribbon to tie it under the chin, and a feather to complete it. This dress is identical to the one that Shirley wore in the movie *The Little Colonel*. Because the dress was so intricate, very few of these were made. Rayon Shirley Temple tag without the NRA logo (this more expensive doll may have been released for Christmas 1935). There were many variations of the Little Colonel fancy dress produced. $3,000.00 and up.

20" Shirley Temple doll in *Little Colonel* dress. Markings from early 1935. Made of organdy, includes matching silk ribbon flowers decorations. Woven cloth NRA tag, and includes white cotton pantaloons with attached long skirt. The bonnet is missing from this doll. $1,200.00. Keith and Loretta McKenzie collection.

25" *Little Colonel* Shirley Temple doll. This doll is wearing a different version of the fancy *Little Colonel* dress. This larger 25" doll has flirty eyes and the lighter hair and coloring of the dolls from early 1935. This version of the *Little Colonel* dress is also commonly seen on look-alike dolls. Because of that, it is not 100% certain that it is a genuine Shirley Temple dress, so it does not have the value that some of the other *Little Colonel* dresses do. The dress is made of taffeta and came in pink or blue. The cotton pantaloons and long skirt have lace edges and picoting. The matching taffeta hat has netting around the edge, silk ribbon to tie around the chin, and a feather to complete it. This dress is not tagged, and has a pin closure in the back (instead of the usual button closure). $1,000.00. Keith and Loretta McKenzie collection.

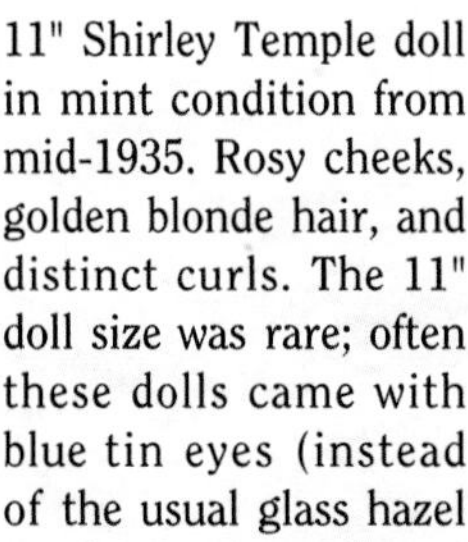

11" Shirley Temple doll in mint condition from mid-1935. Rosy cheeks, golden blonde hair, and distinct curls. The 11" doll size was rare; often these dolls came with blue tin eyes (instead of the usual glass hazel eyes). Wearing a Scottie dog dress from the movie *Our Little Girl.* First version of this dress, with a unique loop pattern going around the bodice. More rare than the later version of this dress. Made of pique and came in either red or blue. Woven cloth NRA tag, was probably one of the last ones tagged in this way. Larger version of this dress came with two other Scottie dogs on the skirt as well as the one on the bodice. Dress alone, $400.00. Doll in dress, $1,500.00 (because of the incredible condition and rare size of the doll).

13" Little Colonel Shirley Temple doll with woven cloth NRA tag. The dress is made of organdy with matching silk ribbon flowers. It has cotton pantaloons with attached long skirt. The pantaloon decorations on the smaller dolls were much less intricate than those on the larger dolls. The 13" size *Little Colonel* outfit did not have the sewn edging around the bottom of the skirt ruffles; the edges were just cut with pinking shears. This dress did not come with a hat. $900.00. Keith and Loretta McKenzie collection.

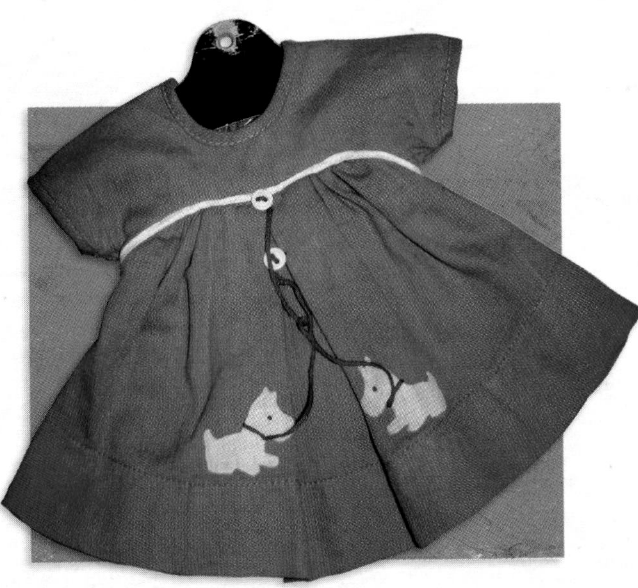

Scottie dog dress with rayon tag (this was the second style of the Scottie dress and was released right around the time that the NRA logo was removed — though some dresses can be found with the NRA tag). More common version of this dress. Came in red, blue, or white. The larger version of the dress came with a third Scottie dog, at the bodice (more like Shirley's own dress in the movie). $250.00. Keith and Loretta McKenzie collection.

Rare size 17" Shirley Temple doll. The hardest size Shirley Temple doll to find. Has light blonde hair and the lighter facial features that are characteristic of the Shirley dolls made in early 1935. Wearing the dimity music note dress, which was made to resemble one that Shirley wore in the movie *Our Little Girl*. Can be found in red, white, or blue. Rayon tag (no NRA logo). Oftentimes, the glued-on music notes have fallen off over the course of time. $850.00. Dress only, $250.00.

Another Shirley Temple dress from the movie *Our Little Girl*. Bolero style with separate pique jacket. NRA woven cloth tag. Dress has been found in a variety of fabric patterns and colors. Very rare. $300.00. Dress without jacket, $200.00.

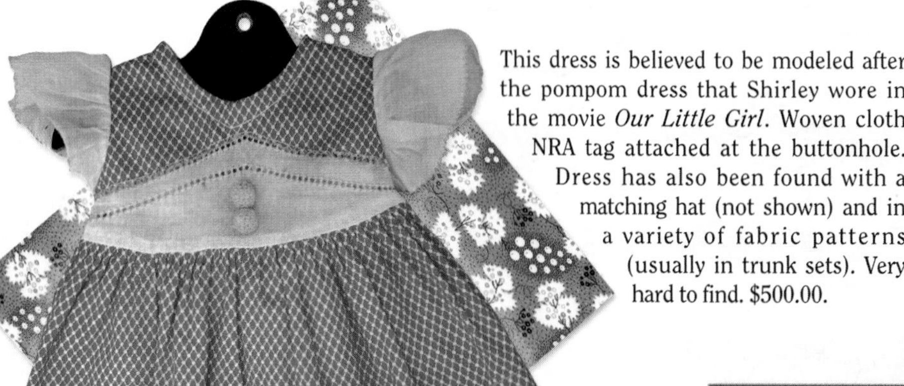

This dress is believed to be modeled after the pompom dress that Shirley wore in the movie *Our Little Girl*. Woven cloth NRA tag attached at the buttonhole. Dress has also been found with a matching hat (not shown) and in a variety of fabric patterns (usually in trunk sets). Very hard to find. $500.00.

18" Shirley Temple doll. Cotton dress from the movie *Our Little Girl*. Unusual because it closes with snaps, instead of the usual button closure in the back. Rayon tag, without the NRA logo. This dress came in both red and blue and is very hard to find. $1,000.00. Iva Mae Jones collection.

Yellow corduroy and plaid coat with matching hat for a 13" Shirley Temple doll. This outfit is from the movie *Our Little Girl* and comes with a rayon NRA tag. This is a very hard- to-find set. $400.00. Keith and Loretta McKenzie collection.

8" x 10" color advertising photo of Shirley Temple and her doll wearing matching duck dresses from the movie *Curly Top* (1935). $25.00. Marge Meisinger collection.

27" Shirley Temple doll wearing rare light blue velvet duck dress from *Curly Top*. Complete with hat. $1,800.00. Rachel Quigley collection.

20" Shirley Temple doll wearing a rare outfit from *Curly Top*. Shirley has the lighter hair color and chubby cheeks of the prototype dolls from 1934, and has the Ideal paper tag inside her head. She may have been re-dressed at a later date. Outfit consists of taffeta dress, separate velvet overlay, and matching velvet hat. Often called the "duck dress" because the larger doll dresses have two ducks sewn onto the velvet overlay (similar to Shirley's own dress is the movie). However, the smaller dolls (20" and under) had a single flower sewn onto the overlay instead of the ducks. Small flowers were also embroidered onto the overlay bodice and sleeves. Very rare, and particularly hard to find with both hat and overlay. Rayon tag with no NRA logo. $1,100.00. Keith and Loretta McKenzie collection.

Pique striped dress from *Curly Top* is very hard to find. Produced in many different fabric patterns and fabric types. Rayon tag, with no NRA logo. For the rest of the production run, the NRA logo was no longer present. The cotton version of this dress has an odd sleeve design, with a flap that was not completely sewn onto the bodice. $300.00.

Sometimes companies were allowed to make their own versions of Shirley's famous dresses. This 20" prototype doll is wearing a very hard-to-find Macy's version of the duck dress. Doll is stamped "Macy's" on the lower torso. This version of the outfit is a single-piece dress consisting of a blue taffeta bodice sewn onto a thick waffle-print fabric skirt. The ducks were sewn onto the blue bodice, along with embroidered flowers. Dress may have come with a straw hat originally. $1,500.00.

20" Shirley Temple doll stamped "Macy's" on her torso and wearing an even rarer version of the Macy's duck dress, with knit hat. $2,000.00. Rachel Quigley collection.

16" Shirley Temple doll with rosy cheeks and golden blonde hair. Wearing one of the most common Shirley dresses. An organdy pleated dancing dress from *Curly Top*, with silk ribbons that tie to the wrists so that Shirley can curtsey. Rayon tag. Dress was produced throughout the rest of the Shirley production run in a variety of different fabric patterns. This particular design is often referred to as the "starburst" design by collectors. Came in a variety of colors: pink, yellow, blue, and green. $700.00.

Pleated dancing dress for a 22" Shirley Temple doll, wearing a common variation of the dancing dress from the movie *Curly Top*. Rayon tag. Often confused with the earlier pleated organdy dress from 1934. The main differences between the two are that this one has a ribbon and bow at the waist, whereas the other one has only a bow on the bib collar, and this one is one solid color, whereas the 1934 dress has a different colored bib and embroidery on the bib. Mint dress, $300.00; dress alone (with pleats washed out), $100.00.

22" Shirley Temple doll wearing a swiss-dotted version of the pleated dancing dress and a white rabbit-fur coat and hat. The fur coat and hat are also from the movie *Curly Top* and are labeled with the rayon tag. This coat and hat set was usually sold separately and is very hard to find. Coat and hat set alone, $400.00; doll, $1,200.00. Keith and Loretta McKenzie collection.

16" Shirley Temple doll wearing embroidered dress from *Curly Top*, made of cotton instead of pique. $900.00. Keith and Loretta McKenzie collection.

18" tall Shirley Temple doll wearing embroidered pique dress from *Curly Top* with matching hat. From late 1935, with rosy cheeks, bright coloring, and four "grown-up" teeth (instead of the smaller baby teeth of the earlier dolls). Her outfit is made of pique. This is a hard-to-find outfit and is even more unusual with the matching hat. Often found with the Shirley doll trunk. Rayon tag. This dress came in blue, pink, and red. Different embroidery was used throughout the Shirley Temple production run. $850.00; dress and hat alone, $350.00; dress alone, $250.00.

Long-style *Littlest Rebel* outfit on a 27" Shirley Temple doll with flirty eyes. Outfit consists of a long dimity dress, cotton pantaloons with attached slip, and gray felt hat. Rayon tag. The long version of the *Littlest Rebel* dress is very hard to find complete with the hat. $2,000.00.

Shorter version of the *Littlest Rebel* dress. Much easier to find than the longer version (but still rare). It came in red, blue, green, and yellow. Rayon tag. This dress did not come with pantaloons or a hat. $350.00.

18" Shirley Temple doll with the rosy complexion and golden curls of the late 1935 dolls and wearing a very rare long fancy dress from *The Littlest Rebel*. It is made of flocked organdy and includes cotton pantaloons and long slip. Tagged with a rayon tag at the waist seam. $2,500.00 and up. Keith and Loretta McKenzie Collection.

Near-mint 16" Shirley Temple doll wearing a slightly different fancy *Littlest Rebel* dress. Rayon tag at waist seam. Also came with pantaloons and long slip. $2,500.00 and up. Rosemary Dent collection.

18" Shirley Temple doll wearing a short version of the fancy *Littlest Rebel* dress. Even rarer than the long version. Rayon tag. $2,500.00 and up. Keith and Loretta McKenzie collection.

13" and 16" Shirley Temple dolls in *Littlest Rebel* outfits. 16" doll has a very rosy complexion and the golden curls of the dolls from late 1935 to early 1936. 13" doll has the lighter complexion and hair color. Dresses are made of cotton with organdy collars and organdy at the bottoms of the long sleeves. They came in a variety of colors and patterns. The organdy aprons fit over the dresses. The 13" doll had a skirt apron only, whereas the larger dolls (16" and up) had bibs attached to the aprons. Both dolls have attached rayon tags at the waist seams. This style is the most common *Littlest Rebel* dress. $800.00 each. Keith and Loretta McKenzie collection.

Specialty Outfits from 1935

In 1935, Shirley became an honorary member of the American Legion, and Ideal made a specialty outfit in honor of it. The coat was made of either black or dark blue velvet and had gold buttons. It came with a matching hat. Woven cloth NRA tag in the back seam of the jacket. $500.00. Keith and Loretta McKenzie collection.

This picture, from May 1935, shows Shirley being made an honorary member of the American Legion. Rita Dubas collection.

Similar to the American Legion outfit with different buttons and trim. $500.00. Lorna Erb collection.

Shirley was featured on the official program for the American Legion convention held in 1936. $30.00. Janet Mitchell collection.

Advertisement that offers children $225.00 in cash prizes for naming the new Shirley Temple doll, released in honor of Shirley's sixth birthday. Janet Mitchell collection.

18" doll wearing the "birthday dress." It is the same style as the dress that Shirley wore in the movie *Now and Forever* (see chapter 1), with a different pattern design. Released for Shirley's sixth birthday on April 23, 1935 (which was really her seventh birthday — Fox altered her birth certificate early in her career to make her seem a year younger than she actually was). Rayon NRA tag in the back seam. One of the last dresses made with the NRA logo. $800.00. Keith and Loretta McKenzie collection.

16" Shirley Temple doll wearing a dress that is very similar to the birthday dress, with a different collar. Very rare. Rayon tag (no NRA logo). $1,000.00. Dress alone, $400.00. Rachel Quigley collection.

Very rare publicity still from the movie *Bright Eyes* shows Shirley wearing the loop dress (1934). $50.00. Rita Dubas collection.

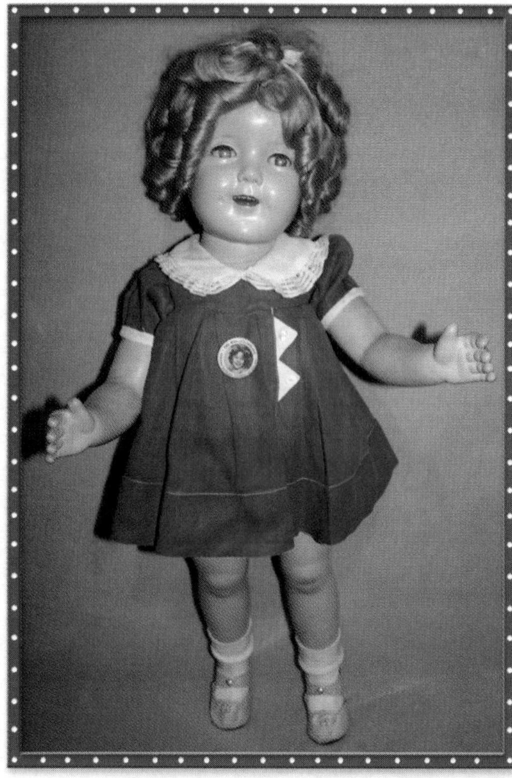

25" tall Shirley Temple doll made in early 1935; it has flirty eyes. She is wearing a dimity dress, commonly known as the "triangle dress" (because of the white triangles on the skirt). Fairly common dress found in many different patterns. NRA cloth woven tag. $1,000.00. Dress alone, $250.00 (in this size).

This dress is modeled after one that Shirley wore in a few rare publicity stills for the movie *Bright Eyes*. Though it was never actually shown in the movie, this dress was very popular throughout the production run of the Shirley dolls and was first advertised in 1935. It can be found in many different pattern variations. This particular loop dress is tagged with the woven cloth NRA tag and came with a matching hat and sunsuit. It was sold in many of the early Shirley Temple trunk sets. $350.00.

13" Shirley Temple doll wearing pink organdy dress and hat. Has the rosy coloring of the dolls from late 1935. Dress is similar to one that Shirley wore in the movie *Dimples*, but labeled with a woven cloth NRA tag, so it must have been made before *Dimples* was released (1936). May have been a party dress and hat outfit that was added to the early Shirley Temple trunk sets. Quite rare. $800.00. Dress alone, $400.00.

13" Shirley wearing a triangle dress with a very unusual fabric pattern. $750.00. Keith and Loretta McKenzie collection.

Organdy dress for a 16" Shirley Temple doll. Common dress found in many different colors: pink, blue, yellow, and green. NRA woven cloth tag on the button, size tag "16" in the back skirt seam. $250.00.

Wool coat for the 18" Shirley Temple doll. This coat was from Shirley's own wardrobe. A paper doll version of this coat can be found in Shirley Temple Dolls and Dresses, #2112, from 1934. Rayon tag. This coat has been found in both navy blue and brown. $250.00.

Green velvet coat and hat set. Woven cloth NRA tag. Most likely sold as a separate clothing set. $300.00.

Early color Shirley Temple cigarette card from the short film *Managing Money* (1933). $10.00.

18" Shirley Temple wearing raincoat and hat set. Made from fragile oilcloth, this set is very hard to find (since oilcloth deteriorates easily over time). This set was sold in the trunk sets. $850.00. Raincoat/hat alone, $400.00. Keith and Loretta McKenzie collection.

Though labeled with the rayon tag of the later doll outfits, this coat and hat set closely resembles one that Shirley wore in *Managing Money*. Set can be found in red, green, blue, and brown. This coat was found in advertising from late 1935 and early 1936. $350.00.

Early advertisement for the Shirley Temple trunk set in the Spiegel catalog, fall and winter 1935. Marge Meisinger collection.

A playsuit tagged with the rayon NRA tag. Commonly found in the Shirley Temple wardrobe trunks. $125.00.

Trunk for the 13" Shirley Temple doll. Dovetailed wood with metal corners, burgundy paper covering, eight pictures of Shirley Temple from her movies, and a key to lock the trunk. The inside of the trunk consists of cardboard lining, metal clothes rack, and one cardboard drawer. $175.00. Keith and Loretta McKenzie collection.

13" Shirley Temple doll in the wardrobe trunk. Near-mint condition Shirley doll with a rosy complexion. She comes wearing a flowered pleated dancing dress from *Curly Top.* The set includes a playsuit and embroidered pique dress, among other outfits. Oftentimes, collectors add dresses to the trunk sets as they accumulate the more rare dresses. This is probably not the original set that the trunk came with, but what a great collection of dresses it is. $2,000.00 and up. Keith and Loretta McKenzie collection.

16" Shirley Temple doll in the wardrobe trunk. Trunk includes the dresses that originally came with the collection: the *Stand Up and Cheer* dress, hat, and sunsuit, a pleated organdy dancing dress from 1934, a playsuit, a cotton print dress, and a coat and hat set. $1,200.00.

Trunk for the 16" Shirley Temple doll. Dovetailed wood construction, painted burgundy color, leather corners, cork decoration going around the middle, eight pictures of Shirley Temple from her movies, and a key to lock the trunk. Inside, there is a cardboard lining, metal clothing rack, and two cardboard drawers. Oftentimes, the stickers from the trunks have peeled off over time. A similar trunk was made for the 17" and 18" dolls. $250.00.

Advertising still of Shirley with a Shirley Temple doll trunk (1935). Reveals many Shirley Temple dresses, including a *Now and Forever* dress, a pleated organdy dancing dress from *Curly Top*, a duck dress and hat from *Curly Top*, a Scottie dog dress from *Our Little Girl*, a playsuit, and lots of other goodies. $20.00. Marge Meisinger collection.

16" molded hair Shirley Temple baby doll in a Shirley Temple doll carriage made by Whitney. 16" baby Shirley is wearing an original pink organdy dress with embroidered flowers on the bodice and puffed sleeves, with a matching original organdy bonnet. The wicker Shirley Temple doll carriage has Shirley Temple hubcaps and hood screws. This set also includes the original Shirley Temple blanket and pillow (see chapter 13 for more information). $2,000.00. Keith and Loretta McKenzie collection.

Closer look at the 16" Shirley Temple baby shown in the buggy. She is wearing all her original clothes. $1,000.00. Keith and Loretta McKenzie collection.

Advertisement for a Shirley Temple baby doll from the mid-1930s. Marge Meisinger collection.

16" bald Shirley baby wearing a mint tagged yellow organdy dress. $1,000.00. Loretta Beilstein collection.

20" wigged Shirley Temple baby doll, all original. $1,800.00. Rosemary Dent collection.

16" Shirley Temple baby doll from 1935. This wigged version (underneath the wig, she has molded hair) is all original and in mint condition. Flirty hazel eyes, open mouth with two upper and three lower teeth. Doll is wearing a simple cotton dress with angel sleeves. Rayon tag in back. Original panties, slip, socks, bonnet, and oilcloth booties. $1,200.00.

20" Shirley Temple doll wearing the original sailor outfit from the movie *Captain January*. Rosy cheeks and very detailed golden curls representative of the dolls made during 1936. Sailor outfit is very sought after, because it is one of Shirley's most recognizable movie outfits. It came in either navy blue or white. Rayon tag at the lower inside seam of the shirt (often missing). $1,100.00. Iva Mae Jones collection.

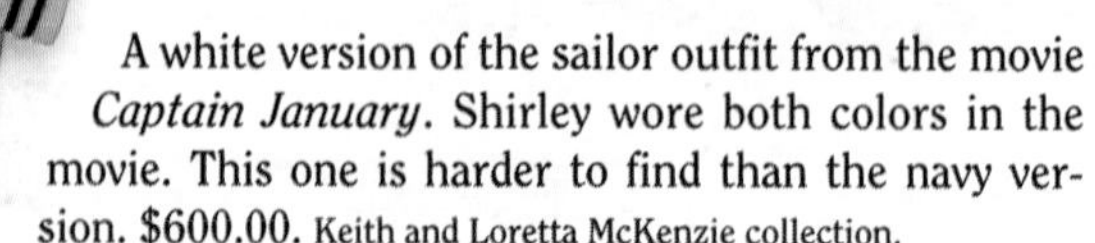

A white version of the sailor outfit from the movie *Captain January*. Shirley wore both colors in the movie. This one is harder to find than the navy version. $600.00. Keith and Loretta McKenzie collection.

Hard-to-find raincoat with matching hat from the movie *Captain January*, with rayon tag at back seam. Made out of oilcloth, which easily deteriorates unless properly preserved (similar to the blue raincoat that came in the trunks). This particular raincoat is in fair condition and has some deterioration to the cloth itself (mainly on the inside) and some staining. Very rare. In this condition, $250.00; mint, $450.00.

Movie poster of Shirley Temple wearing the yellow raincoat and hat in the movie *Captain January*.

Silk pajamas from the movie *Poor Little Rich Girl*. From when Shirley sang "Oh My Goodness" to her dollies. Made of silk and very fragile. Often this outfit is found damaged, because the red felt dots on the material would run if washed. Never put this outfit near water. Rayon tag. Very sought after because it is such a recognizable movie outfit. $500.00. Keith and Loretta McKenzie collection.

27" Shirley Temple doll wearing the red sailor dress from the movie *Poor Little Rich Girl*. This doll has the high color and make-up of the later dolls (see next chapter). Exceptional condition and large size increases its value. $1,800.00. Iva Mae Jones collection.

Dimity dress from the movie *Captain January*, found in many different colors, including light blue, royal blue, red, and green. Rayon tag. $250.00.

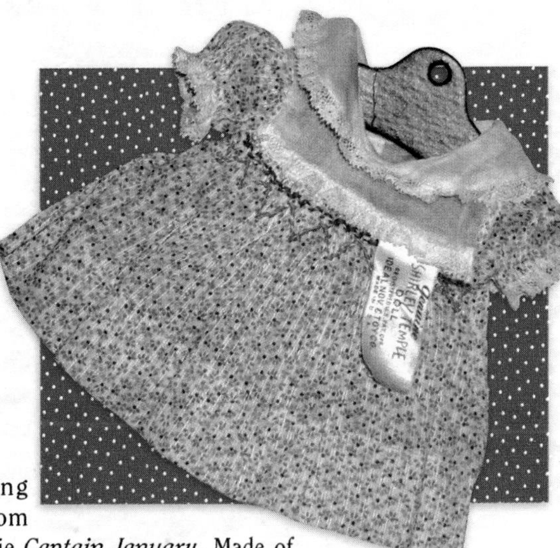

Smocking dress from the movie *Captain January*. Made of dimity. Rayon tag. Came in a variety of different fabric patterns. $300.00. Mary Williams collection.

Wool coat and hat set from the movie *Poor Little Rich Girl* in the original clothing box. Rayon tag in the back of the coat. Offered in a variety of colors. Set includes coat and hat, Shirley Temple doll hanger, Shirley Temple pin, and box with a color picture of Shirley on the top and the color of the outfit marked on the side. $550.00. Coat and hat alone, $300.00. Keith and Loretta McKenzie collection.

This advertisement for a wool coat and hat from *Poor Little Rich Girl* was found in the 1937 catalog for L&C Mayers Co. Marge Meisinger collection.

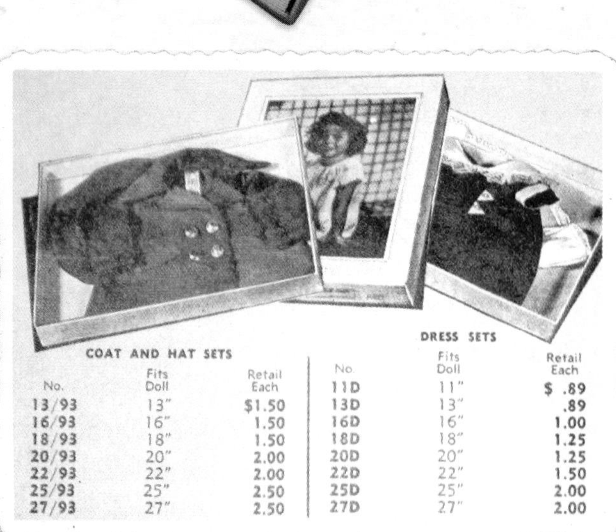

COAT AND HAT SETS

No.	Fits Doll	Retail Each
13/93	13"	$1.50
16/93	16"	1.50
18/93	18"	1.50
20/93	20"	2.00
22/93	22"	2.00
25/93	25"	2.50
27/93	27"	2.50

DRESS SETS

No.	Fits Doll	Retail Each
11D	11"	$ .89
13D	13"	.89
16D	16"	1.00
18D	18"	1.25
20D	20"	1.25
22D	22"	1.50
25D	25"	2.00
27D	27"	2.00

Ad for the outfits sold separately. Sets included outfit, hanger, panties/slip, pin, and box. Value varies greatly, depending on outfit. Marge Meisinger collection.

20" Shirley Temple doll wearing the "emblem dress" from *Poor Little Rich Girl*. Perfect example of what the dolls from 1936 originally looked like, with rosy cheeks, a bright complexion, darker blond hair, and very tight ringlets. Dress has a rayon tag and came in a variety of color combinations. The emblems on the front are also known as "frogs." The larger doll outfits (18" and up) each had three frogs on the bodice, while the smaller doll outfits each had only one frog on the bodice. $1,000.00. Dress alone, $300.00.

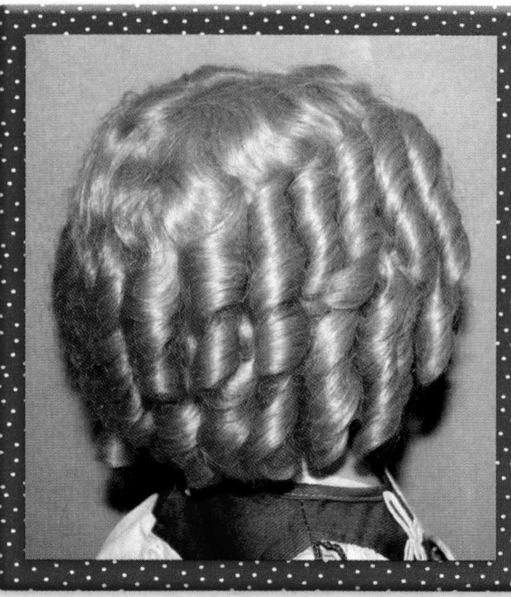

Close-up of the detailed ringlets going around the head of the larger Shirley Temple dolls made in 1936.

Sailor dress from the movie *Poor Little Rich Girl*. Outfit is pique with a matching hat. It was made in a variety of colors: red, royal blue, and navy. $300.00. Dress only, $200.00. Keith and Loretta McKenzie collection.

20" Shirley Temple doll in velvet coat and matching hat from the movie *Poor Little Rich Girl*. This coat was made in a variety of colors, including dark green, dark blue, and red. Rayon tag is attached at the back inside seam. $800.00. Outfit alone, $350.00.

13" Shirley Temple doll wearing a very unusual version of the Chinese outfit from the movie *Stowaway*. This outfit has a very hard-to-find fabric design on the top. $2,000.00. Keith and Loretta McKenzie collection.

18" Shirley Temple doll wearing Chinese outfit from *Stowaway*. This linen outfit consists of yellow pants with suspenders to hold them up, and a dark blue top with frog decorations and button closures. $1,500.00.

Another very rare Chinese outfit from *Stowaway*, this has only been found on the larger-size dolls. Few are known to exist. Outfit only, $800.00. Lorna Erb collection.

22" Shirley Temple doll with flirty eyes and makeup (see more about the makeup dolls in chapter 3), wearing a hard-to-find outfit from the movie *Stowaway*. The outfit is made of flocked cotton and came in red, blue, pink, or yellow. $2,000.00 (because of the incredible condition of the doll). Outfit alone, $500.00.

20" Shirley Temple wearing striped dress from *Stowaway*. This doll has eye shadow and flirty eyes and was probably produced in 1937. Dress came in yellow, blue, and pink. Very rare outfit. $1,600.00. Keith and Loretta McKenzie collection.

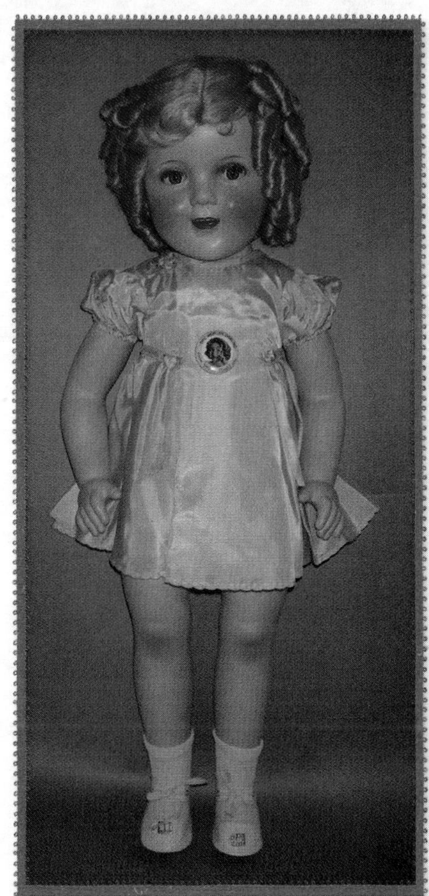

25" doll with makeup, in absolutely mint condition. Wearing a very rare pink taffeta dress from *Stowaway*. $3,000.00 and up (because of the exceptional condition of the doll). Dress only, $500.00 and up. Lorna Erb collection.

Specialty Outfits from 1936

In 1936, Texas marked its first 100 years of statehood with a huge celebration. Shirley Temple's appearance at the Centennial Exposition was commemorated by Ideal with a specialty Shirley Temple Texas Centennial Doll, often referred to as the "cowboy doll." Specially made in the 11", 17", and 27" sizes, though some have been found in other sizes as well. The 27" cowboy doll has a red satin shirt, leather chaps and vest, rayontagged satin bandana, brown socks, oilcloth boots, and a cowboy hat (this one is missing her hat). $1,600.00 and up. Loretta McKenzie collection.

11" cowboy Shirley Temple doll, with a plaid shirt and slightly different style to her leather chaps. Notice how detailed the outfits are. $1,200.00.

Advertisement for the Texas Ranger doll in *Hagn's Annual Counter Gift Catalog.* Marge Meisinger collection.

Publicity still of Shirley Temple playing in the snow (1934). Shown on a postcard from the 1930s. $10.00. Keith and Loretta McKenzie collection.

One of the rarest Shirley Temple outfits. Made to resemble the snowsuit that Shirley wore in publicity pictures from Christmas 1934. It is made of wool and has a matching hat. Rayon tag attached to the top inside collar. This snowsuit very closely resembles a Molly-'es snowsuit of the same time period; however, the quality of the material in the Shirley suit is higher. $2,000.00 and up. Keith and Loretta McKenzie collection.

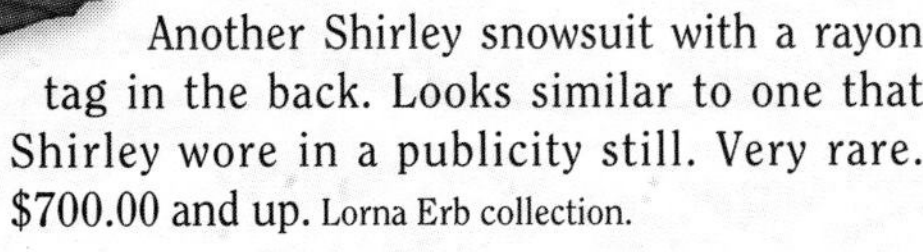

Another Shirley snowsuit with a rayon tag in the back. Looks similar to one that Shirley wore in a publicity still. Very rare. $700.00 and up. Lorna Erb collection.

Other Shirley Doll Accessories

Advertisement for Shirley Temple doll purses.
Marge Meisinger collection.

Shirley doll purses included a Shirley mirror. $60.00. Keith and Loretta McKenzie collection.

Box for doll shoes and socks (socks not pictured) sold separately for the Shirley Temple doll. The shoes themselves do not look like ones that the Shirley dolls originally wore. $80.00. Leslie Tannenbaum collection.

Original clothing rack also came as a stand and was used to display Shirley Temple doll clothing in stores. $300.00 and up.
Leslie Tannenbaum collection.

Doll dress patterns from the 1930s and early 1940s for the "movie" dolls. Not authorized specifically for the Shirley Temple doll, but definitely meant for her. $20.00 – $30.00 each. Janet Mitchell collection.

A smaller doll dress pattern for the movie dolls, from 1937. $20.00. Janet Mitchell collection.

Miscellaneous Doll Items from 1936

This Shirley Temple "dainty flowered organdy dress with ruffles" was advertised in the 1936 Christmas catalog for FAO Schwartz Toy Company. It was not modeled after a movie outfit. Keith and Loretta McKenzie collection.

"Dainty flowered organdy dress with ruffles," for an 18" Shirley Temple doll. Came in either pink or blue. This print pattern was often seen on many of the later Shirley dresses. Rayon tag. $250.00.

25" Shirley Temple doll in hard-to-find embroidered-cherry dress. Made later in the Shirley production run (late 1936). Tagged at the back button with the rayon tag. $1,500.00 (because of large size). Dress alone, $500.00 and up.

22" Shirley Temple doll wearing a printed organdy dress with cherries on the bib collar. Near-mint large-size doll with hard-to-find dress. $1,200.00. Charmaine Euler collection.

Rare terry cloth robe and matching bathing suit with a Vogue tag at the back inside seam. Believed to have been made for the Shirley Temple doll. $300.00. Lorna Erb collection.

16" Shirley wearing a rain cape and hat and holding a matching umbrella. Outfit has a rayon tag at the inside seam. $825.00. Outfit only, $375.00. Rachel Quigley collection.

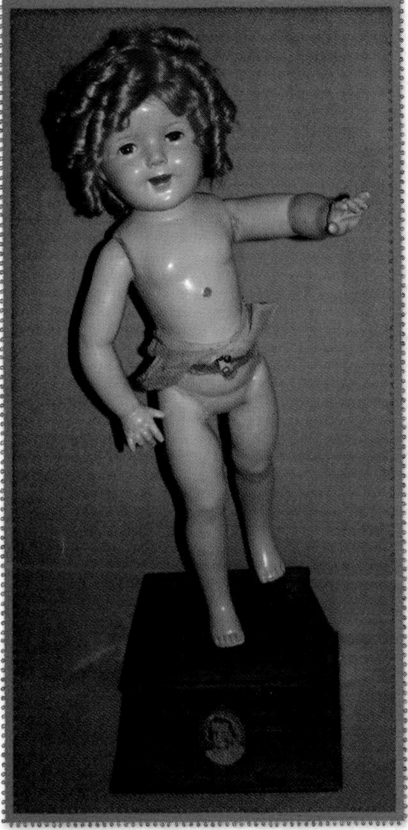

The dancing Shirley Temple doll. 27" tall Shirley Temple doll with a rod that goes from her foot to the top of her head. The rod is attached to a mechanism in the wooden base beneath her that lets the doll "dance" by spinning around in a circle, leaning back and forth, and swinging her leg and arms. Originally came wearing a pleated *Curly Top* dress. $5,000.00 and up. Rachel Quigley collection.

This is a color poster advertisement for the Shirley Temple doll, circa 1935. $250.00. Keith and Loretta McKenzie collection.

In 1936, *Fortune* magazine had an article on how Shirlety Temple dolls were put together. First, composition (a mixture of resin, wood flour, starch, and water) was poured into a mold, and then hardened pieces were dipped in lacquer. Janet Mitchell collection.

The dolls were spray painted. Then the eyes were put in the heads.
Janet Mitchell collection.

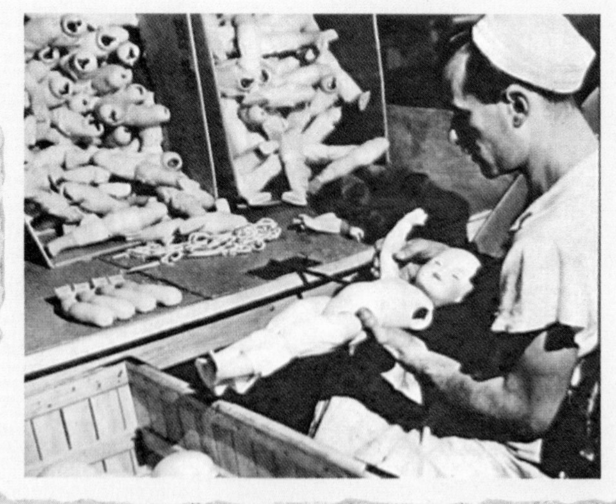

The doll pieces were strung together with elastic.
Janet Mitchell collection.

The mohair wigs were styled.
Janet Mitchell collection.

This unusual color advertisement from 1936 showed many of the different sizes of Shirley Temple dolls that were available at that time, as well as the many outfits that could go with the dolls. 1935 and 1936 were the height of the Shirley Temple doll craze, with a huge assortment of dolls and dresses being produced.

Finally, the wigs were glued on and the dolls were dressed and packed in their boxes.
Janet Mitchell collection.

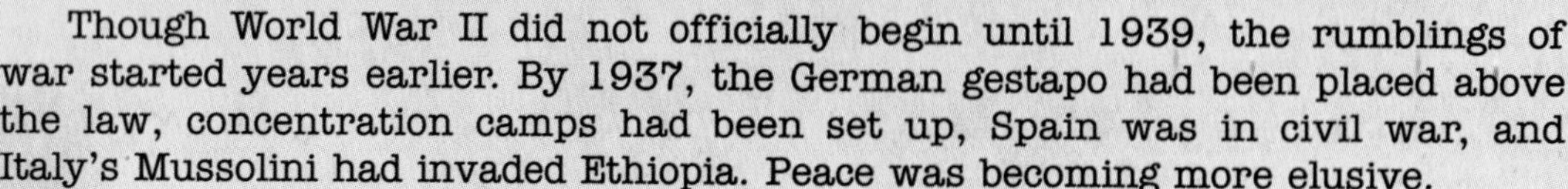

Chapter 3
The End of an Era: Shirley Temple Grows Up (1937 – 1940)

Though World War II did not officially begin until 1939, the rumblings of war started years earlier. By 1937, the German gestapo had been placed above the law, concentration camps had been set up, Spain was in civil war, and Italy's Mussolini had invaded Ethiopia. Peace was becoming more elusive.

In America, the Great Depression was slowly ending and work was becoming more available. As jobs reappeared, people were no longer trying to escape from reality; they were becoming very concerned about the reality of what was happening around the world.

Movies began to echo this change in attitude as well. More dramas were in production, and though comedies were still being made, they were more reflective of real life. Twentieth Century Fox movies began to change as well. Zanuck decided that Shirley Temple's first movie for the year 1937 was to be **Wee Willie Winkie**. It was different from any other movie that Shirley had done, more dramatic. Shirley was also quite different from that little girl audiences had fallen in love with back in 1934. She had grown — she had gained some weight, her hair had darkened, and she didn't look like a baby any more. Shirley Temple was growing up.

Wee Willie Winkie told the story of a young girl living on an army base in India during wartime. For the first time, a Shirley Temple movie did not rely on the Shirley Temple cuteness; in fact, Shirley did not tap dance at all and, other than one small song, hardly sang. **Wee Willie Winkie** was applauded by critics; they were quite impressed that Shirley Temple could do more than just be cute — she could act. The film was also very successful at the box office. About this time, MGM approached Zanuck about allowing Shirley to star in its movie version of the Frank Baum book **The Wizard of Oz**. After intense negotiations, Zanuck agreed to trade Shirley if he could get Jean Harlow and Clark Gable to star in a movie for Twentieth Century Fox. Unfortunately, a short time after the agreement was finalized, Jean Harlow died suddenly. The deal fell through.

Keeping with the more dramatic theme that was such a success in **Wee Willie Winkie**, Zanuck decided that Shirley's next movie would be **Heidi**. Once again, there was more of a focus on the storyline than on Shirley Temple's cuteness. Critics and audiences alike approved, and **Heidi** was also a box-office success. The year 1937 ended with Shirley once again the number-one box office star. However, that year other movie stars were close behind. Shirley starred in only two movies during the year, unlike previous years in which she had starred in four or more. These movies were longer, more expensive to make, and required more time in production.

By 1938, Zanuck had acquired other bankable movie stars for Twentieth Century Fox, including Tyrone Power and Sonja Henie. Though Shirley was still very important to the studio, she was no longer the only star, and her career no longer required Zanuck's constant attention. He decided to go back to the old Shirley formula movies that had been so successful, and so easy and cheap to produce. The first of these was **Rebecca of Sunnybrook Farm**, which reunited Shirley with Bill "Bojangles" Robinson. Completely different from the book of the same name, **Rebecca** was a sweet feel-good story that included a nostalgic radio-show scene in which Shirley sang some of her most famous songs. Possibly the most significant change for Shirley during the filming was her hairstyle. Gone were the 56 curls that she was known for, and in their place were two ponytails full of curls. The audiences appeared to like both the new hairstyle and the film. Rebecca was very well received at the box office. Relieved, Zanuck declared, "Shirley Temple is endless." Movie critics did not seem to think the same. Many wondered how much longer the Shirley formula would be successful. Her next movies, **Little Miss Broadway** and **Just Around the Corner**, had the same storylines as her earlier films, and audiences decided that they'd had enough. Though **Little Miss Broadway** was a moderate success, **Just Around the Corner** was not.

Shirley's next movie, her first in 1939, was **The Little Princess**. Shirley had another dramatic role, and Zanuck was hoping for box-office success comparable to that of her films from 1937. The budget for this film was more than double that of most of her movies, and this was her first movie shot in Technicolor. Zanuck was expecting a blockbuster, and **The Little Princess** was hailed by critics and was well received by audiences. Even today, **The Little Princess** is one of the most popular Shirley Temple movies. After the success of this movie, Zanuck was again hopeful that Shirley would make the transition from child star to adult film star successfully. MGM thought she would too, and made a final bid to get her in its upcoming movie **The Wizard of Oz**, but Zanuck refused.

While Judy Garland was filming **The Wizard of Oz**, Shirley was filming **Susannah of the Mounties**. When released in August of 1939, **The Wizard of Oz** was a huge box-office success, and later proved to be one of the most-beloved movies of all time. Judy Garland became a star. **Susannah of the Mounties** was a box-office failure and was panned by the critics. Many people wonder what would have happened if Shirley had starred in **The Wizard of Oz**.

The end of 1939 brought the official declaration of war against Germany by Britain, France, Australia, and New Zealand. By 1940, most of Europe was at war. Back at Twentieth Century Fox, Zanuck was preparing his answer to **The Wizard of Oz**, a fantasy adaptation of the book **The Blue Bird**. Once again, he greatly increased the budget allotted and filmed the movie in Technicolor. He was hoping for the success of **The Wizard of Oz**. What he received was the opposite — another box-office disappointment, criticized for being too dark and lacking the optimism of **The Wizard of Oz**. This was the beginning of the end of Shirley's relationship with Twentieth Century Fox.

Her final film for Twentieth Century Fox was **Young People**. Ironically, the story centered on Shirley growing up, but it went back to the same formula that she had been using since she was six. Again, she was supposed to be that cute little orphan who fixes every problem. **Young People** was another box-office failure, and shortly after the release — and some intense negotiations with her family — Shirley's contract with Twentieth Century Fox ended.

Shirley was no longer that cute little kid always there to save the day, and movie audiences no longer needed that from her. A war had begun and people were occupied with other things. So was Shirley Temple; she was growing up.

By the late 1930s, Ideal was no longer reliant on the Shirley Temple doll; it had other dolls that were selling very well. These included the Judy Garland and Deana Durbin dolls, the Pinocchio and Snow White dolls, and the many "Mama" baby dolls. In addition, Shirley Temple doll sales were noticeably off. Not only did the drop correspond with Shirley's getting older, it also matched with her move to more dramatic movies in 1937, roles that may have been watched by adults more so than by her usual, younger demographic.

With sales down more than 50% compared to those in 1935, Ideal tried to update the doll so that people would become more interested in it again. It decided to have the doll "grow up" in the same way that Shirley was growing up. It modified the mold, giving the doll a higher forehead and less chubby cheeks, a more grown-up look. It changed the painted facial features, creating a more pale skin, rosier cheeks and knees, darker and more defined eyebrows, gray eye shadow, and darker lip color. It also changed the wig to a more defined side-parted style, with less distinct curls. At the end of 1936, Mollye Goldman stopped designing the Shirley doll outfits. New outfits of Shirley movie costumes were still being produced; however, they were not as detailed as the outfits made by Mollye Goldman, and there were fewer being made. The style of the outfits was also changing, with noticeably longer, more modest skirts to suit the more grown-up Shirley. Ideal also updated some of the doll's most famous earlier dresses again in different styles and fabrics.

For a short time, the new Shirley doll (often referred to by collectors as the make-up doll) was offered in all nine sizes; however, the number of sizes available was reduced when it was apparent that sales were still declining. Soon the prices of the Shirley dolls also started dropping, as Ideal tried to encourage higher sales. Though these dolls were a hard sell at the time, currently they are some of the most sought after by collectors, since they are so hard to find.
In December 1940, the final Shirley dolls were advertised next to the latest popular Ideal dolls, Deana Durbin and Judy Garland. The appropriate description accompanying the doll was, "Shirley Temple has retired...and this is positively the last chance you have to buy a Shirley Temple doll!"

With that ad, the Shirley Temple doll, the most profitable in history to that point, was discontinued, and was not seen again for nearly 20 years.

Shirley Temple embodied the Depression era. With spunk and a smile, she handled any hardship and guaranteed a happy ending. Shirley grew up with the Depression, and as it ended, so did her era as a child star. She had given her audiences what they needed when they needed it, and now a new era had begun.

★ ★

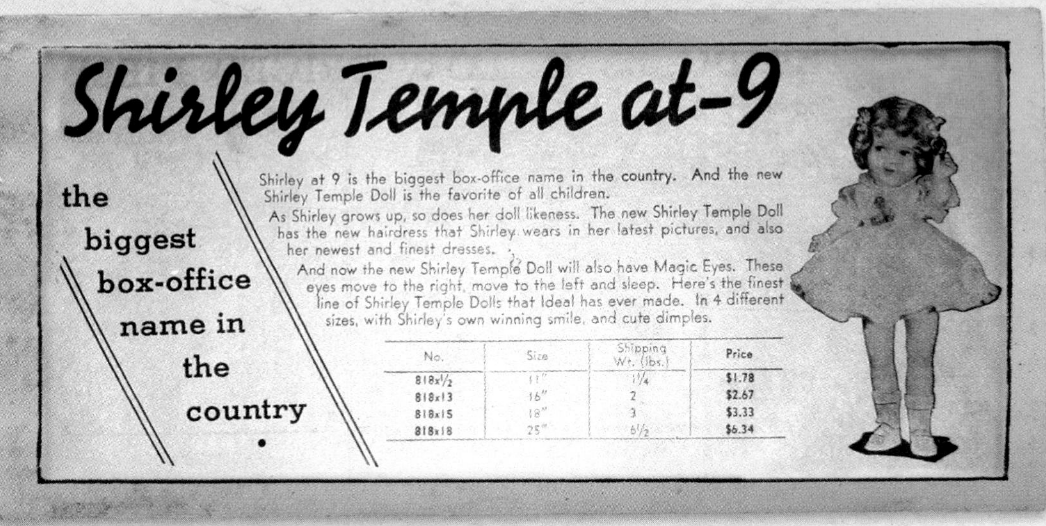

Advertisement from the Hagn Merchandiser, 1938, for the "new" Shirley Temple doll.
Marge Meisinger collection.

Shirley Temple doll (1938), wearing a later version of the pleated *Curly Top* dress, worth $1,200.00.

The face of the later Shirley Temple dolls.

Details

- Darker facial coloring. Rosier cheeks and darker eyebrows, lower eyelashes, and lip paint. Lighter skin tone and oftentimes a thinner coat of paint (which can tend to flake off over time).
- Eye shadow on the lids of the eyes.
- Different eyes that are larger and more blue-green in color than hazel (these seem to be present mainly in the 18" dolls). Also, many of these later dolls had flirty eyes that moved back and forth (previously, only the 25" and 27" dolls had flirty eyes).
- Hair was parted in a side part, with fewer curls, and a more distinct "style" to the hair.
- A larger bow in the hair (of many of the dolls).
- Longer dresses.
- Different oilcloth shoes were sometimes used on the dolls.
- The same style pin and box were used for this doll as were used for the dolls from 1935 and 1936.

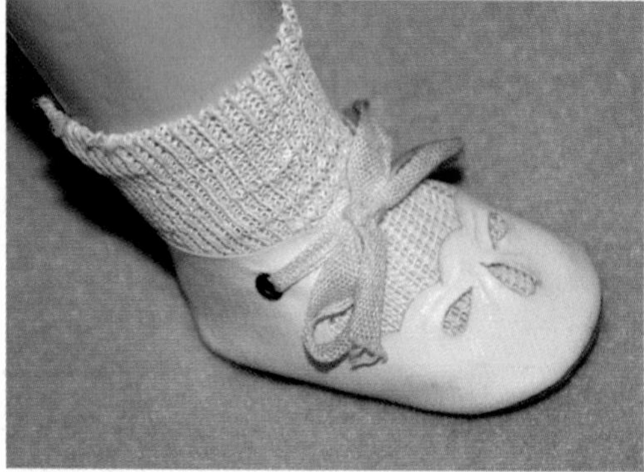

The new-style oilcloth shoes.

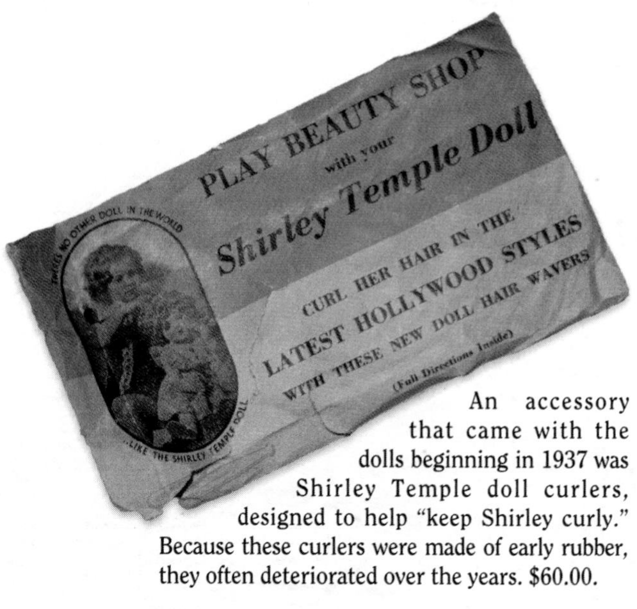

An accessory that came with the dolls beginning in 1937 was Shirley Temple doll curlers, designed to help "keep Shirley curly." Because these curlers were made of early rubber, they often deteriorated over the years. $60.00.

Some of the later dolls were also advertised with this Ideal Dolly Make-up Kit, a very rare find. $125.00 and up. Loretta Beilstein collection.

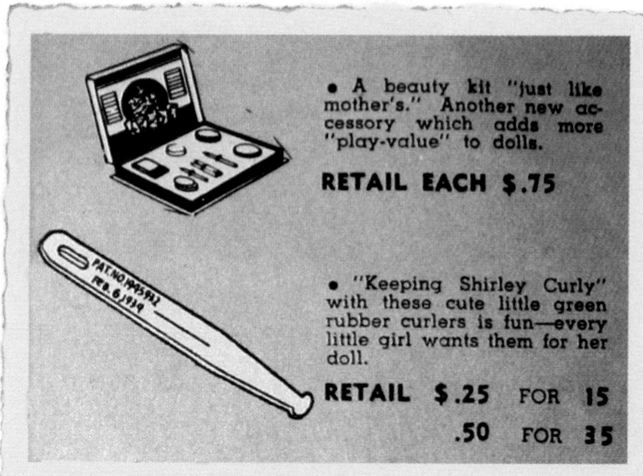

• A beauty kit "just like mother's." Another new accessory which adds more "play-value" to dolls.

RETAIL EACH $.75

• "Keeping Shirley Curly" with these cute little green rubber curlers is fun—every little girl wants them for her doll.

RETAIL $.25 FOR 15
.50 FOR 35

This ad announced the curlers and the makeup kit for the Shirley Temple dolls. Marge Meisinger collection.

Shirley Temple doll (1938), wearing a later version of the pleated *Curly Top* dress.

Details

- Hair in the back was not in distinct curls like it had been previously.
- Dresses were much longer than they had been previously (came down to a bit above the knee). Some were closed in the back with safety pins instead of the usual buttons.
- Dresses were often found without the rayon tag.

18" Shirley Temple doll wearing the complete Scotch military outfit from *Wee Willie Winkie*. Made in early 1937, this doll does not have the makeup of the later dolls. Rayon tag at the back inside top of the jacket. Outfit consists of khaki jacket, plaid skirt (this outfit came in a number of different patterns of plaid; the one pictured here is rare), blue velvet hat with plaid top and blue ribbon going around it, multicolored socks with blue ribbon accent at the top, and black shoes. Very hard to find because there were fewer dolls made — the production of the Shirley Temple dolls was slowing down and the *Wee Willie Winkie* outfit was so intricately detailed and labor intensive. Very valuable because it is such a recognizable movie outfit. $4,000.00. Rachel Quigley collection.

A complete mint-in-box 25" Wee Willie doll, wearing a different plaid pattern on the skirt. This is one of the rarest and most sought-after Shirley Temple dolls. $6,000.00 and up. Rachel Quigley collection.

Advertisement for the Scotch military doll based on the movie *Wee Willie Winkie* and found in the *Ideal Dolls and Doll Accessories Catalog* from 1937. States that the *Wee Willie Winkie* doll came in 18", 22", and 25" size. Currently, only the 18" and 25" sizes have been identified. The 22" size may have never actually been produced by Ideal. Marge Meisinger collection.

This dress came on an 18" Shirley Temple doll and is original. It includes a cotton dress and apron overlay. It is believed to be modeled after an outfit that Shirley wore in the movie *Wee Willie Winkie*. Not tagged. $400.00.

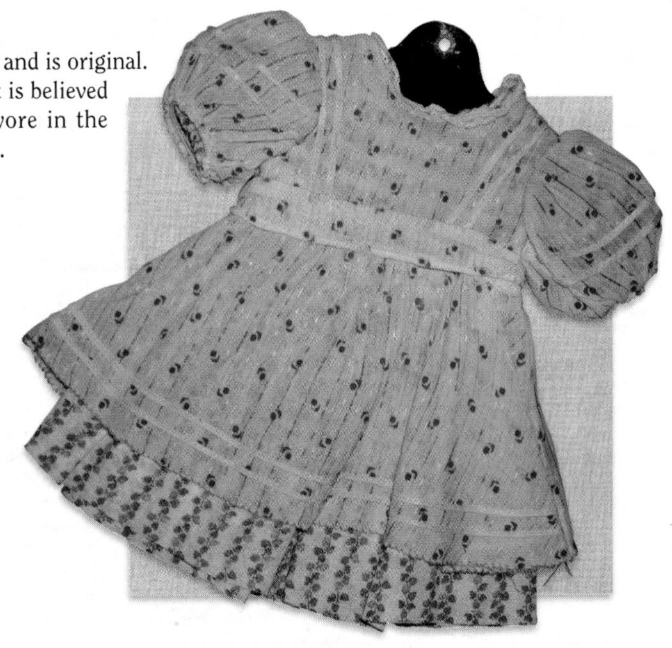

22" Shirley Temple doll is wearing the traveling outfit from the movie *Wee Willie Winkie*. This doll is similar to those made in 1936, without the makeup of the later dolls. The outfit is made of flocked cotton and came in peach or blue. Consists of dress, jacket, and hat. Rayon tag. Very sought-after outfit because it is so recognizable and so few were made. $4,000.00. Keith and Loretta McKenzie collection.

Factory outfit found on a 16" Shirley Temple doll. Closely resembles one that Shirley wore in *Heidi*; however, it is unknown whether it is original, since it does not have a tag and is not documented in any Shirley advertisements. $75.00. If originality could be determined, it would be worth significantly more.

20" Shirley Temple doll wearing the Dutch outfit from *Heidi*. Shirley wore this outfit in a dream sequence in which she had a wig of blond braids (instead of her signature curls) and was dancing to the song "In Our Little Wooden Shoes." This doll has the dark facial paint and eye shadow of the later dolls from 1937 to 1940. There are only a few dolls known to exist in this outfit. It is one of the most sought after sets. Consists of a dress with a velvet bodice and striped skirt, separate apron, rayon socks, wooden shoes, and organdy Dutch hat. Rayon tag at the skirt seam. $5,000.00 and up. Keith and Loretta McKenzie collection.

18" Shirley Temple doll wearing a slight variation of the *Heidi* Dutch dress; this one has a multicolored skirt. Shoes are not original. $3,000.00.

16" mint Shirley Temple doll in printed organdy "hearts dress." This doll has the coloring of the 1936 Shirley. The outfit was a party dress and was not made to resemble one from her movies. It was often shown in advertisements from 1937. This doll was found in the original box, which came with an original curler set. $1,800.00. Dress alone, $500.00. Keith and Loretta McKenzie collection.

An advertisement for a Shirley Temple doll wearing the hearts dress, in *The John Plain Book* from 1939. This doll outfit was used in many advertisements from 1937 to 1939. Marge Meisinger collection.

Rare doll curler box that was released in the late 1930s, featuring a little girl holding a Shirley Temple doll. $75.00. Leslie Tannenbaum collection.

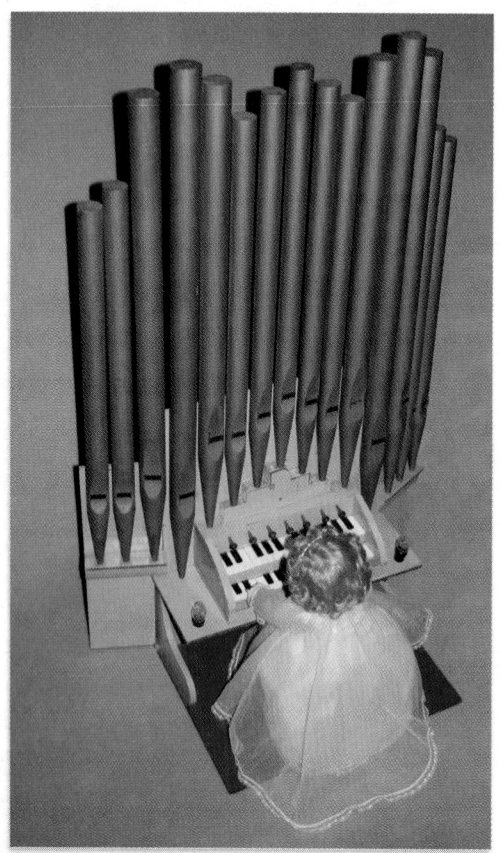

A beautiful example of the Shirley Temple doll playing the organ. The organ set was released in three different sizes; this is a smaller version. The dress Shirley is wearing is not original. Complete, $5,000.00 and up. Iva Mae Jones collection.

Close-up of the original organ. Iva Mae Jones collection.

A side view of the larger organ doll. As the record played music, Shirley's hands moved across the organ. All original. $6,000.00 and up. Rachel Quigley collection.

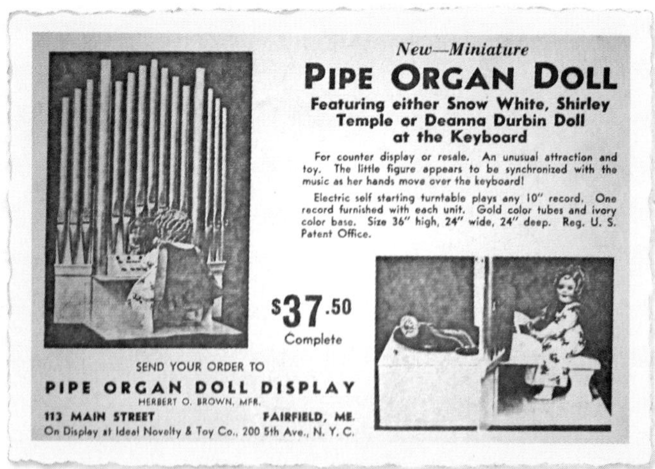

Advertisement in the 1937 edition of *Playthings* magazine, featuring a Shirley Temple doll playing the organ. The set was offered with a Shirley Temple, Deanna Durbin, or Snow White doll. Marge Meisinger collection.

16" Shirley Temple organ doll with original velvet outfit, light blond wig, cloth body, and metal rods in her hands and bottom. She was found in a regular Ideal box (without the Shirley Temple label). $1,000.00 and up.

A close-up of the hands and body rods on the Shirley organ doll.

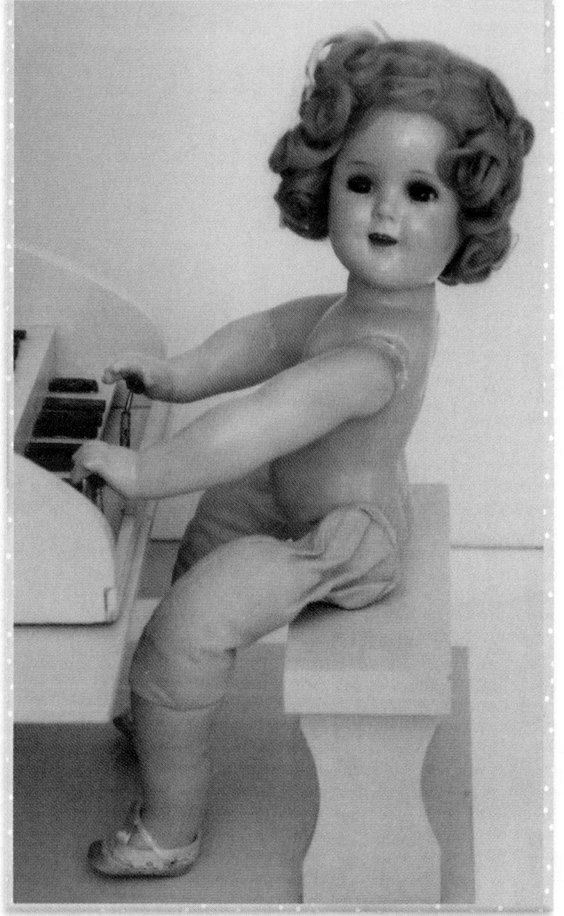

This is how the organ doll sat at her organ. Rachel Quigley collection.

The back of the doll with pigtails has a center part going all the way down the back of her head. Hair style makes this a very rare doll. Rachel Quigley collection.

18" made around the time of *Little Miss Broadway*, with pigtails instead of the usual curls. In the original box and wearing a starburst *Curly Top* dress. $1,500.00 and up. Rachel Quigley collection.

18" Shirley Temple doll is all original and from the movie *Rebecca of Sunnybrook Farm*. The overalls have a rayon tag at the side seam. Also includes a plaid cotton shirt and buckram hat. Incredibly rare and very recognizable from the movie, very valuable to collectors. $5,000.00 and up. Lana and Neal Fisk, Keith and Loretta McKenzie collection.

20" Shirley Temple doll with makeup is wearing a very rare jumper dress from the movie *Little Miss Broadway*. The outfit consists of a dimity shirt and cotton jumper with crisscross detail and is just like the one Shirley wore in the movie. Only a few of these dresses are known to exist. $2,500.00 and up. Keith and Loretta McKenzie collection.

16" Shirley Temple doll is wearing the "zipper dress" from the movie *Little Miss Broadway*. This doll has the eye shadow and bright coloring of the later dolls. Her wig is very unusual and is styled into two separate ponytails (similar to Shirley's own hairstyle in that movie). Dress has hand-painted leaves going down the front. It has been found in orange and blue, very hard to find (mainly because so few were produced). Rayon tag. $1,500.00 and up; dress alone, $800.00 and up. Keith and Loretta McKenzie collection.

18" Shirley Temple makeup doll wearing one of the hardest to find outfits, the "Lucky Penny dress" from *Just Around the Corner*. Doll also has hard-to-find flirty eyes (only seen on the smaller-size dolls — 22" and under — released late in the production run). Only a few dolls were released in this outfit, incredibly rare and sought after by collectors. $2,000.00 and up. Keith and Loretta McKenzie collection.

18" Shirley Temple doll is wearing a very hard-to-find jumper outfit that was made in the late 1930s. It was modeled after a jumper in Shirley's own wardrobe; she was often pictured in a similar outfit during that time period. Only a few of these are known to exist. $2,500.00 and up. Rachel Quigley collection.

18" doll is in one of the only known examples of the birthday party dress from the movie *The Little Princess*. Satin dress with lace overlay and flowers on the bodice. $3,000.00 and up. Rachel Quigley collection.

Gorgeous example of the later 27" doll with dark eye shadow and facial features. The woman I bought this doll from said that she got it directly from the original owner, who was given the doll as a gift by George Temple (Shirley Temple's father). I cannot verify that this is true, but it is a wonderful story. She stated that the dress was original and from the dream sequence from the movie *The Little Princess*. Again, origin can't be verified, as the dress is not tagged. $1,500.00, based on the gorgeous condition of the doll. If the authenticity of the dress could be confirmed, it would be worth significantly more.

Ad for a doll in the flocked organdy-style dress was found in *The John Plain Book*, 1940. Marge Meisinger collection.

18" Shirley wearing a printed organdy dress with a flower decoration on it. This fabric design was found on many of the later Shirley dresses. Not much is known about this outfit. It is not tagged, but does seem original. $1,200.00. Rachel Quigley collection.

Matching 13" Shirley Temple dolls show the two different types of makeup dolls produced in the late 1930s. The doll on the left has sleep eyes, light eye shadow, and rosy skin coloring. Her wig has a distinctive side part and a large hair bow. The doll on the right has flirty eyes, dark eye shadow, and pale skin, and has a wig that is styled in the earlier Shirley hair set. The dolls are wearing similar dresses that were featured in many advertisements from 1939 to 1940. Dresses are of flocked organdy in different patterns (the one on the left has a leaf print, and the one on the right has a dove print) and have slightly different decorations on the bodices. Dresses are very hard to find. Rayon tag on each. $1,000.00 each. Keith and Loretta McKenzie collection.

Rare 16" doll wearing a dress that is often featured in many of the later Shirley Temple doll ads. The dress is made of printed organdy with a flower decoration at the waist. Only a few examples of this outfit are known to exist, because at the time it was made, so few Shirley dolls were being sold. $2,000.00 and up. Rachel Quigley collection.

18" Shirley doll wearing a printed organdy dress with braided trim, found in many ads from 1939 and 1940. $850.00. Keith and Loretta McKenzie collection.

18" with makeup and flirty eyes, wearing another version of the printed organdy dress with braided trim, this time with a printed bluebird pattern (which was probably released after the movie *The Blue Bird* came out in 1940). $850.00.

18" Shirley Temple doll wearing a very rare dress and jacket set from the movie *The Blue Bird*. The dress is made of cotton and consists of a knee-length dress and a jacket. Not tagged; it seems that many of the later dresses were not. Only a few of these are known to exist, found in red and blue. Doll is posed in a doll stand that was used to hold Shirley's own dolls when they were displayed at the Children's Hospital at Stanford University. At the time that the dolls were removed from display in the early 1990s, Shirley's husband allowed some of the helpers to take home the stands. One of the helpers later gave the extra stands that she had received to those in attendance at the 2002 Shirley Temple Collector's Convention. $4,000.00 and up. Keith and Loretta McKenzie collection.

This is the only doll known to exist in this dress from the movie *The Blue Bird*. The blue cotton dress has netting overlay and a felt bluebird on the bodice. It may have been a salesman sample. $5,000.00 and up. Rita Dubas collection.

16" doll wearing another rare outfit from the movie *The Blue Bird*. Cotton dress and felt vest. At the time, the dolls were not selling well, and only two are known to exist. $5,000.00 and up. Rachel Quigley collection.

This jumper looks exactly like the one that Shirley wore in the movie *Young People*; however, it is not tagged and its authenticity cannot be verified. As is, it is valued at $100.00 to $150.00. If the jumper was determined to be authentic, the value would greatly increase. Rita Dubas collection.

18" Shirley wearing the Spiegel bolero dress, which closes in the back with button closure and has attached matching panties (instead of the usual organdy panties/slip combination). This dress was not modeled after one from a Shirley movie, but it was a popular style of dress at the time. Dress not tagged. $1,000.00. Rachel Quigley collection.

18" Shirley Temple makeup doll wearing a fancy dimity dress with a knee-length skirt. Resembles some of the outfits from Shirley's own wardrobe at the time. Rayon tag. $1,200.00. Keith and Loretta McKenzie collection.

The last advertisement for the Shirley Temple doll, featured in Spiegel's winter catalog, 1940. Marge Meisinger collection.

20" Shirley Temple doll, the last Shirley Temple doll produced. Marked "SHIRLEY TEMPLE COP IDEAL N&T Co." on the head and "IDEAL" on the body. She has the makeup of the later dolls, but she has a very different hairstyle, with curly bangs and the longer hair popular during 1940. Outfit consists of a bolero (one piece) dress and a matching straw hat. $1,200.00.

Chapter 4
Foreign Shirley Temple Dolls: Shirley Temple around the World

Shirley Temple was not only popular in the United States during the 1930s, she was well known throughout the world. People around the world watched Shirley Temple movies and became Shirley Temple fans. Some of the largest Shirley Temple fan clubs of the 1930s were formed in England and other parts of Europe. Shirley Temple fans around the world also wanted Shirley Temple dolls. The Ideal Novelty and Toy Company sold its Shirley Temple doll molds to companies in other countries that put together, dressed, and distributed the dolls. The Reliable Doll Company sold Shirley Temple dolls in Canada. The Reliable Shirley Temple doll looked similar to the Ideal doll, but had a slightly different paint color and style of painted facial features, and some slightly different outfits. Ideal also distributed doll molds to Australia and Latin America. These countries produced dolls that looked very similar to the Ideal dolls, with only slight variations in the paint color, painted features, and doll outfit styles.

In some countries, doll companies produced their own authorized versions of the Shirley Temple doll. In England, the authorized Shirley Temple dolls were produced by Allwin. These dolls were 18" tall, with a cloth body and a pressed felt face "mask" with painted features. In France, Raynal created a Shirley Temple "bebe" that also had a cloth body and pressed felt face mask with oil-painted features. Germany produced two versions of the Shirley Temple doll. One was made by Carl Bergner and marked "CB Germany" on the back of the head. It was made of composition, and had bright blue sleep eyes and a curly blond wig. The other version was also made of composition, but was only marked with the height on the back of the head. Poland's Shirley Temple doll was made of celluloid, with a mohair wig and stationary blue eyes, and was marked "Shirley Temple" on the back of her head. A similar celluloid doll was released in Holland and other countries throughout Europe. The doll resembled Shirley Temple and had an open mouth and dimples. Some of these dolls were dressed like Shirley; others had hair and clothing that corresponded to the styles of the cultures of the countries producing the dolls. Japan produced many small all composition dolls resembling Shirley, though these dolls were not authorized Shirley Temple dolls. These were commonly sold in the United States during the 1930s.

From Europe to Australia, Asia to South America, Shirley Temple fans could buy their very own Shirley Temple dolls. Compared to those of the Ideal Toy Company, which sold more than six million Shirley Temple dolls in the United States, the foreign doll sales were relatively small, estimated to be in the thousands to tens of thousands. Because of this, the authorized foreign Shirley Temple dolls are very hard to find and are some of the most valuable to Shirley Temple collectors.

Close-up of the Reliable tag and pin. Pin, $125.00.

16" Shirley Temple doll produced by the Reliable Doll Company, of Canada. Paint is thinner, and slightly browner in color than that of the Ideal dolls. Lip paint is more orange, lower eyelashes are thinner, and cheeks are rosier than on the American dolls. Marked "SHIRLEY TEMPLE 14" on her head and back (only the Canadian dolls can be found marked "14" — dolls are similar to the 16" Ideal dolls). Wearing the Reliable version of the *Littlest Rebel* dress, very similar to the Ideal version. Woven cloth Reliable tag. Reliable pin attached to the front of the dress. $800.00.

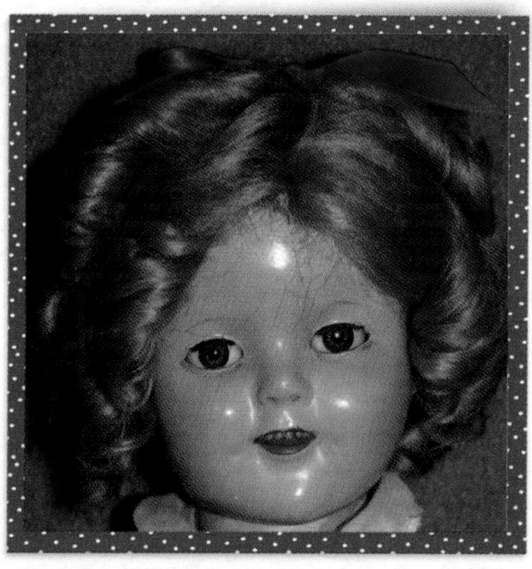

Close-up of the face of the 16" Reliable Shirley Temple doll.

Close-up of the label on the end of the Reliable Shirley Temple box.

Printed organdy dress for a 13" doll, with Reliable tag. Similar in style to the hearts dress from 1937 that was produced by Ideal. $400.00. Keith and Loretta McKenzie collection.

22" Shirley Temple doll by Reliable. Wearing unusual and very rare Canadian variation of the *Littlest Rebel* dress and apron. Reliable dress tag and pin. $1,800.00.

18" Shirley Temple doll by Reliable, wearing the Reliable version of the *Heidi* dress. Reliable dress tag. $3,000.00 and up. Rachel Quigley collection.

18" Shirley Temple doll by Reliable, wearing the Reliable version of the *Wee Willie Winkie* outfit. Very rare. $3,000.00 and up. Rachel Quigley collection.

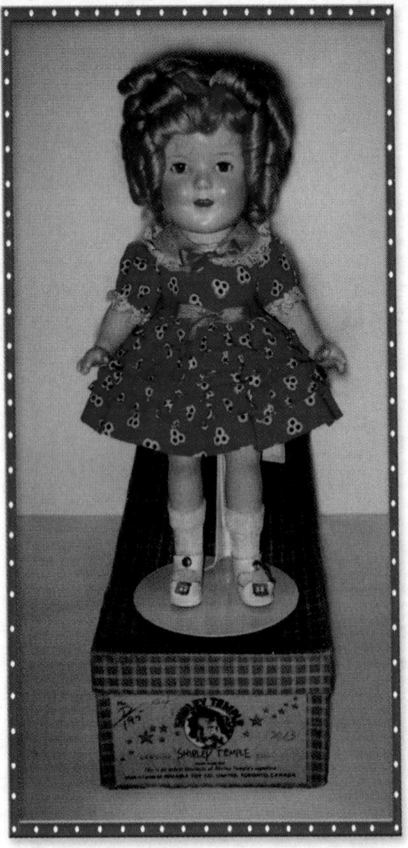

Mint-in-box 13" *Littlest Rebel* by Reliable, with unusual dress and box. $2,250.00. Rachel Quigley collection.

13" Reliable doll wearing a dress that is similar to the late 1930s printed organdy dove dress from Ideal. $800.00. Iva Mae Jones collection.

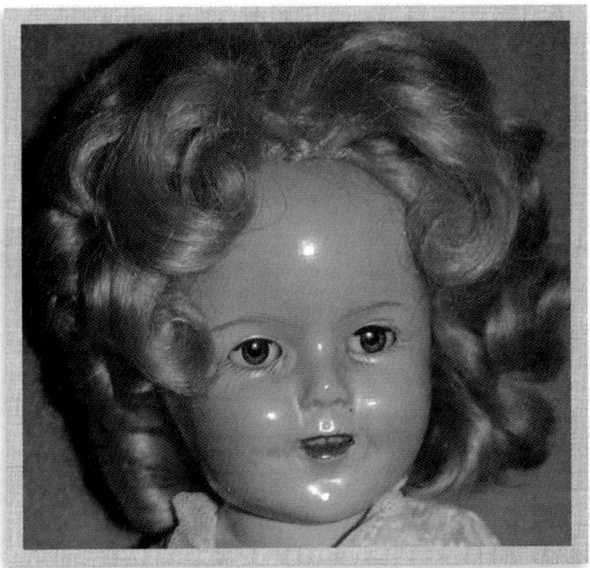

The face of this 13" distinguishes it from the Ideal version of the Shirley Temple doll. The Canadian version is a bit more angular. Iva Mae Jones collection.

Fox publicity still showing many of the foreign Shirley Temple dolls. From left: Australian Shirley Temple doll, Raynal French Shirley Temple doll, Allwin English Shirley Temple doll, Polish celluloid Shirley Temple doll, and South American Shirley Temple doll. Rita Dubas collection.

Another ad from Printemps (late 1935) features a Shirley doll wearing a *Curly Top* duck dress. Marge Meisinger collection.

20" doll is marked "Ideal"; however, it was produced in Australia. It has the eye shadow of the later dolls and is wearing a very unusual dress, similar to the *Poor Little Rich Girl* dress from Ideal that has three bows going down the bodice. Unusual pin from Australia that identifies it as a genuine Shirley Temple doll. $1,200.00.

The French Shirley Temple dolls were made by Raynal and were sold exclusively by Au Printemps. This advertisement found in *Au Printemps* catalog from 1935 introduces a cloth Shirley Temple doll wearing clothes from *The Little Colonel*. Marge Meisinger collection.

This Shirley Temple "bebe" doll was made by Raynal. This doll has a molded cloth face and body. Very rare, $3,000.00. Rosemary Dent collection.

Close-up of the Raynal Shirley Temple bebe doll. Rosemary Dent collection.

SHIRLEY TEMPLE

DOLLS

"THE WORLD'S DARLING"
IN 18 CHARACTER STUDIES

These life-like Dolls are charming reproductions of "The World's Darling" and are giving thousands of delighted children great pleasure in all parts of the Country.

A "Shirley Temple" Doll is always a favourite birthday present and there are 18 different character studies from which to choose. Write to Allwins who are the sole British makers for illustrated list.

PRICES RANGE FROM 10/6 to 32/6

OBTAINABLE FROM LEADING STORES AND TOY DEALERS THROUGHOUT GREAT BRITAIN

THE ONLY AUTHORISED BRITISH REPRODUCTION OF "THE WORLD'S DARLING"—AND MADE SOLELY BY:—

RICHARDS SON & ALLWIN, LTD., GREAT BRIDGE, TIPTON, STAFFS.

Allwin produced all of the genuine Shirley Temple dolls that were made in England. This ad from a 1936 *Film Pictorial* magazine shows that there were 18 different outfits available for these dolls, ranging from a plain striped schoolgirl dress to the fancy *Little Colonel* dress. Marge Meisinger collection.

Genuine Shirley Temple doll from England, produced by Allwin. Shirley has a pressed cloth face with painted eyes and open mouth showing her teeth. She has a mohair wig in Shirley-style curls and is wearing the *Little Colonel* dress (missing the hat). It is a pajamas doll; the body is cloth and there are no legs (just an opening in the back of the dress in which a little girl could put her pajamas). Very hard to find. $2,000.00.

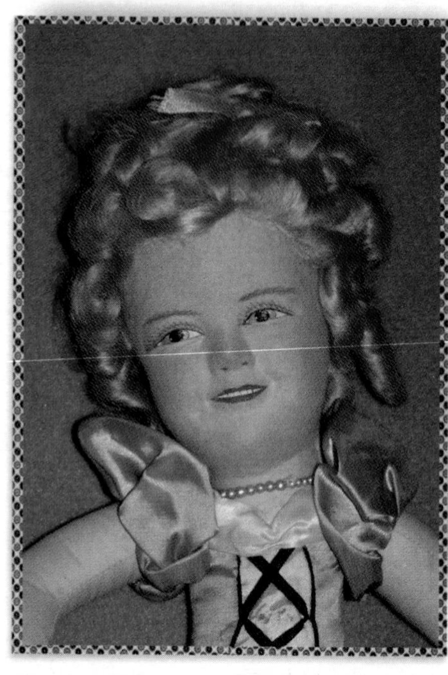

Close-up of the pressed cloth face of Allwin's version of the Shirley Temple doll. Notice the hand-painted detailing.

Another Allwin Shirley Temple doll, wearing a slightly different dress. This one has a pin on the front that reads "The World's Darling Genuine Shirley Temple British Doll." This doll is somewhat dirty. $1,600.00. Rachel Quigley collection.

12" doll made of celluloid, marked "SHIRLEY TEMPLE Poland" on the back of her head. Her blue eyes are stationary and she is wearing a dimity dress with matching hat. Her wig is mohair, a very light blonde with bangs. Though the face of this doll resembles Shirley Temple, the outfit and hairstyle do not. The Polish doll also came with a curled golden blonde mohair wig and wearing a red and white polka-dot dress that resembled one of Shirley's. $800.00.

Close-up of the face of the celluloid Shirley Temple doll from Poland.

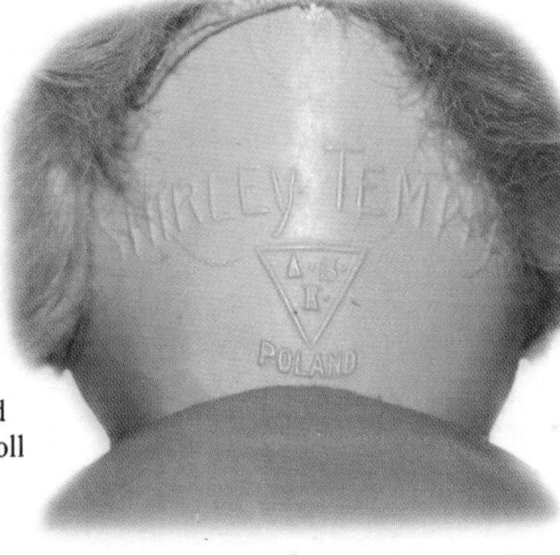

Close-up of the markings on the back of the celluloid Shirley Temple doll from Poland.

12" doll is very similar to the one made in Poland, with similar markings; however, the doll states on the back that it was made in Holland. Again, the face resembles Shirley Temple; however, the Dutch outfit is not a Shirley outfit and the dark brown hair is not Shirley's color. $800.00.

6" bisque doll was made in Japan and has very unusual sleep eyes. She is not marked "Shirley Temple" and is not authorized. $100.00. Marge Meisinger collection.

6" bisque Shirley Temple doll marked "Made in Japan." It is not marked "Shirley Temple" and may not be an authentic version, but it clearly was made to resemble her. These dolls are more common than many of the other foreign Shirley Temple dolls and may have been a cheaper import to the United States during the 1930s. $35.00.

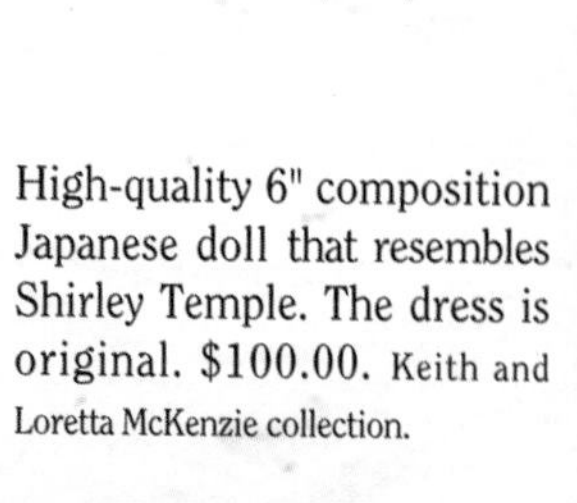

High-quality 6" composition Japanese doll that resembles Shirley Temple. The dress is original. $100.00. Keith and Loretta McKenzie collection.

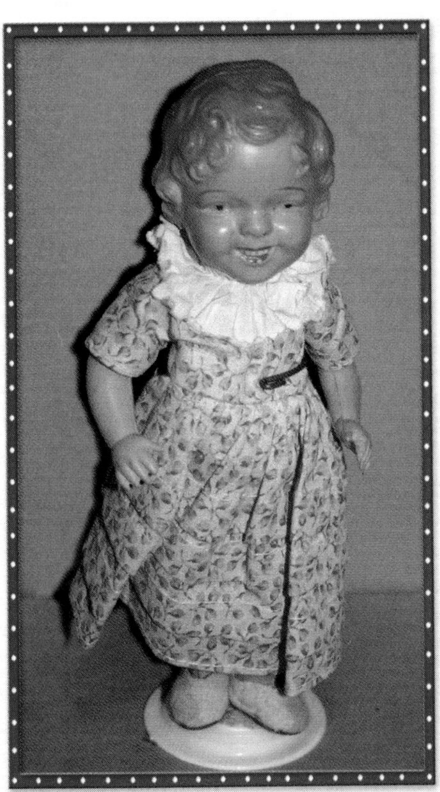

Small 7" celluloid doll that resembles Shirley Temple, most likely from Japan. The dress is not original. A very unusual find. $150.00. Courtesy of Kathy Evans, doll dealer.

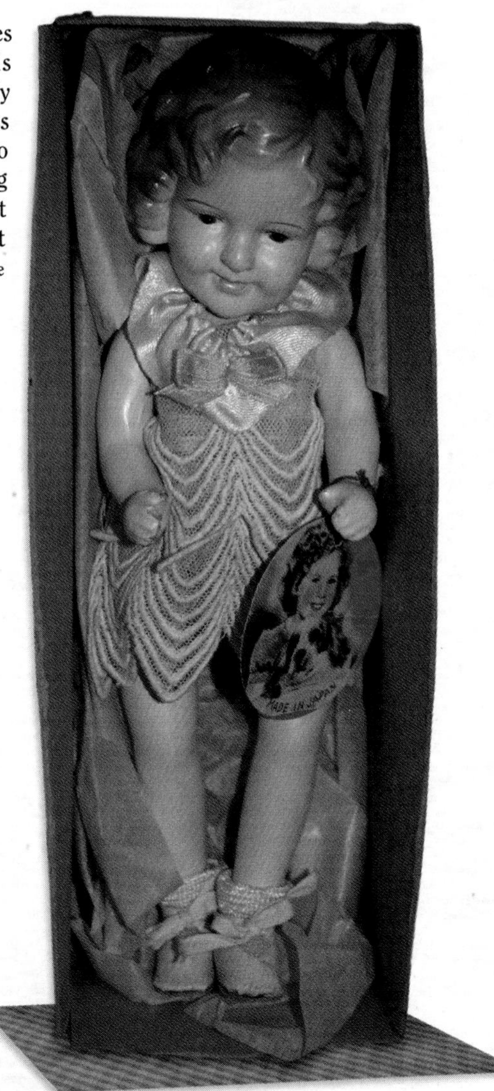

7" Japanese doll that resembles Shirley Temple. This doll is very unusual, because not only does it have the original dress and original box, but it also has a Shirley Temple hangtag stamped "Made in Japan" that clearly indicates it was meant to be Shirley. $300.00. Leslie Tannenbaum collection.

Tiny 4" bisque doll that resembles Shirley Temple is marked "Germany" on her back. Though she was found without clothes, she is now wearing an adorable *Curly Top* dress. $50.00. Marge Meisinger collection.

18" Shirley Temple doll made in Germany. She has blue eyes that open and close. She is marked "S.T. CB Germany" on the back of her head and was made by Carl Berger. This doll is wearing an Ideal pleated dress that is not original to her. $600.00 (because of condition).

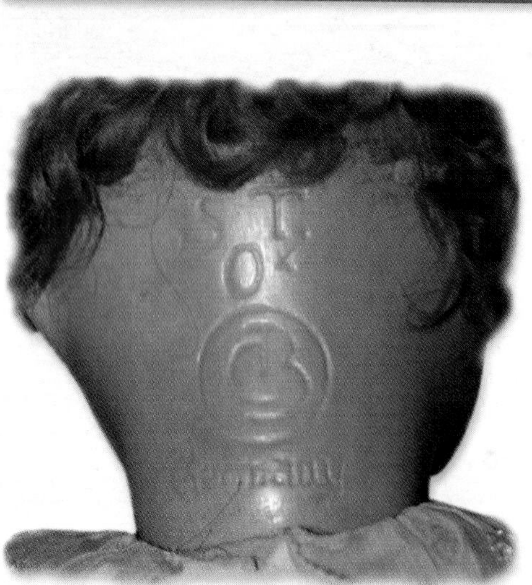

Markings on the back of the German Shirley Temple doll.

Small 13" German Shirley Temple doll by Carl Berger. Mint condition with original *Curly Top* outfit. $1,200.00. Rachel Quigley collection.

Mint-condition 22" German Shirley Temple doll from Carl Berger. All original outfit. Marked "CB" and "Germany" on the back of the head. $1,500.00.

16" Shirley Temple doll made in Germany (not by Carl Berger) of high-quality composition. Blue eyes (most of the foreign Shirley dolls had blue eyes, though Shirley herself had hazel and Shirley's mother insisted that the Ideal dolls have hazel) that sleep and flirt back and forth, an open mouth with teeth, and a blonde mohair wig. Shirley is wearing an organdy dress, most likely original. This doll is not marked, but is a genuine Shirley Temple doll. Interestingly enough, the quality of the composition is higher than that of the German dolls that were marked. $750.00. Marge Meisinger collection.

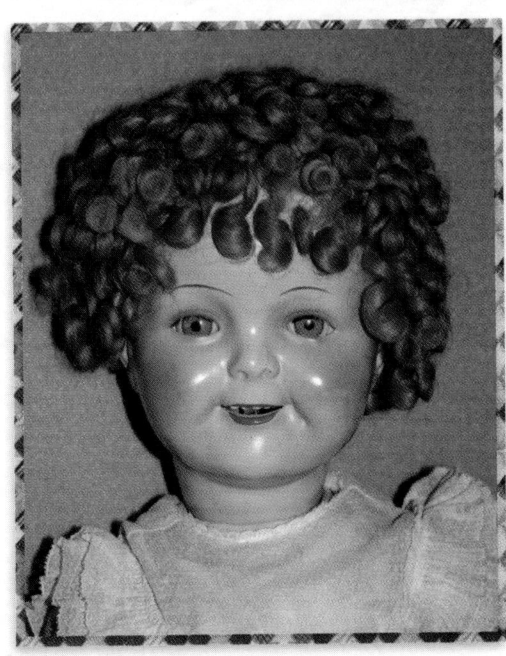

Close-up of this mint-condition German Shirley Temple doll.

Huge 28" Shirley Temple doll made in Germany. Wearing a Shirley Temple Nannette dress (for children) from the 1930s. Marked only with the size in centimeters ("71") on the back of the head. $1,500.00. Suzi Reed collection.

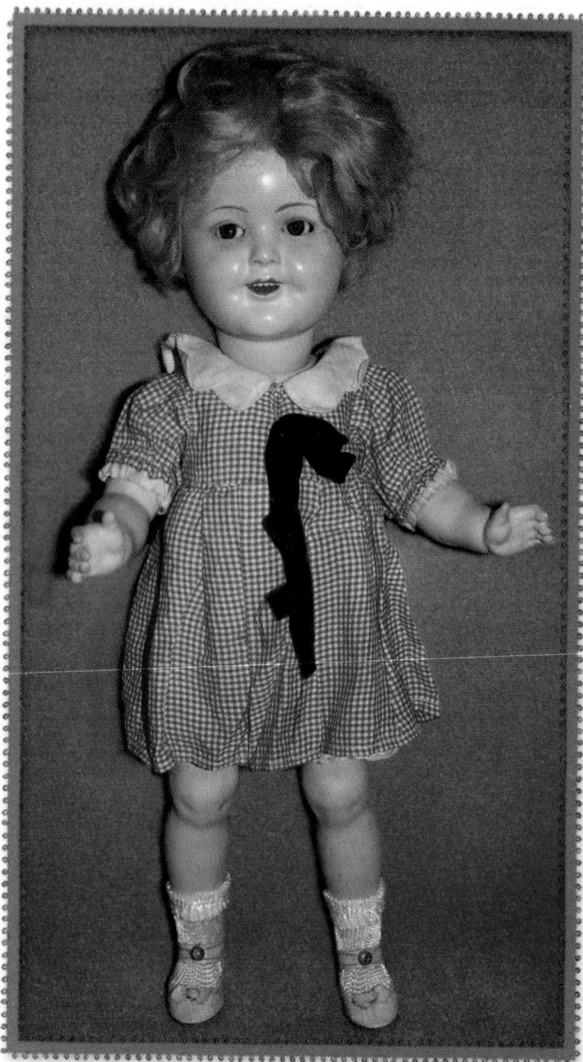

18" tall Shirley Temple doll was also made in Germany and is marked only with the size in centimeters on the back of her head. She has flirty sleep eyes and a mohair wig (which has been cut). She is wearing an original dress that very closely resembles the "Got Milk" dress from 1934. $600.00 (because of condition).

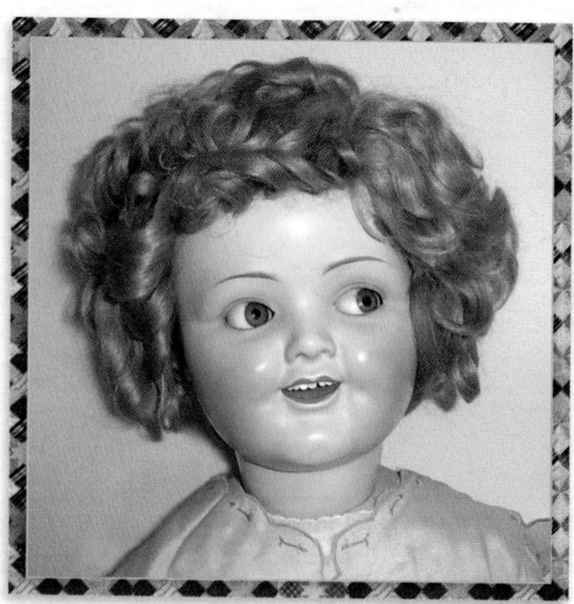

Close-up of the 28" tall German Shirley Temple doll. Suzi Reed collection.

13" Shirley Temple doll made in South America and sold in South and Central America as well as Mexico. It is believed that the Ideal doll molds were shipped down to South America. Dolls are made of composition and fully articulated. The facial coloring is much more distinct on this doll than on the American dolls, and she has blue eyes. The rayon tag on the dress is original and attached loosely to the bottom of the skirt (most likely to make it easy to remove). $1,200.00. Rita Dubas collection.

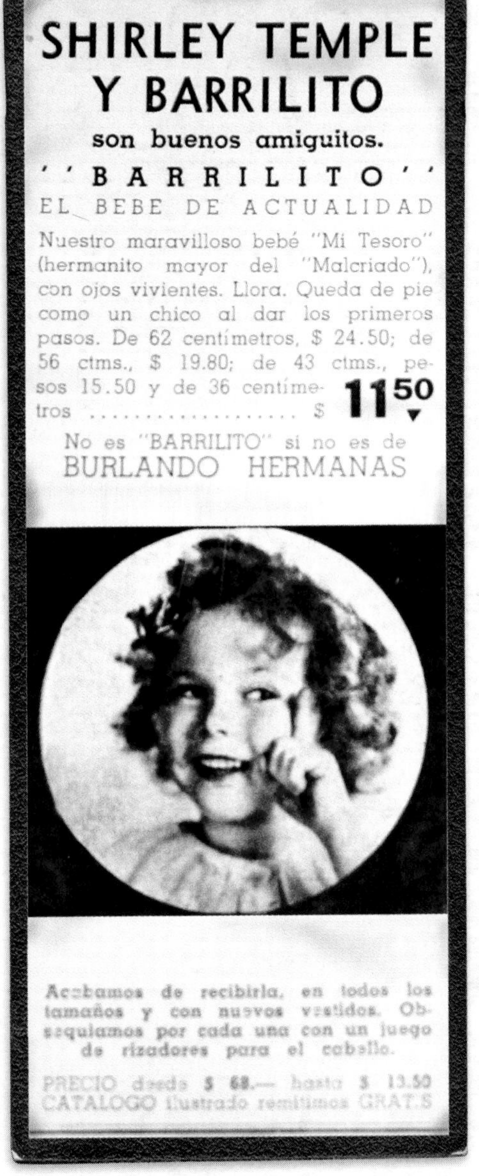

Rare ad for a Shirley Temple doll from Argentina. Marge Meisinger collection.

Close-up of the face of the South American Shirley Temple doll. Notice the differences in the facial features and eye color. Rita Dubas collection.

Chapter 5
Profiting from the Magic: Shirley Temple Look-alike Dolls

The Ideal Novelty and Toy Company was the exclusive authorized manufacturer of the Shirley Temple doll in the United States. When the Shirley Temple doll became popular, it was incredibly profitable for Ideal. The dolls were so successful that other doll companies wanted to capitalize on the profits as well, rushing to make their own versions of the Shirley Temple doll. Since they could not use the Shirley Temple name, nor the Shirley doll mold, they had to come up with their own creative names and make their own similar molds. Some of the names chosen were Bright Eyes, Miss Charming, Little Miss Movie, and The Movie Queen. All of these dolls were unmistakably Shirley, with chubby cheeks, golden curls, dimples, and outfits that were very similar to the ones that Shirley wore in her movies. The major distinction was that these dolls did not have the hazel eyes that the genuine Shirley Temple dolls had; Ideal had specially made the hazel eyes at Shirley's mother's request.

Since most toy companies that were producing dolls at the time made an attempt to create a version of the Shirley Temple doll, by 1935 Ideal was placing notices in sales catalogs and newspapers telling the public that Ideal produced the only genuine Shirley dolls and not to be fooled by the imitators. Ideal also launched many lawsuits against the other companies for violating Ideal's Shirley Temple doll copyright.

Perhaps the Madame Alexander doll company had the most creative way of avoiding copyright laws. In 1935, when Fox Films released **The Little Colonel**, Ideal produced its Shirley Temple dolls in outfits corresponding to the ones that Shirley wore in the movie. The Madame Alexander doll company copyrighted the book **The Little Colonel** by Anne Fellows Johnston. It was able to release its own official **Little Colonel** doll. This doll just happened to closely resemble Shirley, and the outfits were very similar to the ones that Shirley wore in the movie. The **Little Colonel** doll was very successful for Madame Alexander. Afterwards, Ideal bought the copyrights to all the books that Shirley's movies were based on. Despite Ideal's efforts to the contrary, the look-alike dolls were prevalent throughout the Shirley movie era.

Though the look-alike dolls did not have the beauty, details, or the quality workmanship of the Ideal Shirley Temple dolls, they did look similar and they were significantly cheaper than the genuine Ideal Shirley Temple dolls. Little girls all over America dreamed of having their own Shirley Temple doll. For families that could not afford the genuine Ideal version, the look-alike dolls were a very close alternative. Even today, many women mistake their look-alike dolls for the originals.

To add to the Shirley doll confusion, Ideal also used its Shirley doll molds to create other dolls. The three most well-known dolls made with the Shirley molds were the Marama doll, the Snow White doll, and the Cinderella doll. The Marama doll, also referred to as the "Hawaiian Shirley Temple doll," was not meant to resemble Shirley at all. It was modeled after a Hawaiian child from the 1937 movie **The Hurricane**. The doll had painted side-glancing eyes and a painted mouth. It wore a black yarn wig, a grass hula skirt, and flowered leis. The Snow White doll had a black mohair wig and dark painted features resembling the Shirley makeup dolls. It was made to correspond with the release of the Disney

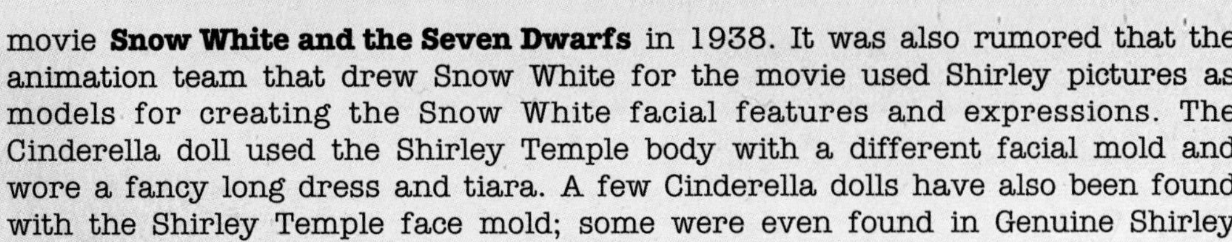

movie **Snow White and the Seven Dwarfs** in 1938. It was also rumored that the animation team that drew Snow White for the movie used Shirley pictures as models for creating the Snow White facial features and expressions. The Cinderella doll used the Shirley Temple body with a different facial mold and wore a fancy long dress and tiara. A few Cinderella dolls have also been found with the Shirley Temple face mold; some were even found in Genuine Shirley Temple boxes.

Because these three dolls were marked "SHIRLEY TEMPLE" on the backs of the head and/or backs, and closely resemble the Shirley dolls, they are very popular with Shirley Temple doll collectors.

After the Shirley doll was phased out, the Shirley doll molds were sold to other doll companies. During the late 1930s and early 1940s, quite a few dolls resembled the compo Shirley Temple dolls, and many even had the markings of the Shirley dolls.

An ad for the Miss Charming dolls from 1935 (notice that the button says "Little Miss Movie"; this was another name for the Miss Charming doll). This doll was offered in many sizes and outfits and cost noticeably less than the Ideal genuine Shirley Temple doll. Marge Meisinger collection.

17" Miss Charming doll, one of the prettiest look-alike dolls. All-composition body, golden mohair wig, blue tin eyes that open and close, and an outfit that closely resembles one that Shirley wore in her movies. This dress looks very similar to the original triangle dress from 1935. $250.00. Loretta Beilstein collection.

17" tall Miss Charming Shirley Temple look-alike with painted tin eyes. Wearing a plaid schoolgirl dress very similar to the *Bright Eyes* Shirley dress. Also shown are punch card games from the 1930s, with pictures of the winning prize — a Miss Charming doll. $200.00. Suzi Reed collection.

Close-up of Miss Charming.
Suzi Reed collection.

20" Shirley Temple look-alike doll by the Arranbee Doll Company. She is a Miss Charming doll. Marked "Nancy" on the back of her head, she has glass eyes (only some of the larger Miss Charming dolls had glass eyes). Her dress resembles the Shirley dancing dress and is shown in the Miss Charming ad; she also has her "Little Miss Movie" pin. $250.00. Suzi Reed collection.

Close-up of the "Nancy" doll. Suzi Reed collection.

Some of the different original pins for the Shirley Temple look-alike dolls. $30.00 each. Janet Mitchell collection.

20" unmarked look-alike Shirley doll, mint in her original plain brown box, wearing a pink pleated dress that very closely resembles the one that Ideal produced for the genuine Shirley dolls. She also has a bright blue fake fur coat and a handbag. She has a golden mohair wig and blue tin eyes with painted and hair upper lashes and no lower lashes. She is most likely the Bright Star doll produced by Horseman Dolls, Inc. $600.00 (because of the pristine condition). Courtesy of Peggy Ann Bealefield, Doodlebug Dolls.

This is a close-up of the face of the Shirley look-alike. Courtesy of Peggy Ann Bealefield, Doodlebug Dolls.

This ad from 1935 shows a similar look-alike doll for sale. Notice that this 13" doll cost $1.49. The 13" Shirley Temple doll sold for $3.00 at the time. Marge Meisinger collection.

This ad from the 1936 Larkin catalog features a similar look-alike doll in a dress that very closely models Shirley's *Stand Up and Cheer* dress. Marge Meisinger collection.

17" Shirley look-alike wearing a dress and hat very reminiscent of the *Stand Up and Cheer* outfit. This is the doll shown in the Larkin ad (above right). $200.00. Loretta Beilstein collection.

Another ad from the 1936 Larkin catalog featured a large Shirley look-alike doll with composition head, shoulder plate, arms, and legs, and a cloth body. If a doll looks like Shirley and is unmarked and has a cloth body, it is a look-alike. The Shirley babies had cloth bodies, but they were marked "Shirley Temple." Marge Meisinger collection.

18" cloth doll made by the Blossom Doll Company. She has a cloth body, a molded cloth face with dimples and painted features, and a mohair wig. She is unmarked and is wearing a cowboy outfit similar to the 1936 Texas Centennial cowboy outfit. Another cloth Shirley look-alike (not pictured) was made by the Wacker Manufacturing Company and was known as Our Girl Shirley. $400.00.

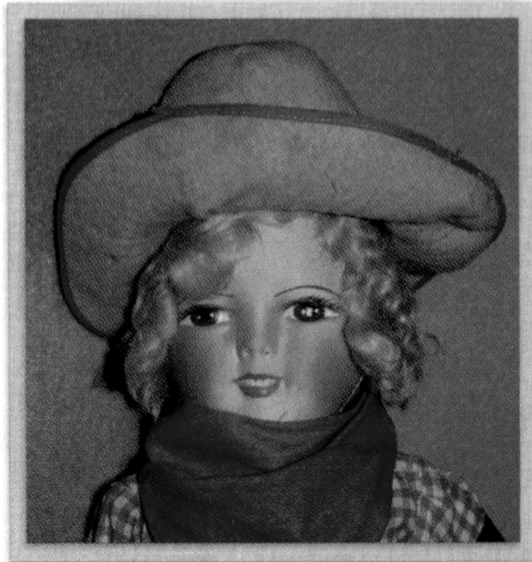

Close-up of the Blossom doll.

Close-up of the Reliable bride doll. Keith and Loretta McKenzie collection.

20" Shirley look-alike by the Reliable Doll Company of Canada. Wearing original (though wrinkled) bride outfit. $300.00. Keith and Loretta McKenzie collection.

18" *Little Colonel* doll from Madame Alexander, wearing the military outfit. Looks very similar to the outfit that Shirley wore in the movie. $400.00. Rachel Quigley collection.

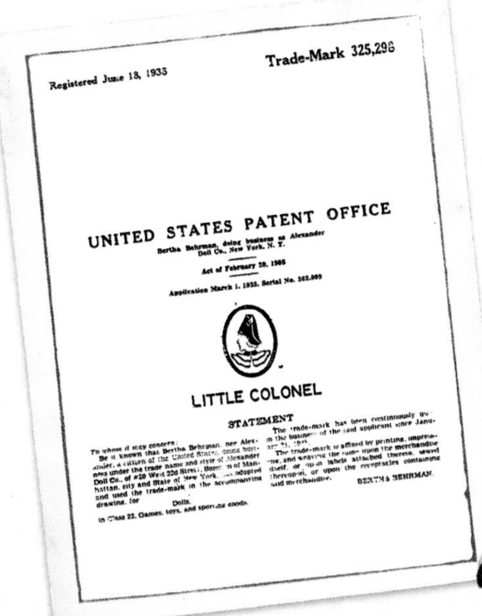

Registered June 18, 1935 — Trade-Mark 325,296

UNITED STATES PATENT OFFICE

Bertha Behrman, doing business as Alexander Doll Co., New York, N. Y.

Act of February 20, 1905

Application March 1, 1935, Serial No. 362,009

LITTLE COLONEL

STATEMENT

To whom it may concern:

Be it known that Bertha Behrman, nee Alexander, a citizen of the United States, doing business under the trade name and style of Alexander Doll Co., of #20 West 33d Street, Borough of Manhattan, city and State of New York, has adopted and used the trade-mark in the accompanying drawing, for Dolls, in Class 22, Games, toys, and sporting goods.

The trade-mark has been continuously used in the business of the said applicant since January 21, 1935.

The trade-mark is affixed by printing, impressing, and weaving the same upon the merchandise itself, or upon labels attached thereto, sewed thereupon, or upon the receptacles containing said merchandise.

BERTHA BEHRMAN.

Patent that Madame Alexander obtained to make *Little Colonel* dolls. Marge Meisinger collection.

In 1935, the Alexander Doll Company obtained the copyright for the Anne Fellows Johnston book *The Little Colonel*. It proceeded to produce its own version of the *Little Colonel* doll, which wore outfits that closely resembled Shirley's outfits in the movie. This doll is wearing the Alexander version of the fancy long organdy dress. Very rare. $400.00. Courtesy of Joan Kaaihue, doll dealer, Kaaih7@aol.com.

Close-up of the Madame Alexander *Little Colonel* doll. Courtesy of Joan Kaaihue, doll dealer, Kaaih7@aol.com.

20" tall black Shirley temple look-alike, not marked. All original, with organdy dress in Shirley style. $150.00. Iva Mae Jones collection.

SNOW WHITE

Beautiful Dolls 13 And 18½ in. Tall

The beautiful Princess we all loved in the picture has come to life in these two gorgeous new dolls. The doll shown above at the left is 18½ in. high, dressed in a court gown of satin trimmed net over taffeta, with silk mantle. She has real hair and lashes, sweetly goes to sleep when you lay her down. The 13-inch size is shown above at the right. That doll has flirting eyes that roll from side to side; she also goes to sleep when you put her to bed. Real hair and lashes; pearly teeth. She is dressed in a taffeta gown decorated with her friends, the Seven Dwarfs, and her forest animal friends; she wears a jacket of Royal Red velvet, trimmed with a bouquet. Each doll has movable head, arms and legs, and is completely and beautifully dressed, exactly as shown.

K26075 13 In. High, PRICE.................... **$4.20**
K26076 18½ In. High, PRICE.................... **9.50**

In 1938, Ideal began advertising its Snow White doll. Marge Meisinger collection.

11" Snow White doll with the Shirley Temple mold, marked "Shirley Temple" on head and back. Black mohair wig and pale paint color. Her facial features are darker than those on the Shirley Temple doll. Her dress has a velvet bodice and taffeta skirt with screen-printed dwarfs on it, button closure in back, and an "Ideal" tag. This dress came in either red or blue velvet, with matching velvet cape. $800.00. Rachel Quigley collection.

18" Snow White doll was made by Ideal in honor of the Disney movie *Snow White and the Seven Dwarfs* from 1937. She is marked "Shirley Temple" on her back and is unmarked on her head. The head mold on the larger Snow White dolls is not the Shirley mold. All original. $650.00. Keith and Loretta McKenzie collection.

In 1937, the Shirley Temple doll mold was used to produce a Hawaiian girl doll resembling a child who costarred in the movie *Hurricane*. Because it used the Shirley mold, this doll is often sought after by Shirley Temple collectors. Marked "Shirley Temple" on her head and back. She is painted golden brown and has painted brown side-glancing eyes and a painted open mouth. She has a black yarn wig and a Hawaiian grass skirt and leis, and flowers in her hair. The doll was made in a number of different sizes; shown are the 18" and 13". $650.00 each. Iva Mae Jones collection.

Larger 18" Cinderella doll, with the Shirley face mold. Very unusual to find a Shirley head mold on a Cinderella doll. $800.00. Rachel Quigley collection.

13" Cinderella doll by Ideal using the Shirley Temple body mold and a different head mold. Marked "Shirley Temple" on her back. This doll came with a number of different dress designs. All original. $350.00. Keith and Loretta McKenzie collection.

18" Cinderella doll using the Shirley Temple body mold. $350.00. Iva Mae Jones collection.

13" Cinderella doll that came in a Shirley Temple box. $450.00. Rosemary Dent collection.

Close-up of the Cinderella face shows a close resemblance to the Shirley Temple face mold. Rosemary Dent collection.

Mollye Goldman Outfits

In the mid-1930s, Mollye Goldman designed all of the outfits for the Shirley Temple doll. She also fashioned her own doll creations, tagged "Created by Molly-'es." These were very well-made outfits for the composition dolls of the day. Most of her designs fit the Shirley Temple doll perfectly, and many closely resemble the original Shirley Temple outfits. Because of this, oftentimes Shirley doll collectors also collect Molly-'es clothing. The more a Molly-'es outfit resembles an original Shirley outfit, the more valuable it is. This is a picture of an original Molly-'es display from the 1930s. Notice the Shirley Temple clothing rack at the right-hand side. Marge Meisinger collection.

Registered Oct. 6, 1936

Trade-Mark 339,303

UNITED STATES PATENT OFFICE

Molly-'es Doll Outfitters, Inc., Philadelphia, Pa.

Act of February 20, 1905

Application April 1, 1935, Serial No. 363,290

HOLLYWOOD CINEMA
FASHIONS
FOR DOLLS

STATEMENT

To the Commissioner of Patents:

Molly-'es Doll Outfitters, Inc., a corporation duly organized under the laws of the State of Pennsylvania and located at Philadelphia, Pennsylvania, and doing business at 2139-45 S. 48th Street, Philadelphia, Pa., has adopted and used the trade-mark shown in the accompanying drawing, without waiving any of applicant's common law rights, exclusive use of the words appearing on the drawing, with the exception of the name "Molly-'es" is disclaimed apart from the mark shown, for DOLLS AND DOLL CLOTHES, in Class 22, Games, toys, and sporting goods, and presents herewith five specimens showing the trade-mark as actually used by applicant upon the goods, and requests that the same be registered in the United States Patent Office in accordance with the act of February 20, 1905. The trade-mark has been continuously used and applied to said goods in applicant's business since March, 1935. The trade-mark is applied or affixed to the goods, or to the packages containing the same, by placing thereon a printed label on which the trade-mark is shown.

The undersigned hereby appoints Lester L. Sargent, of 1115 K Street, N. W., Washington, D. C., its attorney to prosecute this application for registration, to make alterations and amendments therein, to receive the certificate and to transact all business in the Patent Office connected therewith, and to represent it in any interference, opposition or cancellation proceedings.

MOLLY-'ES DOLL OUTFITTERS, INC.,
By MEYER GOLDMAN,
Pres.

Original Molly-'es patent for Hollywood Cinema Fashions for Dolls, from 1936. Marge Meisinger collection.

Printed organdy dress with large Peter Pan collar, tagged "Molly-'es," displayed on an original Molly-'es hanger. $40.00. Hanger, $15.00. Keith and Loretta McKenzie collection.

Coat and hat set tagged "Molly-'es." $50.00. Keith and Loretta McKenzie collection.

A very Shirley-looking red dress with matching hat, tagged "Molly-'es." $50.00. Keith and Loretta McKenzie collection.

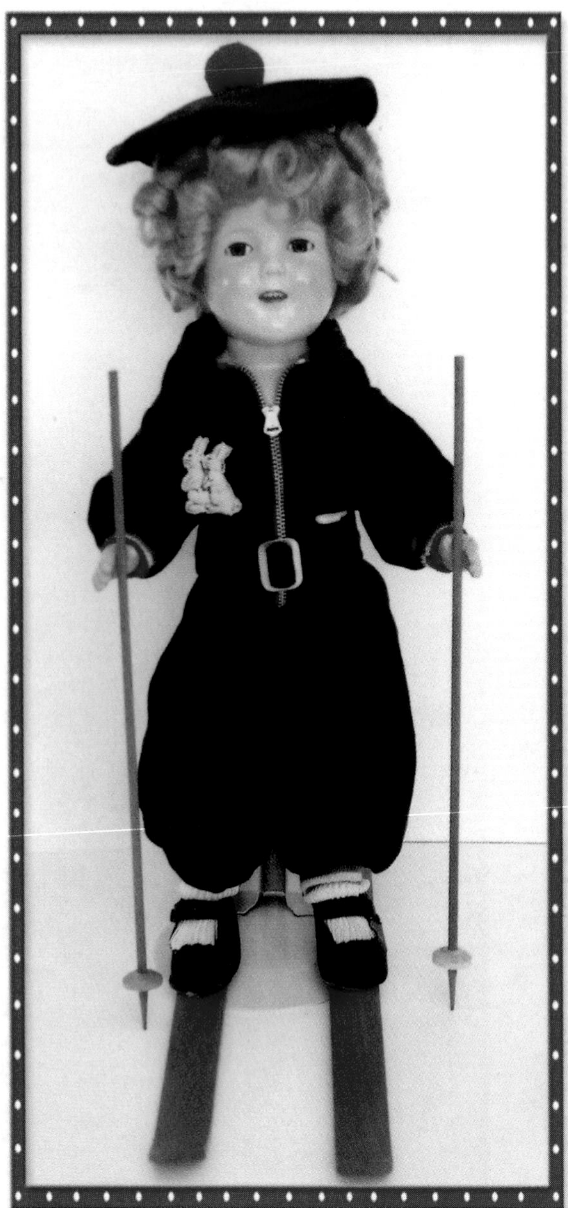

17" Shirley wearing a high-quality Molly-'es tagged snowsuit that is almost identical to the genuine Shirley snowsuit; suit also includes matching hat. Skis and poles were added later. $1,000.00 and up. Outfit only, $600.00 and up. Rachel Quigley collection.

Blue and white school dress, tagged "Molly-'es." $30.00. Keith and Loretta McKenzie collection.

Molly-'es tagged snowsuit, resembles a very rare Ideal Shirley Temple tagged one (see chapter 2). $100.00. Keith and Loretta McKenzie collection.

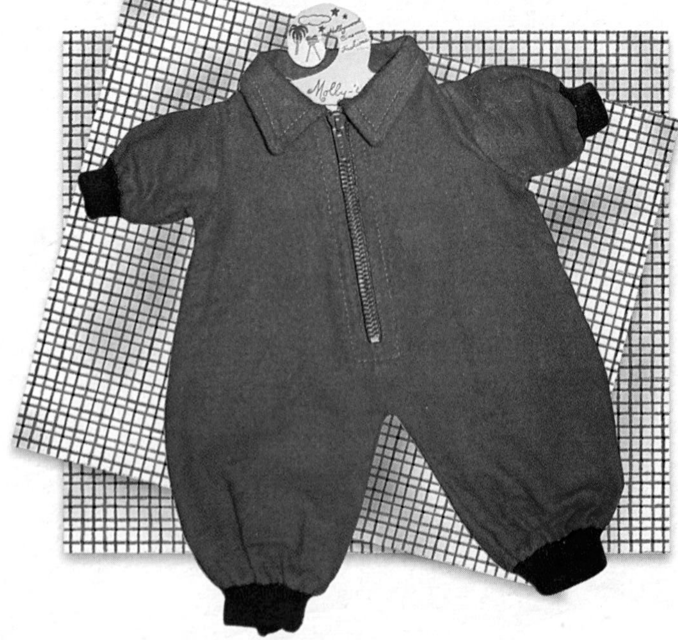

18" Shirley wearing a fancy riding outfit tagged "Molly-'es" (with original hangtag). Outfit comes complete with coat, pants, hat, scarf, and mittens. $550.00. Outfit only, $200.00. Keith and Loretta McKenzie collection.

18" Shirley doll wearing a tagged Molly-'es riding outfit with matching hat. $550.00. Outfit alone, $200.00. Rachel Quigley collection.

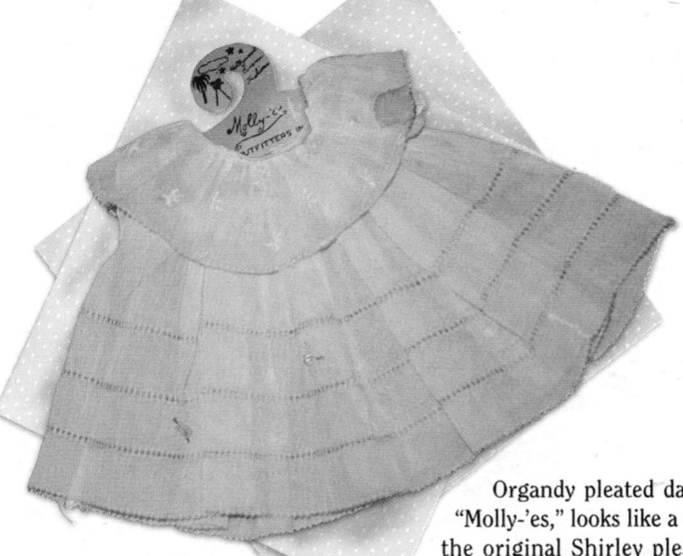

Organdy pleated dancing dress, tagged "Molly-'es," looks like a very fancy version of the original Shirley pleated dancing dress. $150.00. Keith and Loretta McKenzie collection.

Gorgeous quilted coat with lined interior and tagged "Molly-'es." Extravaluable because it looks similar to a coat that Shirley herself wore in publicity stills. $300.00. Lorna Erb collection.

Another tagged riding outfit by Molly-'es. $150.00. Lorna Erb collection.

Pink checked school dress tagged "Molly-'es." $30.00. Keith and Loretta McKenzie collection.

Cute red sundress with sailboats on it, by Molly-'es. $40.00. Lorna Erb collection.

Very unusual green riding outfit by Molly-'es. $125.00. Lorna Erb collection.

Organdy party dress with matching bonnet, tagged "Molly-'es." $65.00. Keith and Loretta McKenzie collection.

20" Shirley Temple doll wearing a tagged Molly-'es dress that is made of the same coin-dotted fabric that Shirley's *Stand Up and Cheer* dress was made of. $500.00. Outfit only, $150.00. Rachel Quigley collection.

Party dress with the same coin-dotted fabric that the first Shirley Temple *Stand Up and Cheer* dresses had, tagged "Molly-'es." $100.00. Keith and Loretta McKenzie collection.

Molly-'es tagged coat with matching hat and rabbit-fur muff. $80.00. Lorna Erb collection.

Molly-'es tagged wool coat. $40.00. Keith and Loretta McKenzie collection.

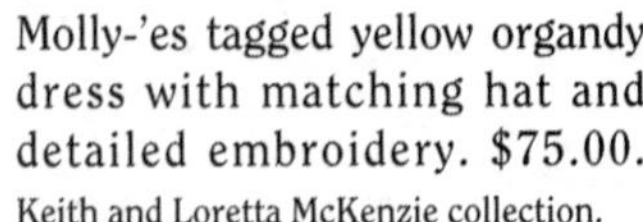

Molly-'es tagged yellow organdy dress with matching hat and detailed embroidery. $75.00. Keith and Loretta McKenzie collection.

Coat and matching hat, tagged "Molly-'es." $50.00. Keith and Loretta McKenzie collection.

Adorable nightgown, bathrobe, and matching slippers by Molly-'es. $80.00. Lorna Erb collection.

Blue striped school dress, tagged "Molly-'es." It has also been found with matching hat. $30.00. Keith and Loretta McKenzie collection.

Molly-'es tagged pink coat with matching hat. $60.00. Keith and Loretta McKenzie collection.

Molly-'es tagged "Little Colonel" dress. Exactly like the original Shirley outfit. $500.00. Lorna Erb collection.

Beautiful printed organdy fancy party dress, tagged "Molly-'es," with matching bonnet and in the original Molly-'es outfit box. Fits the baby Shirley doll perfectly. $150.00. Keith and Loretta McKenzie collection.

This poncho and umbrella set is often advertised as original Shirley; however, it is not. A similar plaid raincoat and hat set has been found tagged "Molly-'es," but this poncho is not tagged. $35.00. Iva Mae Jones collection.

Molly-'es tagged embroidered chick dress on a 13" Shirley Temple doll. Came in either red or blue. This dress is very rare and sought after, because it is similar to one of Shirley's own dresses. $650.00. Outfit only, $225.00 and up. Iva Mae Jones collection.

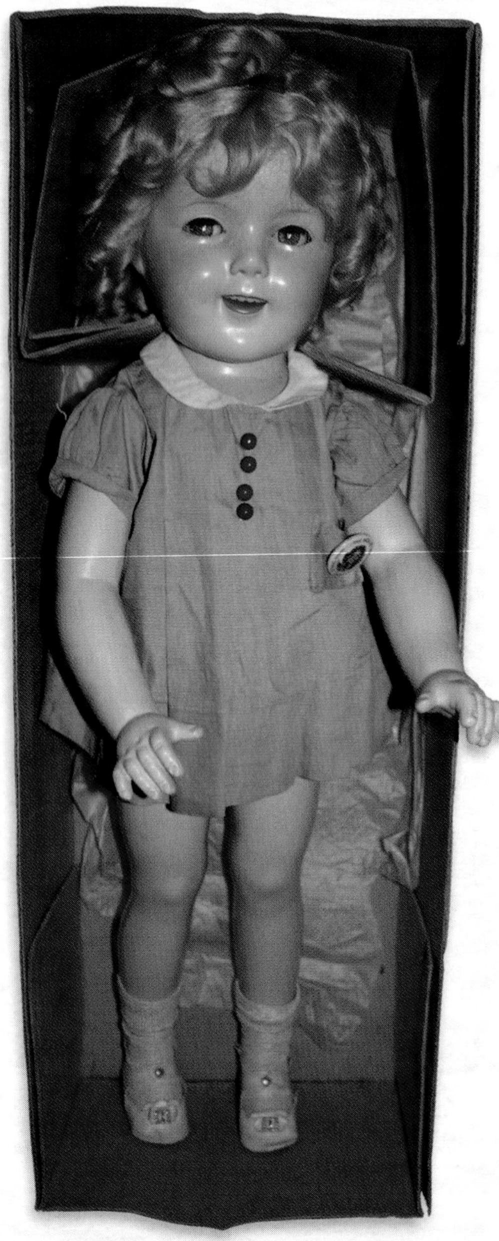

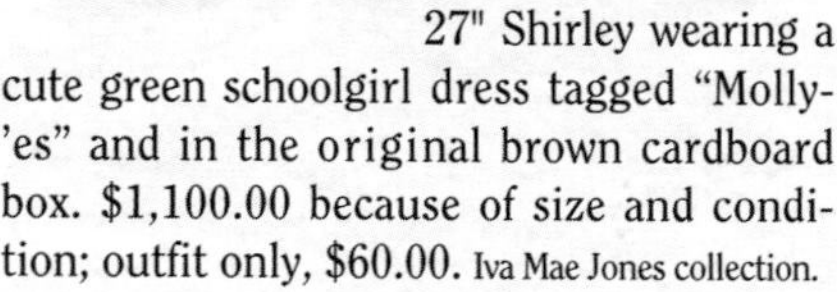

27" Shirley wearing a cute green schoolgirl dress tagged "Molly-'es" and in the original brown cardboard box. $1,100.00 because of size and condition; outfit only, $60.00. Iva Mae Jones collection.

Molly-'es tagged taffetta and netting dancing dress that is very similar to the original Shirley *Curly Top* pleated dancing dress. Shown on an 18" prototype Shirley Temple doll. $750.00. Outfit only, $150.00. Keith and Loretta McKenzie collection.

22" Shirley wearing a cute Molly-'es schoolgirl dress. $500.00. Outfit only, $80.00. Iva Mae Jones collection.

17" Shirley doll wearing an outfit that looks exactly like the rare "Littlest Rebel" dress. It is not Molly-'es, but it is definitely a Shirley look-alike. $700.00. Outfit only, $400.00. Rachel Quigley collection.

18" Shirley wearing a Molly-'es tagged sailor playsuit. $400.00. Outfit only, $60.00. Rachel Quigley collection.

Very sought-after Molly-'es tagged dress that resembles the original Shirley military outfit from *The Little Colonel*. Shown on a 13" doll. Doll in dress, $700.00. Outfit only, $250.00. Iva Mae Jones collection.

Composition was made of pressed sawdust and had characteristics similar to those of wood. It would crack, craze, and/or bubble under different conditions. Finding a Shirley Temple doll in mint condition, with clear eyes, bright coloring, and no crazing, is very difficult. This is the reason the mint dolls are so much more valuable than dolls in good condition. When you buy a Shirley Temple doll, one of the most important things to do is to make sure that the condition of the doll when you bought it is either maintained or even improved a bit.

Wear from play, along with changes in temperature and humidity levels, can flaw the composition of the Shirley Temple doll. Wear often signifies that a doll has been loved over the years. It can result in matted or brushed-out doll curls (or even cut hair), faded coloring, paint rubs to the joints and appendages, and broken fingers or toes. Changes in temperature and changes in or extreme humidity levels can do even more damage. Even small changes in temperature can cause the fine-line crazing and cloudy eyes that are often found on even the best dolls. Excessive changes can result in cracks to the composition itself; large cracks usually have to be fixed at a doll hospital.

The most frustrating flaw to the composition Shirley Temple dolls is paint bubbling. A paint bubble is a small separation, or "lift," between the composition and the paint of the doll. Bubbling can occur because of small flaws created when the doll was produced at the factory. It often occurs on the face, at the dimples or the inside of the eyes. Paint bubbling distorts the features of the doll itself, which takes away from the detailed beauty of the doll's expression. It often occurs even on the dolls that are in the best condition. Unfortunately, there are no easy fixes for it. If the doll is otherwise in good condition, it is best to leave the doll in its original condition with the paint bubbling.

There are a few very easy-to-follow suggestions for keeping the composition Shirley Temple dolls beautiful. First, make sure that the room in which you store your Shirley dolls is kept at a constant temperature; usually 68°F to 72°F is best. Second, be sure that an air-conditioning vent is not blowing directly on the Shirley dolls. Third, keep the dolls out of direct sunlight; this can fade the coloring of the hair and paint. It is easiest to just keep the blinds or curtains in the room shut. Fourth, the dolls should be enclosed in a vented glass or plastic case to keep them shielded from dust and dirt. Fifth, try to keep the humidity of the room constant. High humidity is a big problem for my dolls. My solution was a dehumidifier, which I simply keep at the normal humidity setting. If you live in a dry location, you may want to do the same with a humidifier in the room. Sixth, never smoke near your dolls. These suggestions should preserve your dolls for years to come.

Though some collectors can afford the most pristine Shirley Temple dolls, such dolls are not affordable to everyone. A few easy tips can turn a reasonably priced Shirley Temple doll into a wonderful displayable doll that appears to be in excellent condition. There are, however, two criteria such dolls must meet. First, you do not want a doll with a lot of facial paint bubbling. Second, you do not want a doll with excessive cracks on the face. Personally, I focus on the face of the doll itself. I don't mind missing toes (they can be covered with shoes), missing fingers (they can be rebuilt), or even some cracking to the body (it can be hidden with clothes). Over the next few pages, I will go over some very quick fixes that can help make your Shirley Temple dolls look their best.

These quick fixes are not solutions for every problem that you may come across with a Shirley Temple doll; more detailed repairs should be done at a reputable doll hospital (see appendix). If you need to take a doll to a doll hospital, be sure to ask to see before and after pictures of other dolls that have been restored there before you leave your Shirley Temple doll. Always try to have your restorations done by a place that first tries to keep the doll as close to the original as possible. Dolls should only be restored as a last resort; original condition is always better in everything but the most extreme cases.

In the following pictures, we are looking at the doll face; if there was significant damage to the body of a doll, the price would go down accordingly. 22" Shirley Temple doll is in mint condition (10), with no crazing, no paint bubbling, and clear eyes. Also notice the very rosy coloring, original paint, and matte finish to the compo. Her wig is completely in the original curl set. Without clothes, this doll is worth $1,500.00. Larger dolls are worth more than smaller dolls in general (except for the 11", which is more rare and valuable).

Condition Up Close

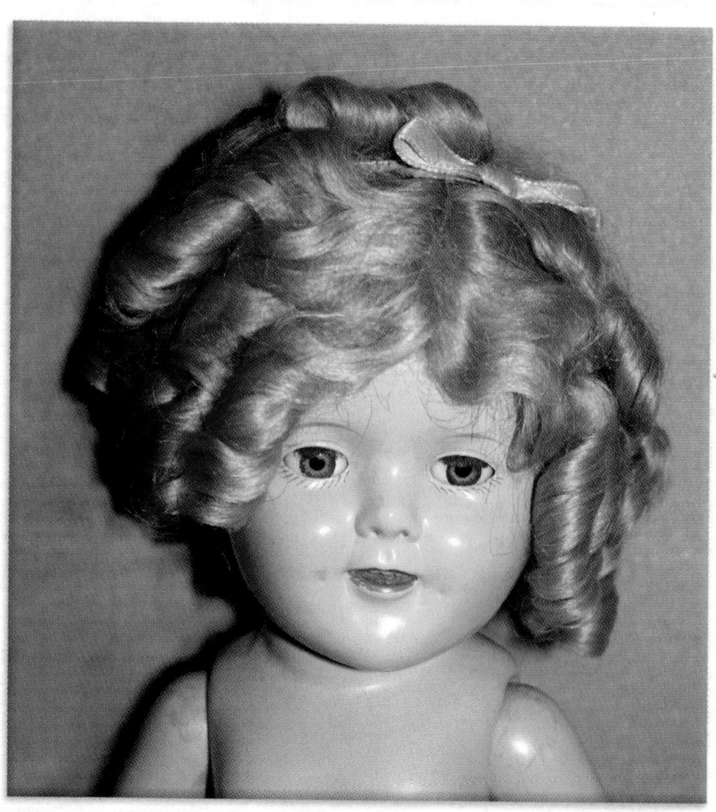

16" Shirley Temple doll is in near-mint condition (9+), with almost no crazing and clear eyes. Her coloring is not as rosy as it was originally (though it could be enhanced; see Quick Fixes), but her wig is in the original curl set. She is less valuable than the preceding doll but still very close to mint and is very rare. This doll, without clothes, is valued at $800.00.

This Shirley Temple doll is in excellent condition (8+), with few light craze lines. Her eyes were cloudy, but have been enhanced (see pp. 125 – 126) so that they now look clear. She has good coloring and original facial paint. Her wig is a bit messy but is mostly in the original curl set. Most values in this book assume dolls are in this condition or better. Without clothes, she is worth approximately $450.00. Notice how much a doll depreciates between mint condition and excellent condition.

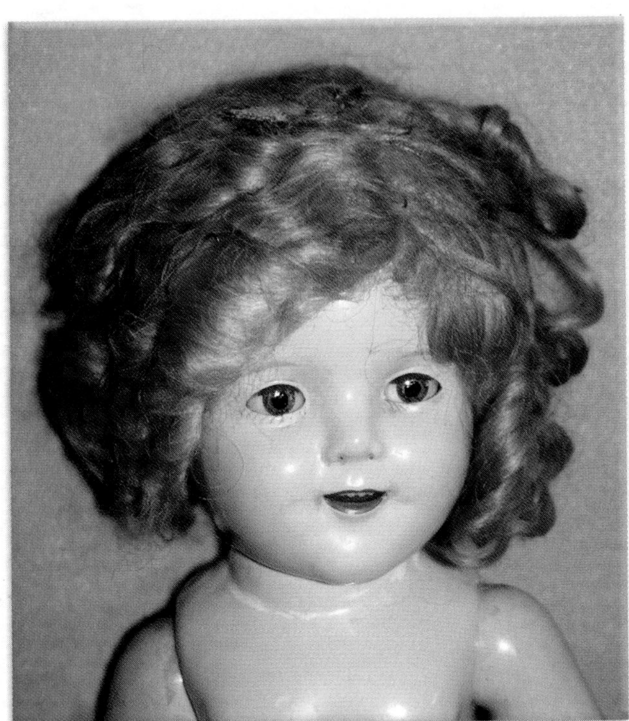

18" Shirley Temple doll in very good condition (6 – 7). She has light crazing, or superficial cracking, to her face paint and over her entire body, and cloudy eyes (which have been enhanced to look clear; see pp. 125 – 126) that have yellowed slightly. She also has a small amount of paint bubbling around her dimple. Her coloring is not very rosy, but she has her original facial paint. Without clothes, she is worth approximately $250.00.

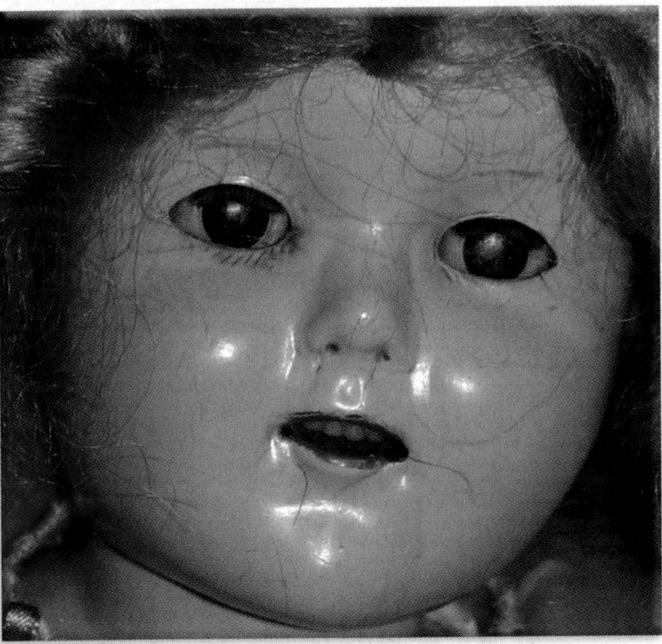

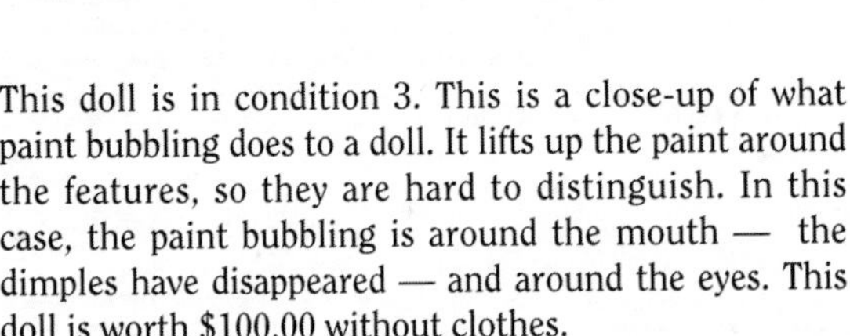

This doll is in condition 3. This is a close-up of what paint bubbling does to a doll. It lifts up the paint around the features, so they are hard to distinguish. In this case, the paint bubbling is around the mouth — the dimples have disappeared — and around the eyes. This doll is worth $100.00 without clothes.

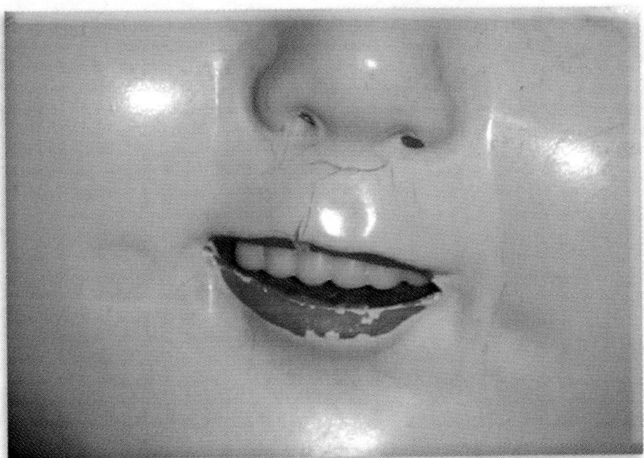

Another example of paint bubbling around the mouth.

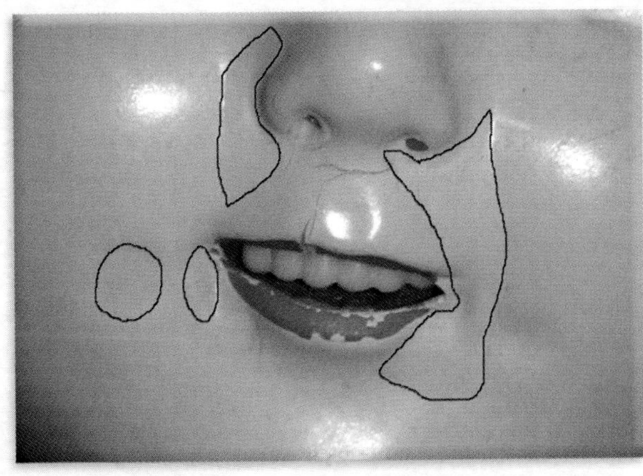

The black lines show where the paint bubbling is located.

13" Shirley Temple doll in good condition (5 – 6). She has allover light crazing, superficial cracking of the paint of the doll likely caused by the composition expanding and contracting over time. She also has cloudy eyes. Her coloring is not very rosy, but she does have most of her original facial paint. Without clothes, she would be worth approximately $150.00 (worth less than some other dolls because of her small size).

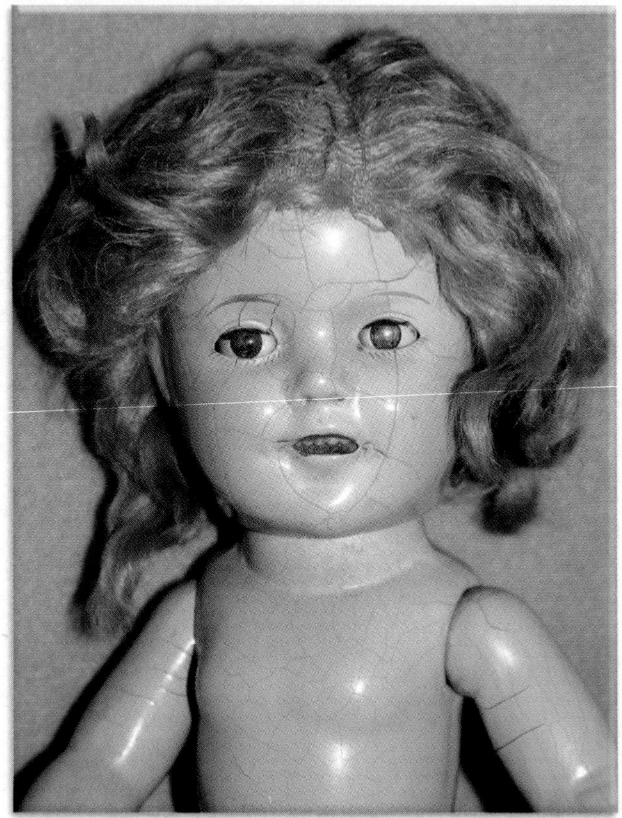

13" Shirley Temple doll in poor condition (2 – 3). She has crazing, cracking, and cloudy eyes. Her wig is original; however, it has been cut. Without clothes, she is worth approximately $100.00. It would be appropriate to have a doll that looks like this completely restored to her original beauty.

This unusual Shirley baby is in fair condition (3 – 4). She has no paint bubbling. However, she has a lot of crazing, a cloudy eye, and a crack over the cloudy eye. The crazing can be well hidden (see p. 129) with a $1.00 colored pencil. In this photo, half of the crazing has been concealed so that you can see the difference. Quick fixes can increase the value of this doll by at least $200.00.

16" Shirley Temple doll that has been restored. She also has an appropriate replaced mohair wig. This is a good restoration, and the paint closely resembles the original paint. Without clothes, this doll is valued at $300.00.

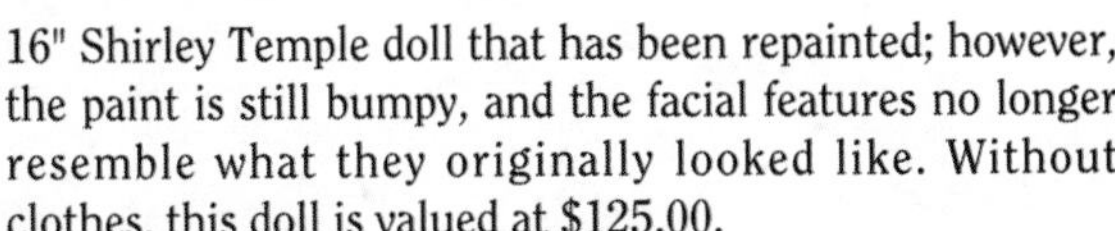

16" Shirley Temple doll that has been repainted; however, the paint is still bumpy, and the facial features no longer resemble what they originally looked like. Without clothes, this doll is valued at $125.00.

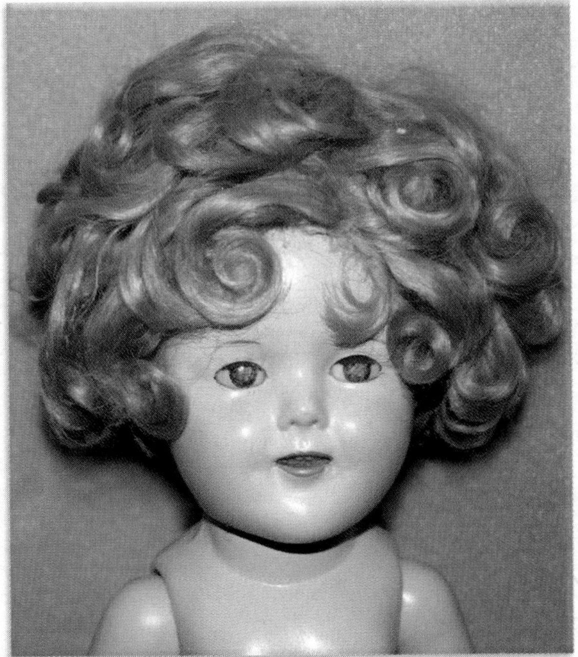

13" Shirley Temple doll that has been restored. The restoration is not a good one. Shirley is yellow, her eyes don't look right, and her synthetic wig does not look anything like the original. Without clothes, this doll is valued at $75.00.

Quick Fixes for the Shirley Temple Dolls

Quick Fix #1

The products required to fix up this Shirley Temple doll include bobby pins, pen, comb, clear nail polish, black and yellow acrylic paint; red, yellow, and brown oil paint; cotton Q-tips, Elmer's wood filler, Nivea cream, replica pin, outfit, shoes, and socks.

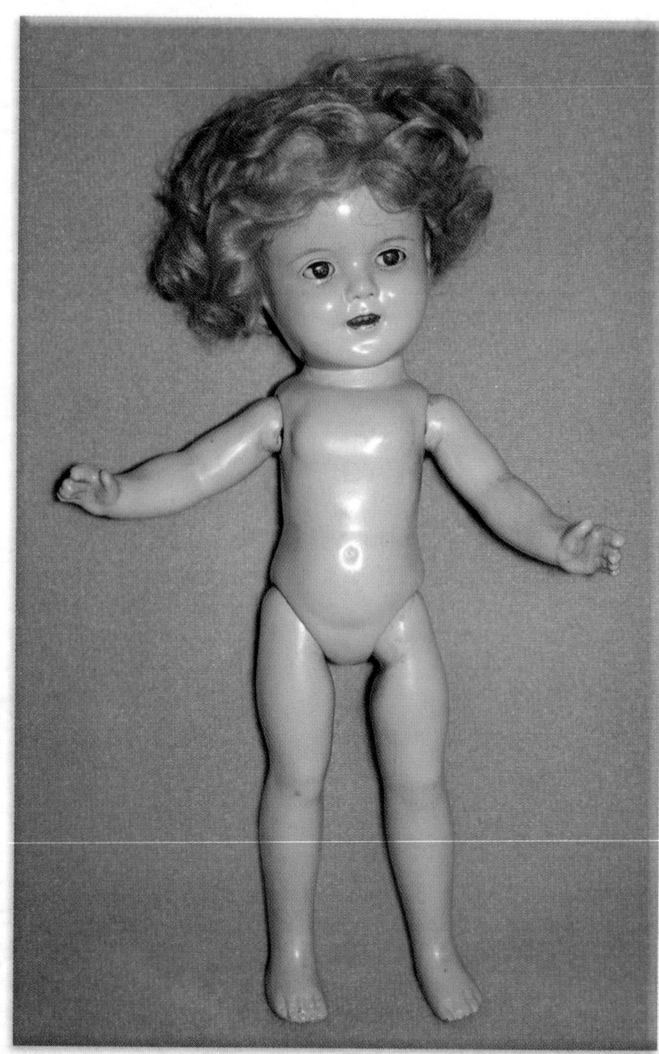

13" Shirley Temple doll. I bought her from eBay because she has almost no crazing, no cracking, and no paint bubbling, and she has her original wig. This is what I look for in a Shirley Temple doll. Unfortunately, she is very dirty, has cloudy eyes, and her wig is very matted. She is also missing her clothes. This doll originally sold for $150.00.

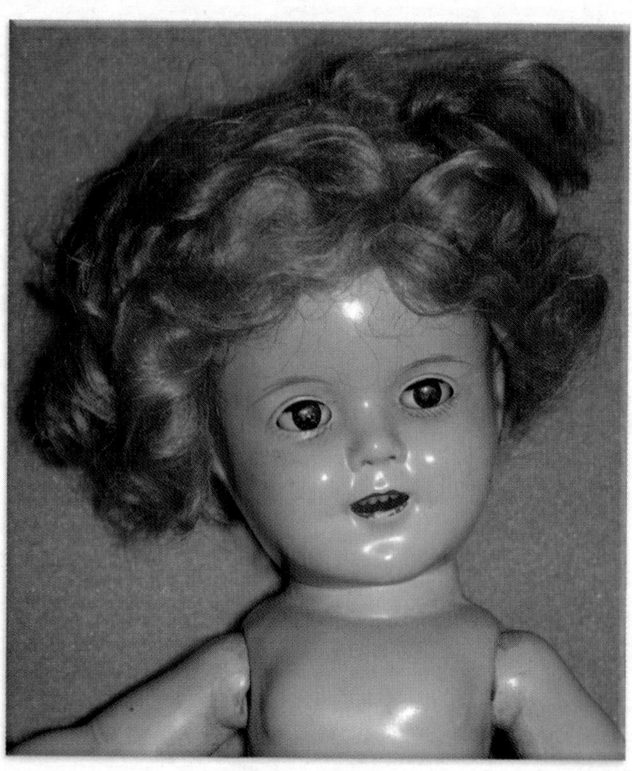

Close-up of the 13" Shirley Temple doll.

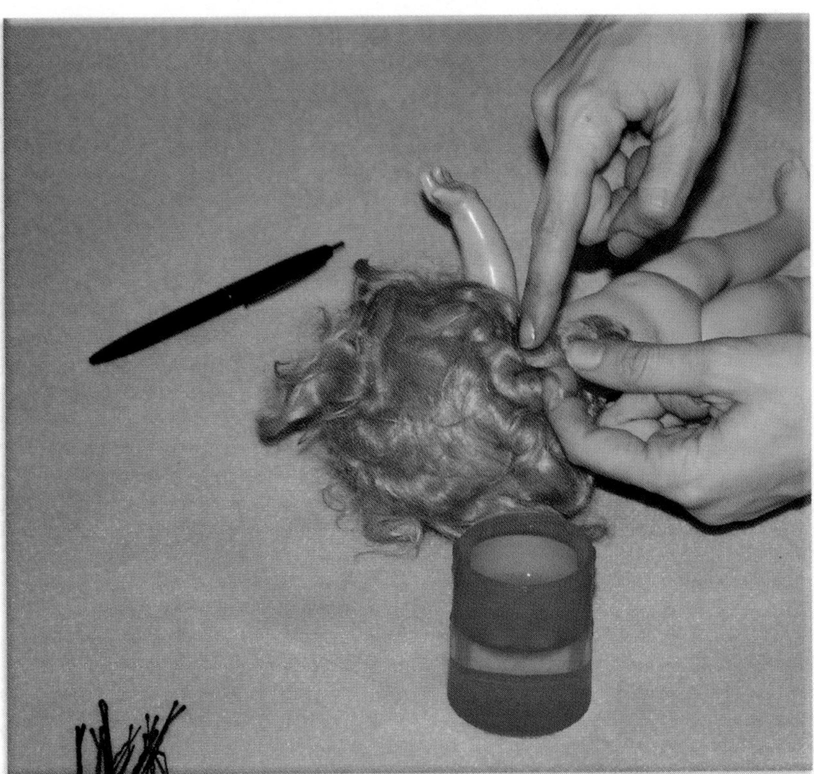

To begin, each curl was reset one at a time. First, a small amount of water was applied with fingertips to dampen the curl (be careful, do *not* get water on the compo — if you do, wipe it off immediately or else the paint will bubble up).

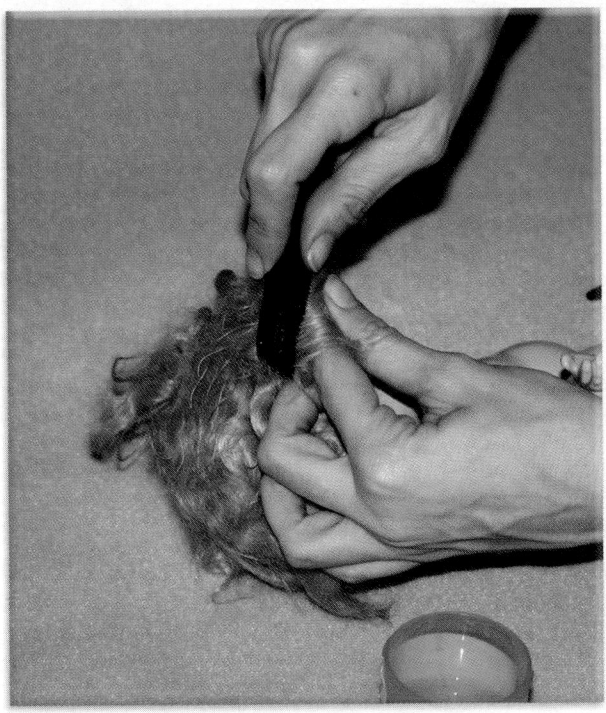

Then, the curl was gently combed out.

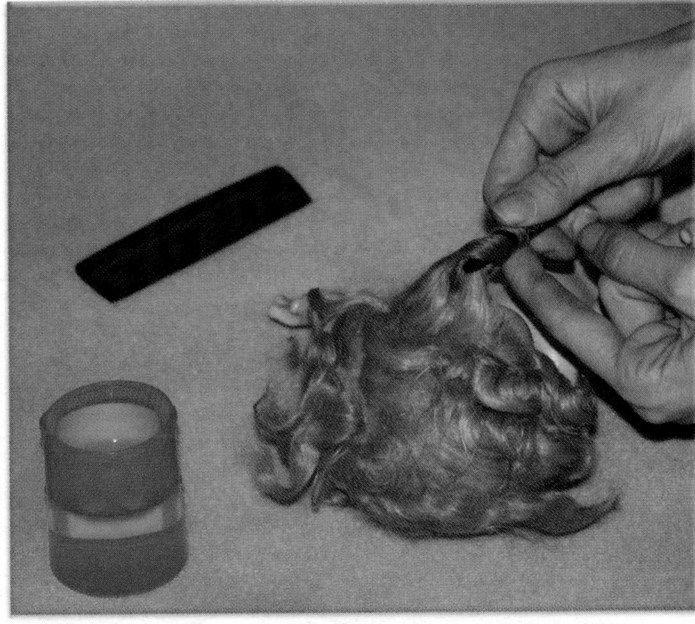

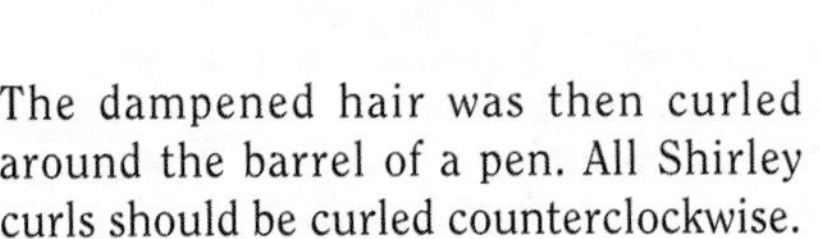

The dampened hair was then curled around the barrel of a pen. All Shirley curls should be curled counterclockwise.

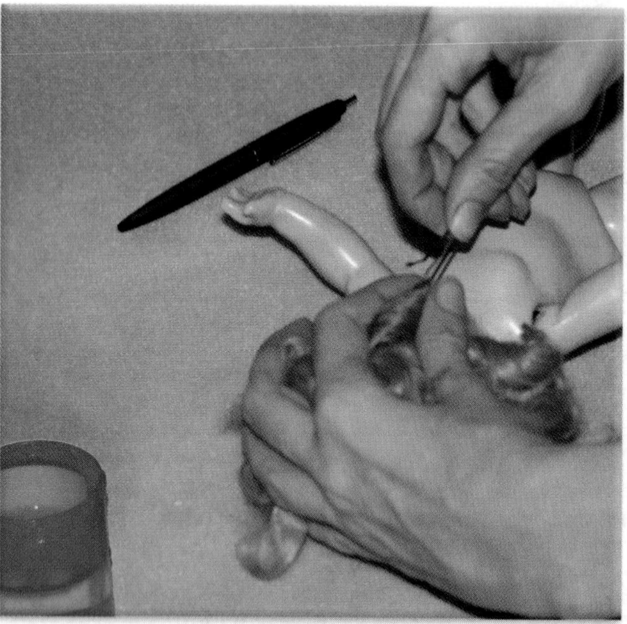

Fingers held the curl together as the pen was removed, and then two bobby pins (on either side of the curl) were used to secure the curl in place. This process was continued around the entire head, one curl at a time.

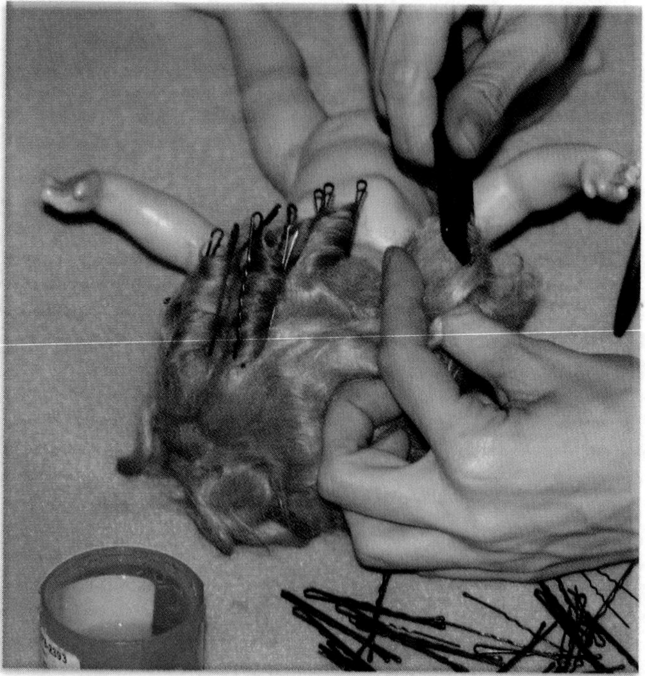

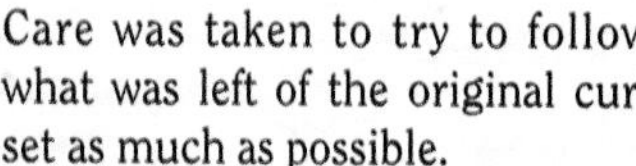

Care was taken to try to follow what was left of the original curl set as much as possible.

After all of Shirley's curls were finished, her hair was left in bobby pins to air dry.

The doll was then cleaned with Q-tips. Clean in small circles, first with Elmer's wood filler (gets the dirt right off) and then Nivea cream (found in the soap aisle of your local supermarket) to shine up the composition. Be careful to avoid cleaning any painted features (or they could come off). Any really dirty areas can be erased using a pen eraser.

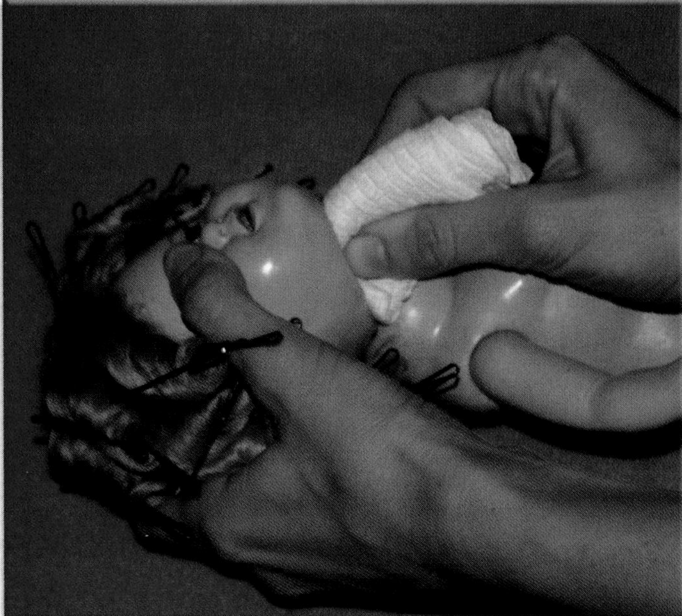

Holding the eyes open with my thumb, I stuffed a paper in the head to keep the eyes open (the eye closes on a weight inside the head and the towel keeps the weight from moving — closing the eye).

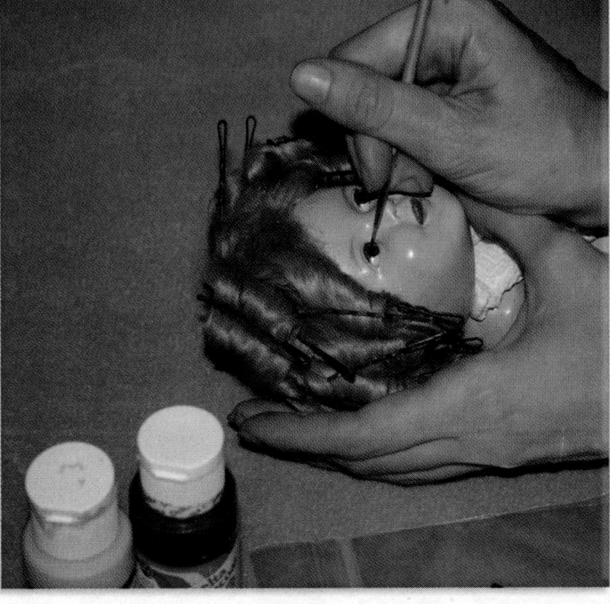

The doll's eyes were painted with acrylic paint. First, a mixture of yellow and black (looks almost green) was lightly applied in a star pattern, a bit larger than the pupil would be. Then the black pupil was painted on the eye.

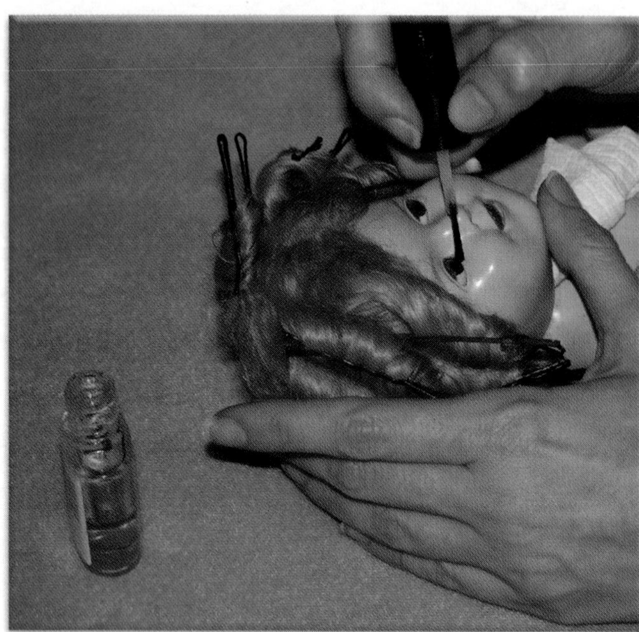

The eye was then sealed with clear, long-lasting nail polish and left to dry overnight.

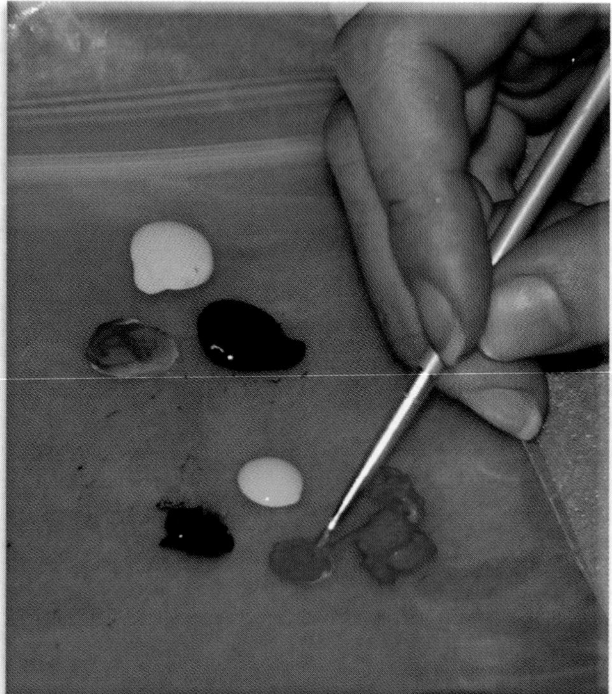

The doll's lips were painted with oil paint. The original paint color is a red-orange. The easiest way to get the color is to look at the paint of an original Shirley while you are doing it. I mix together about ⅓ yellow and ⅔ red, and then mix in a hint of brown (the brown makes the color just right).

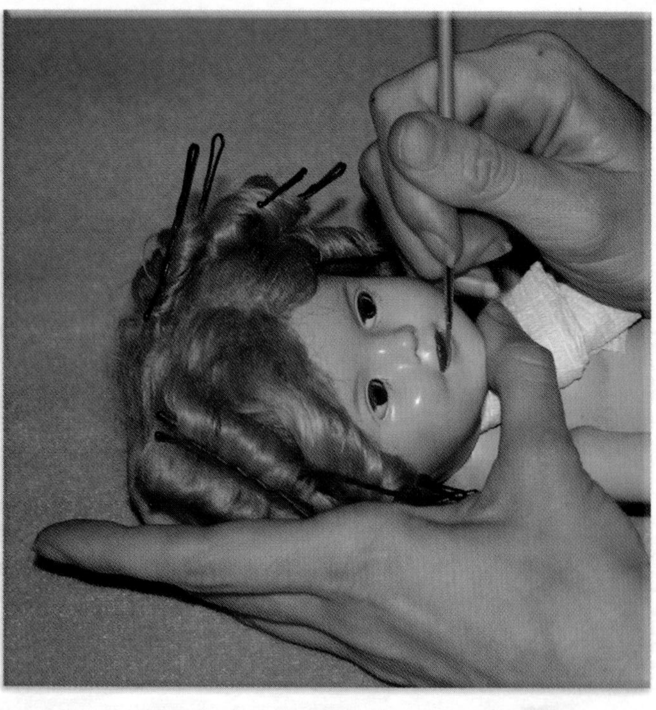

Care was taken to closely follow Shirley's original lip line. Also, be careful — oil paint takes a few days to dry, so don't smudge it!!

A fingertip of red oil paint was blotted on the cheeks and then blended with soft tissue to make the cheeks appear lightly rosy. Please note, you can only do this if the doll has almost no crazing; if there is crazing, the red paint will highlight the lines.

At this point, Shirley's facial makeup looked beautiful.

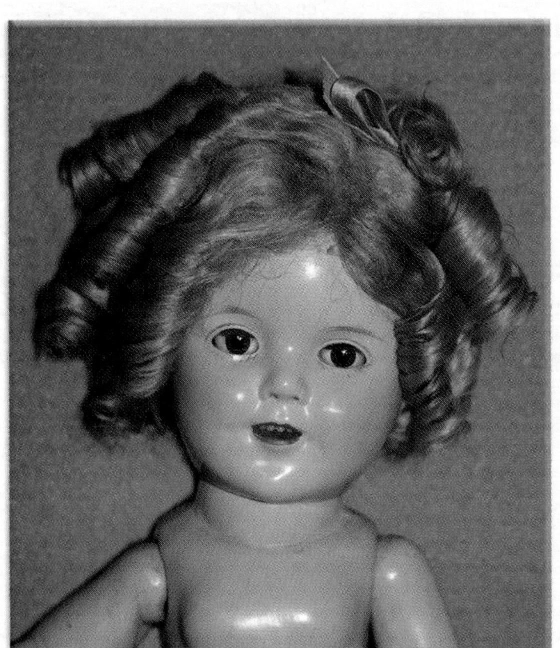

The bobby pins were taken out of her hair, which was finger styled appropriately before a hair ribbon was added.

Pattikins combo onesie and Scottie dog dress from Old B Dolls (oldbdolls.com), rayon socks and real leather doll shoes from Dollspart Supply Catalog, and a reproduction pin were added to complete the look of the doll. Now she displays perfectly and is worth a lot more than $150.00!

Quick Fix #2

The products used for this quick fix were Elmer's wood filler, Nivea, Q-tips, a Prismacolor colored pencil (Orange Deco; a small jar of flesh-colored oil paint could also have been used), bobby pins (two kinds), Sandra Lee doll cleaning solution, doll elastic from Dollspart Supply Catalog, yellow and black acrylic paint, clear nail polish, and bent-nose pliers.

16" Shirley Temple doll has light crazing, unruly hair (in mostly original set), cloudy eyes (with yellowing to the whites of the eyes), and no clothes. Her stringing is so loose that she can no longer stand up. She cost approximately $200.00 in this condition.

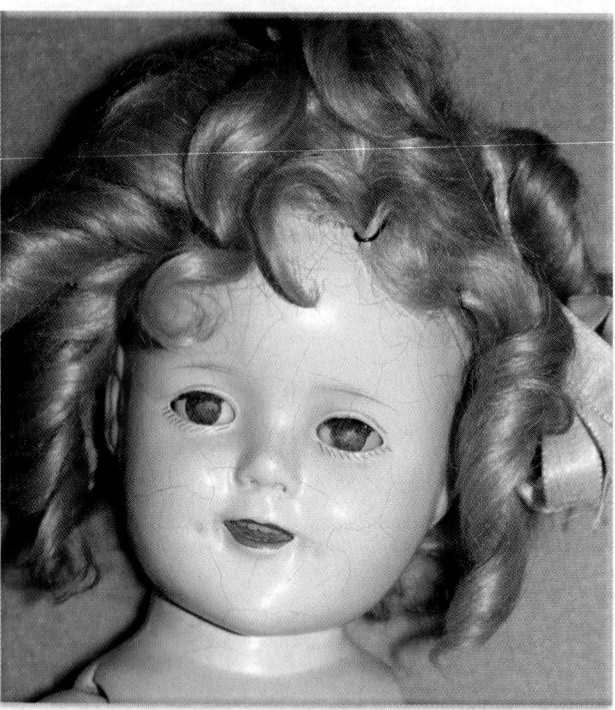

This is a close-up of her face.

The first thing to do was clean her. She was cleaned with Elmer's wood filler, and then Nivea, on Q-tips.

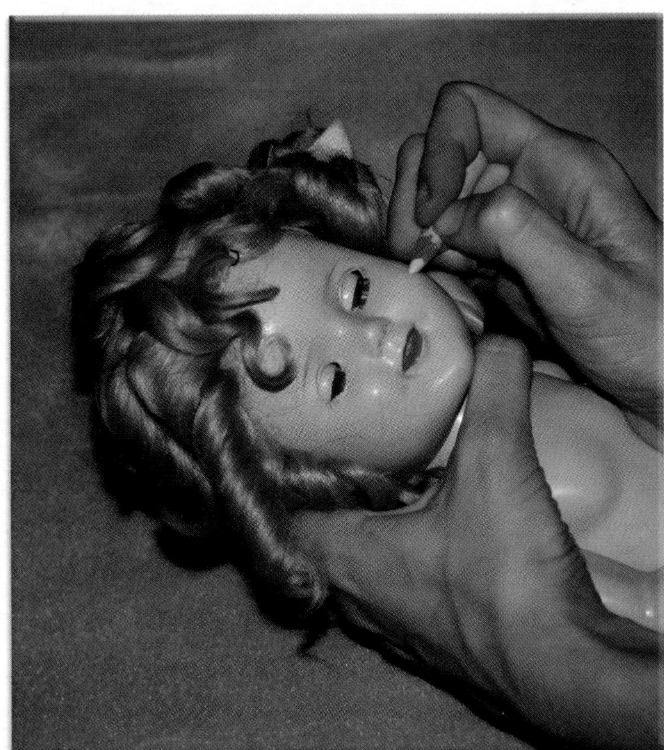

Once she was clean, a Prismacolor colored pencil (in the color Orange Deco) was used to color in her crazing. Once the coloring was finished, the excess pencil residue was wiped off with a tissue. You may also choose to use oil paint to cover the craze lines. Personally, I only use the paint on dolls with heavier crazing (it also acts as a sealant). The best way to use it: paint match (at your local hardware store) a pint of oil paint to a Shirley doll, dab a fingertip of it onto the crazing, rub it in gently to cover the crazing (avoid all painted features when you do this), wait five minutes for it to set, and then rub the excess paint off of the doll.

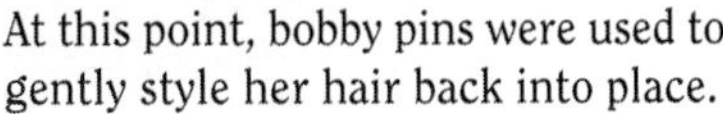

At this point, bobby pins were used to gently style her hair back into place.

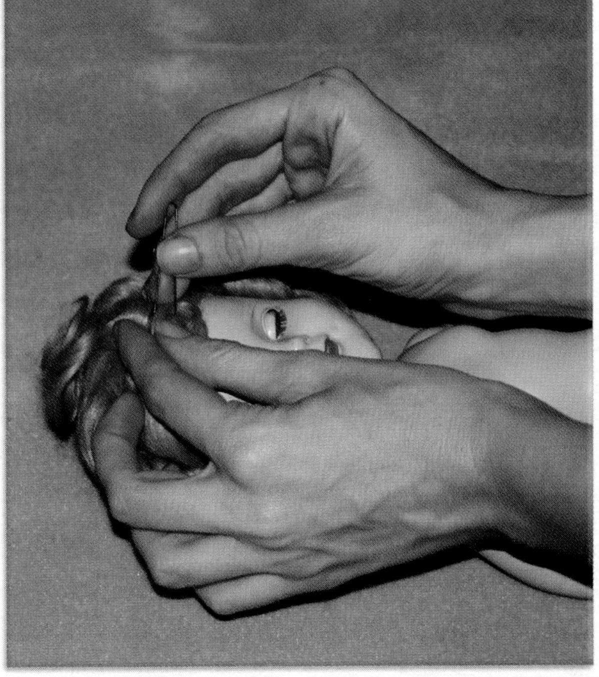

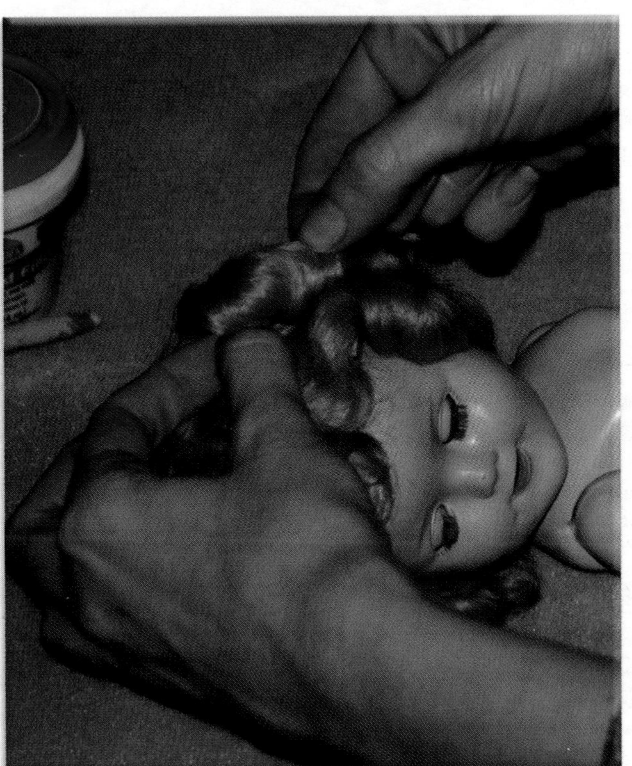

Flattened curls were separated (pull either end of the curl gently) to refresh them. Then, the whites of the eyes were cleaned with Sandra Lee doll cleaning solution (on a Q-tip) to decrease the yellowness (be very careful to avoid the painted lower lashes). The pupil was then painted on the eyes and sealed.

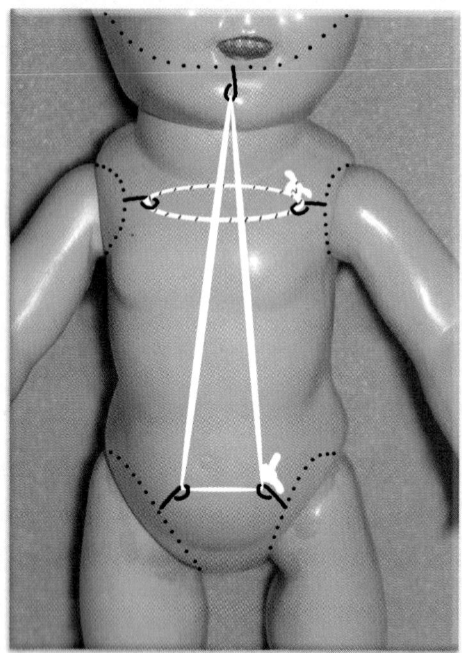

Shirley was then taken apart, and her pieces were strung back together using bent-nose pliers and doll elastic from Dollspart Supply Catalog. First the arms were strung together, then a hemostat clamp (you can get one on eBay) was used to hold the elastic tight while a knot was tied in the elastic (you can tie without a clamp, but the elastic may not be as tight). Then, the head was strung to the legs, and the elastic was tied off with a knot.

A clean but very faded original pleated organdy dancing dress for this size doll was found on eBay for around $80.00.

The dress was dyed blue with Rit dye, silk ribbons were added, and it was put on the doll. A reproduction pin was added, and a silk hair ribbon was tied in the doll's hair. Now the doll displays perfectly. At this point, her value is approximately $500.00, an increase of almost 100%. I recommend dying the pleated organdy dancing dress or the pleated organdy dress from *Curly Top* only, and *only* if the dresses are very faded.

A close-up of the doll's face.

A very pretty 11" Shirley was wearing a very dirty pleated organdy dancing dress.

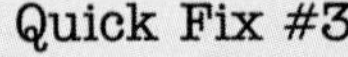
Quick Fix #3

The product used for this quick fix was Staintique (from Sandra Lee Products).

This is Staintique, from Sandra Lee Products, one of the first products I found that really works to clean the old dresses safely, though denture cleaner works very well also.

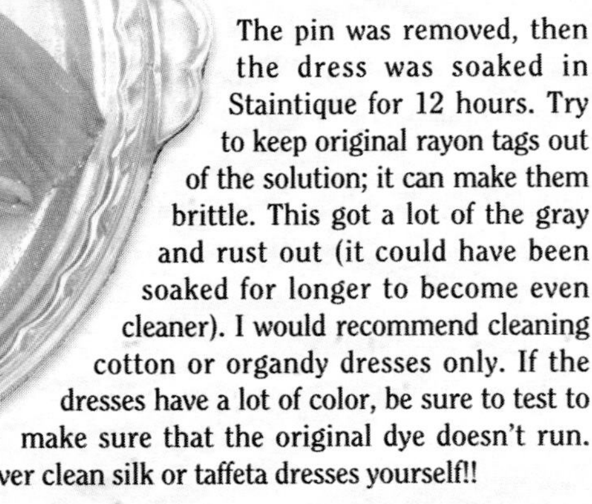

The pin was removed, then the dress was soaked in Staintique for 12 hours. Try to keep original rayon tags out of the solution; it can make them brittle. This got a lot of the gray and rust out (it could have been soaked for longer to become even cleaner). I would recommend cleaning cotton or organdy dresses only. If the dresses have a lot of color, be sure to test to make sure that the original dye doesn't run. Never clean silk or taffeta dresses yourself!!

After being rinsed in cool water, the dress was laid out on a towel and left to air dry.

The dress looks so much better now.

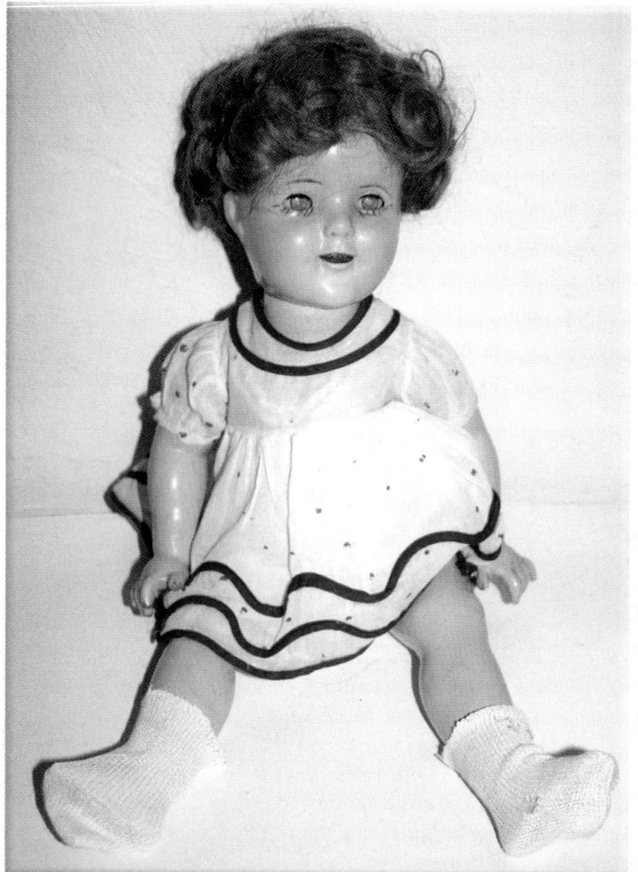

Before: Shirley Temple doll that needs some fixing. She is wearing her original dress, but she is very dirty, has a synthetic wig that is not appropriate, and has pencil marks all over her face. This doll cost around $150.00.

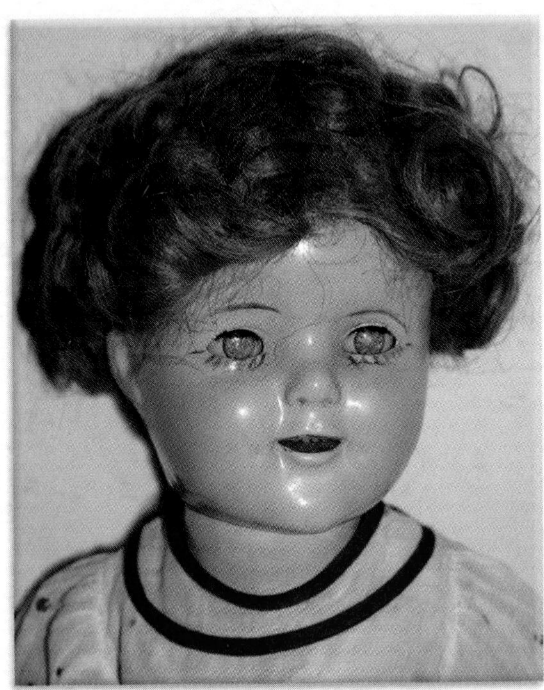

Close-up of the doll before she is cleaned up.

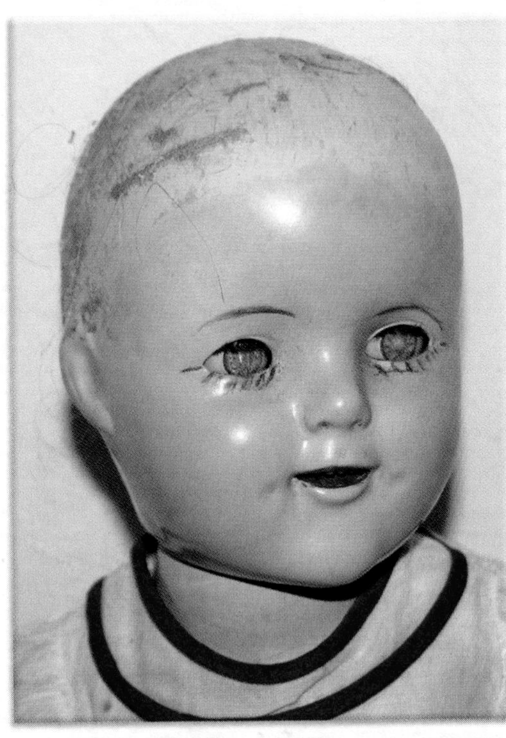

First, the wig is removed from the doll. This is usually fairly easy to do by moving your fingers slowly under the base of the wig and pulling up to remove it. The new wig from Dollspart catalog will be glued onto the head with Elmer's glue.

After: The doll has been cleaned, her eyes and facial coloring have been enhanced with paint, and her wig has been replaced. She looks much better.

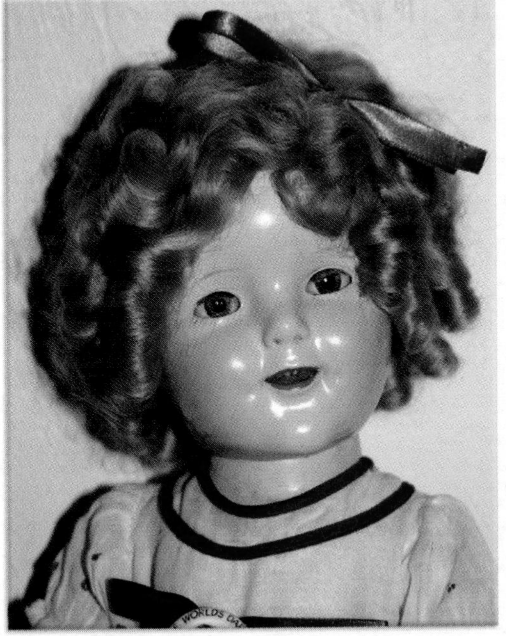

Close-up of the doll after her quick fix.

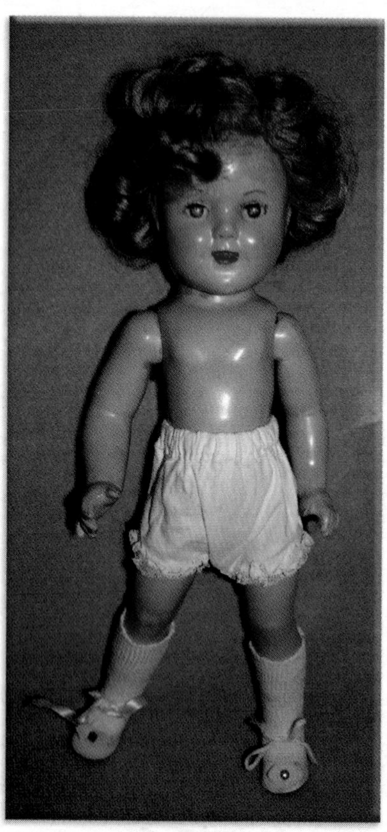

Before: Shirley Temple has a replaced wig and many odd marks on her face; she also needs clothes and a new wig. This doll was bought for $80.00 on eBay.

After: Shirley was cleaned and a pen eraser was used to erase the stubborn marks on her face. Her facial features were enhanced with oil paint, a mohair wig from the Dollspart catalog was glued on her head, and finally, leather shoes from the Dollspart catalog and Pattikins panties/slip, pique sailor dress, and matching hat from Old B Dolls (oldbdolls.com) were added.

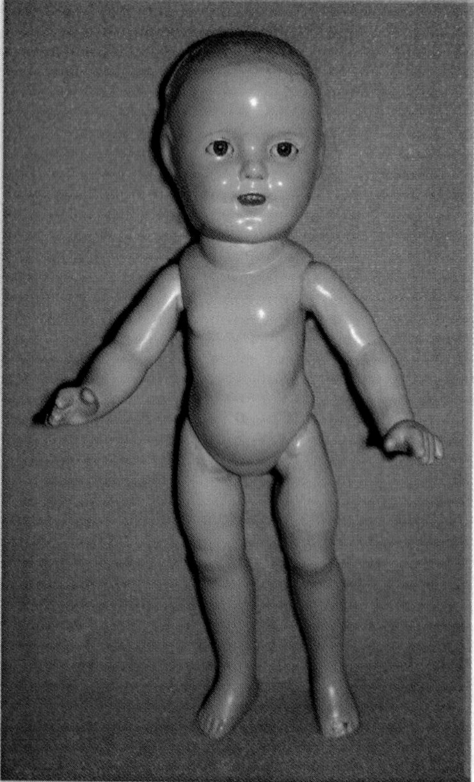

Before: A naked and bald Shirley Temple doll, bought for less than $100.00.

After: A proper mohair wig, rayon socks, leather shoes from Dollspart, a Pattikins panties/slip, an organdy dress, and a silk hair ribbon from Old B Dolls (oldbdolls.com), and a reproduction pin can turn any old doll into a beautiful doll. Always try to get the most authentic materials, to make the doll look her best!

Before: Pleated dancing dress in pretty bad shape.

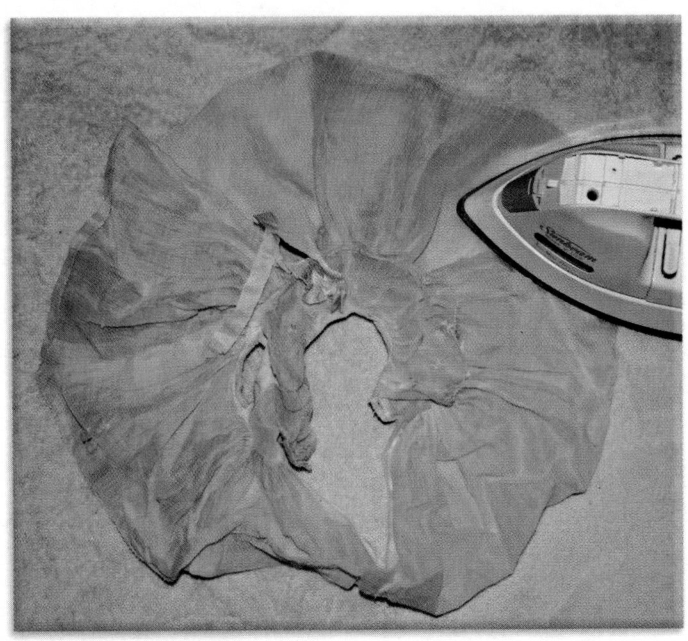

After being cleaned with Staintique, the dress was ironed on the lowest setting.

After: What a difference; the dress looks significantly better!

Though Shirley Temple's contract with Twentieth Century Fox ended in 1940, she remained in the public eye, becoming active in public service drives, including advertisements and publicity for the Red Cross, for war bonds, and for Christmas Seals. Though she attended Westlake High School, an exclusive all-girls school (her first time in a real classroom setting), Shirley's fans were still able to keep up with her. Many movie magazines closely followed her dating escapades and charity work. She was also active in radio programs and had a recurring role as "Junior Miss" Judy Graves.

She first returned to movies in late 1941, with the MGM release of **Kathleen**. Though Shirley's performance was well received, the attack on Pearl Harbor coincided with the movie's release and people had other things to be concerned about. In 1942, Shirley tried again with **Miss Annie Rooney**, in which she had her first screen kiss, but again, this light-hearted comedy was not what audiences were looking for at the time. Shirley was contracted to David Selznik in 1943. He starred her in the war drama **Since You Went Away** as Brig, a teenager dealing with life in wartime. This was her teenage breakout movie, and many critics believed that she might be able to make the transition to adult star. Her next few movies were also fairly successful and included **I'll Be Seeing You** (another wartime drama), **Kiss and Tell** (a light-hearted comedy that was probably her most successful starring teenage role), **Honeymoon**, and **The Bachelor and the Bobbysoxer** (in which she costarred as a teenager infatuated with a much older Cary Grant). However, Shirley was no longer a teenager, she was almost a mother.

Shirley married John Agar in 1945, at the age of 17, and in 1948 she gave birth to a daughter, Linda Susan. At the time, Ideal wanted to produce a "Shirley Temple Mother and Daughter Dolls" set, but Shirley would not agree to it. Shirley continued to star in movies while she was pregnant and after her daughter was born; her husband also acted in a few movies with her. There were small roles for both in **Fort Apache**, and starring roles in the box-office flop **Adventures in Baltimore**. More box-office failures followed with the release of **That Hagen Girl** (with Ronald Reagan), **Mr. Belvedere Goes to College**, and **A Kiss for Corliss**. Shirley's marriage was failing as well. She later described the marriage by simply saying, "It [the marriage] just should never have happened."

In October 1949, Shirley Temple filed for divorce from John Agar; soon after, she officially retired from the movies. At that point, Shirley began a completely new phase of her life, a truly private life. On a vacation to Hawaii in early 1950, she met Charles Black and fell in love. They married in December of that year. Soon, with the addition of son Charles Alden in 1952 and daughter Lori in 1954, her family was complete.

Around this time, the television was becoming a fixture in the American household. With the introduction of TVs came the reintroduction of Shirley Temple to the American public. Shirley gained a whole new generation of fans when her most famous movies began airing on TV. This led NBC to offer Shirley her own television series, and it also led Ideal to offer to reintroduce the Shirley Temple doll.

Shirley agreed to both, and in January 1958, **The Shirley Temple Storybook** premiered. In the series, Shirley introduced, and occasionally starred in, lavish adaptations of fairy tales and classic children's stories. Episodes included "Rapunzel," "Rumpelstiltskin," "Mother Goose," and "Beauty and the Beast," among others. Sixteen programs were shown throughout 1958. The success of the series was due, in many ways, to Shirley's own publicity savvy. During that year, she was the focus of more than a dozen TV and magazine articles. In 1959, the series was renamed **The Shirley Temple Show** and was produced for another season. Unfortunately, stiff competition from programs on other networks led to low ratings and the eventual cancellation of the show.

In the winter of 1957, the first new vinyl Shirley Temple dolls were released. These dolls had hazel sleep eyes and rooted saran wigs. Originally, 17" and 19" dolls were offered; each wore a **Stand Up and Cheer** dress and came with a curler box. The 17" doll sold for $10.47, and the 19" for $13.47. By early 1958, Ideal also released a 12" doll in a pink taffeta slip and matching panties, and a 15" doll. An assortment of outfits was sold separately for the 12" doll. A 26" Shirley Temple doll, shown in a few publicity stills at the time, was never released to the public. A black Shirley Temple doll was also planned, but was never produced (though a few have been found). Ideal advertised the new Shirley Temple dolls during Shirley Temple's television program and when her old movies were shown on TV. The new vinyl dolls were quite successful. Each year, Ideal produced new clothes for the Shirley dolls. These included contemporary outfits from the 1950s, movie outfits from Shirley's most famous childhood movies, and storybook outfits modeled after the stories that were told on her television series.

Shirley herself was very active in the production and promotion of the dolls. She often went to the factory to inspect the quality of the dolls, and she made several special appearances at department stores to sign the dolls and other assorted Shirley Temple collectibles that were being sold at the time. During one of those appearances, in March 1959, Shirley introduced the Shirley Temple Playpal doll to the public. This doll was a huge 36" tall and was modeled after the Patti Playpal dolls that were successful for Ideal at the time. When Shirley Temple was chosen to lead the 1959 Macy's Thanksgiving Day Parade, her daughter Linda Susan accompanied her carrying a 36" Shirley Playpal doll. Once Shirley's television series ended, interest in the dolls faded. In 1963, the last of this series of vinyl Shirley Temple dolls was produced.

Television solidified and expanded the fan base of Shirley Temple. Not only was she seen as the beloved child star, but she was also known to children and adults alike as the fantastic storyteller that visited them on their TV sets. The new Shirley Temple dolls led many adults to reminisce about their old Shirley Temple dolls and collectibles from the 1930s. In 1960, the first Shirley Temple Collectors Club was established, which allowed Shirley Temple fans to seek out old and new Shirley Temple items and to correspond with each other. Shirley Temple collections started springing up as fans began communicating — buying, selling, and trading Shirley Temple items with each other.

1957

The first vinyl Shirley Temple doll was offered in the 1957 *Sears Christmas Book* wearing a nylon dress that resembled the one that Shirley wore in the movie *Stand Up and Cheer*. The dress came with an attached half-slip, panties, shoes, and socks. A box of curlers was also included in this set. The original value of the 17" doll was $10.47, and the original value for the 19" doll was $13.47. Marge Meisinger collection.

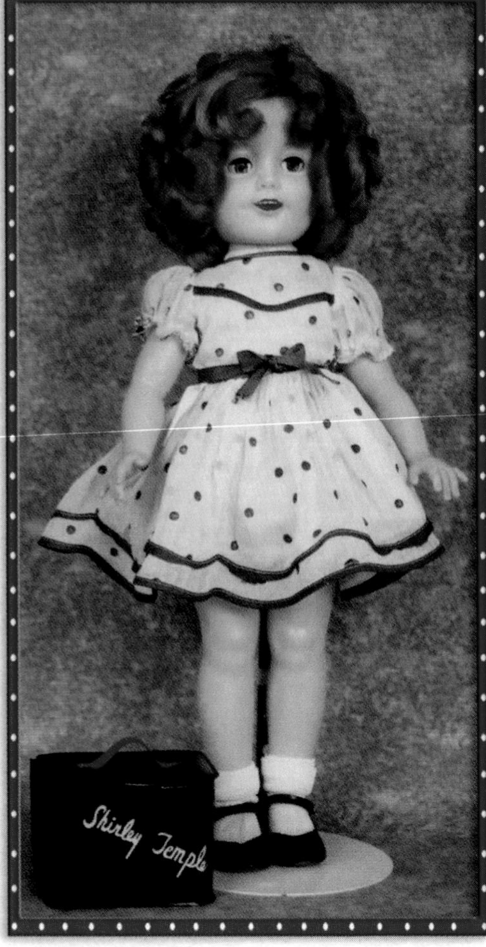

19" Shirley Temple doll wearing a *Stand Up and Cheer* dress. Marked "ST-19" on the back of her head and on her back (*ST* is for *Shirley Temple*, *19* is her size in inches). This picture also shows a box of curlers that was produced later in the production run. $200.00. Karen Holich collection.

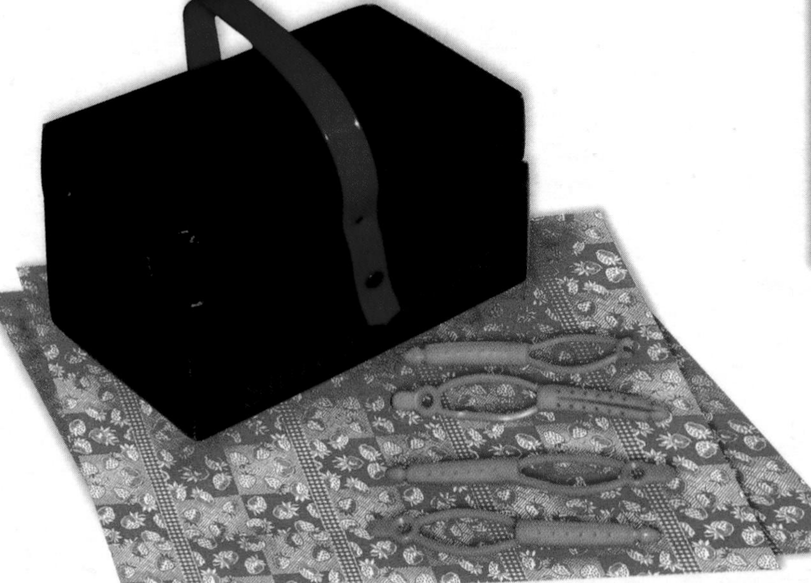

This is a close-up of the box of curlers that came with the first vinyl Shirley Temple dolls. Very rare. $75.00. Keith and Loretta McKenzie collection.

Shirley was very proactive in the vinyl Shirley Temple doll production. This publicity still shows her inspecting some of her dolls. Notice the size of the doll on the right, a 26" Shirley that was never released to the public (a few are currently known to exist and are very valuable). $10.00. Marge Meisinger collection.

First version of the original box (though this one has seen better days).

Close-up of the tag on the original Shirley Temple dresses from the 1950s. Keith and Loretta McKenzie collection.

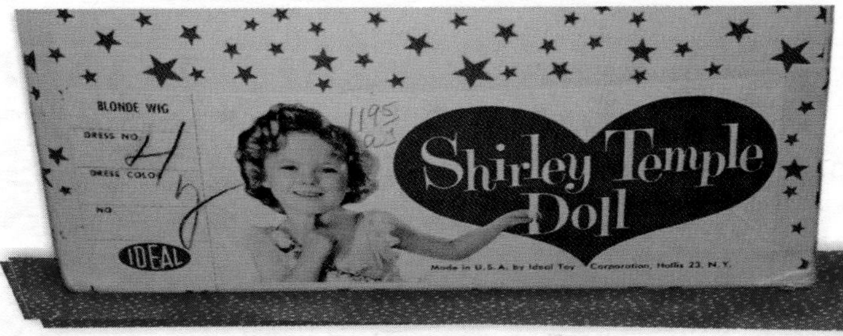

Close-up of the original label on the box. Iva Mae Jones collection.

1958

12" Shirley Temple doll, Ideal item #9500. Marked "ST-12" on the back of her head and on her back. The basic doll, wearing a pink satin slip with matching panties. Her slip is tagged at the waist. Also includes "Shirley Temple" silver script pin, socks, black plastic shoes (first production dolls have black patent leather with snap closures and are more rare), and pink hangtag. Mint in box, $200.00. Keith and Loretta McKenzie collection.

Many detailed outfits were sold separately so that the 12" Shirley Temple doll would have a large wardrobe to be dressed up in. Two-piece pajama set for the 12" doll, Ideal #9501. Consists of a red or blue shirt and striped pants. $40.00. Keith and Loretta McKenzie collection.

Close-up of the original Shirley Temple script pin is on the left, and a reproduction pin is on the right. The original pin is much more silver-gold in color; the reproduction is more silver-blue in color. Original pin, $25.00; reproduction pin, $5.00. Keith and Loretta McKenzie collection.

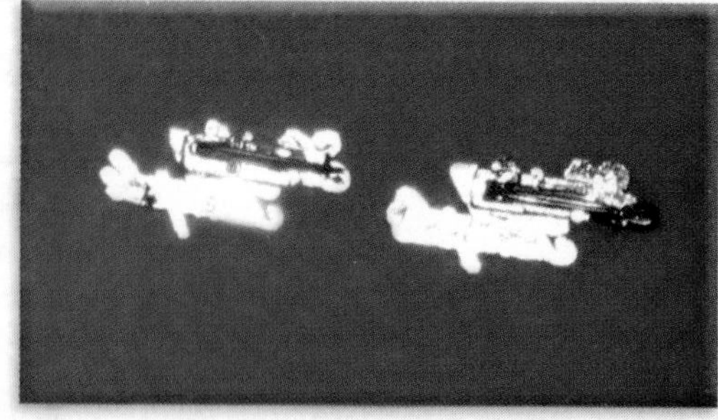

The backs of the pins. The original is on the left, the repro is on the right. The latch is different; the reproduction has more of a loop at the pin closure. Keith and Loretta McKenzie collection.

Close-up of the label on the side of the dress box. Keith and Loretta McKenzie collection.

Bolero dress for the 12" doll, Ideal #9504. Came in a variety of colors and fabric patterns. Includes an attached slip and rayon tag. Came in a small white window box with gold stars on it. Mint in box, $70.00. Keith and Loretta McKenzie collection.

Cotton dress for the 12" doll, with loops on bodice. Ideal #9503. Came in a variety of colors. Most of the dresses made for the vinyl dolls have an attached slip with a rayon tag, and a two-snap closure in the back. $30.00. Keith and Loretta McKenzie collection.

Quilted coat for a 12" doll, Ideal #9505. Came in either pink or blue. Currently worth $50.00 (outfit only). Ideal catalog.

Insignia dress for the 12" doll, Ideal #9506. Came with a plastic signature purse (not pictured). $50.00 complete. Keith and Loretta McKenzie collection.

Dress with patterned pinafore attached, for a 12" doll. Ideal #9507. Released in 1958, with a variety of fabric patterns. $35.00. Keith and Loretta McKenzie collection.

School dress with embroidered trim on the bodice and skirt, for a 12" doll. Ideal #9509. Has an unusual style of signature purse. $60.00. Keith and Loretta McKenzie collection.

Patterned raincoat for a 12" doll, with attached hood and matching belt. Ideal #9510. Came in different pattern designs. $60.00.

Lined coat and matching cap for a 12" doll, Ideal #9511. In the original box. $70.00. Keith and Loretta McKenzie collection.

12" Shirley Temple doll wearing pedal pusher outfit, Ideal #9526. Complete with cutoffs, a striped shirt, and plastic glasses. $300.00 in box. $70.00 complete outfit only. Iva Mae Jones collection.

Overalls, checked shirt, and straw hat for a 12" doll, Ideal #9525. $55.00. Keith and Loretta McKenzie collection.

Tagged purple fuzzy coat that was advertised in 1958 catalogs. $15.00. Keith and Loretta McKenzie collection.

12" Shirley Temple doll wearing a nylon party dress with embroidered trim, Ideal outfit #9532. Came with a straw hat with veil and plastic signature purse. Doll includes original hangtag and script pin. $225.00. Keith and Loretta McKenzie collection.

This 12" Shirley Temple doll is wearing an unidentified tagged dress. The dress was pictured in the 1958 Sears Christmas catalog. The signature purse is a different style than the usual one the 12" dolls came with. The gold star box is also unusual; the 12" Shirley Temple dolls are usually seen in the red box with Shirley's picture on it. The socks are longer than the normal socks and have two bands around the top, and the shoes are sandals (original and rare). $350.00. Keith and Loretta McKenzie collection.

Close-up of the unusual gold star box for the 12" doll (shown top right). Keith and Loretta McKenzie collection.

Ad from 1958 Sears Christmas catalog showing this rare Shirley doll. Marge Meisinger collection.

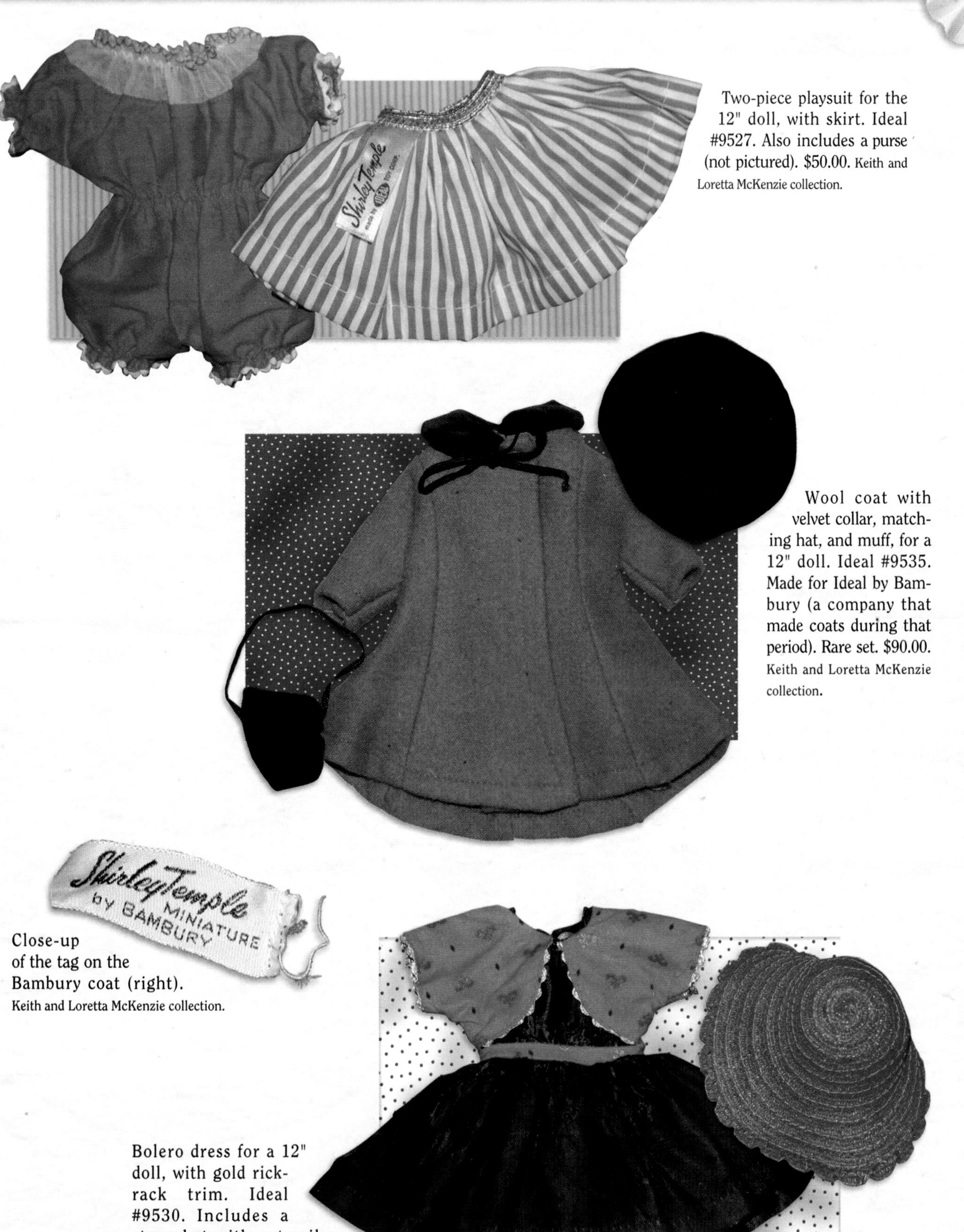

Two-piece playsuit for the 12" doll, with skirt. Ideal #9527. Also includes a purse (not pictured). $50.00. Keith and Loretta McKenzie collection.

Wool coat with velvet collar, matching hat, and muff, for a 12" doll. Ideal #9535. Made for Ideal by Bambury (a company that made coats during that period). Rare set. $90.00. Keith and Loretta McKenzie collection.

Close-up of the tag on the Bambury coat (right). Keith and Loretta McKenzie collection.

Bolero dress for a 12" doll, with gold rick-rack trim. Ideal #9530. Includes a straw hat with net veil (veil not pictured). $50.00. Keith and Loretta McKenzie collection.

12" Shirley Temple gift set in gold star box. Production began in 1958. This particular doll set was made later in the production run (probably 1961 – 1962), based on the outfits in it. $500.00. Iva Mae Jones collection.

The Marshall Fields catalog from December 1958 advertised a steel-covered trunk for that store's Shirley Temple doll (made exclusively for it). The trunk came complete with a doll and an assortment of clothes. This is thought to be that trunk. Since it is not marked "Shirley Temple," it is hard to identify it for certain. $400.00 as a set, if original. Keith and Loretta McKenzie collection.

Complete Outfit . . 12-inch Shirley Temple Doll with 4 outfits in a gift box. Same doll as described at left. Includes: cotton dress with cotton panties, "pearl" necklace, soft fleecy coat, "straw" hat; 2-pc. cotton pajama set; 3-pc. blouse, shorts and skirt ensemble of cotton. All outfits highly styled with careful detailing, snap closures. Buy extra outfits at left.
49 M 3950

The first advertisement for the Sears Shirley Temple gift set from the 1958 Sears Christmas catalog. This gift set was sold in the Sears catalog through the end of the Shirley Temple run. Marge Meisinger collection.

17" Shirley Temple doll released in 1958. Sleep eyes (not flirty). Wearing a nylon flocked dress with red velvet vest and carrying a white plastic signature purse (with strap). Mint in gold star box. This dress is similar to the one produced for the 1972 Ward's Yesterday's Darling doll. $250.00.

Close-up of the 17" vinyl Shirley Temple doll.

Back of the 17" vinyl Shirley. The hair at the back was not in distinct curls, but instead was a curled mass. This dress has buttons in the back, but most vinyl-doll outfits had snap closures.

Advertisement for this doll in the 1958 Ideal catalog.
Loretta Beilstein collection.

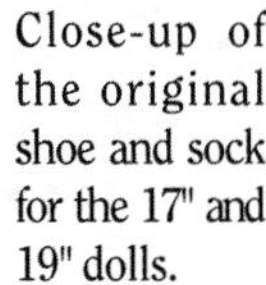

Close-up of the original shoe and sock for the 17" and 19" dolls.

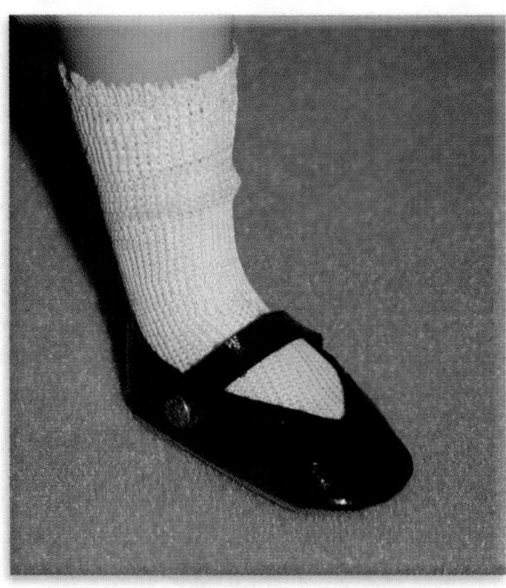

School dress for 12" doll, with nylon apron and embroidered decoration on bodice. Ideal #9542. This dress was also made for the 15" and 17" dolls. Made in a variety of colors, it also came with a signature purse. $40.00. Keith and Loretta McKenzie collection.

Three-piece raincoat set for the 12" doll. Ideal #9540. Also released in 1960 as outfit #9711, with a tote bag made of clear plastic. Outfit came in a variety of colors and consists of plastic raincoat with matching headscarf (with visor), matching tote bag, and belt (not shown). $50.00. Keith and Loretta McKenzie collection.

Three-piece cotton knit pajamas set for a 12" doll, Ideal #9541. Outfit includes pants, long shirt, and matching stocking cap. Mint in box, $75.00. Iva Mae Jones collection.

Sailor dress for the 12" doll, Ideal #9543. Includes a matching cap. $45.00. Keith and Loretta McKenzie collection.

Mint-in-box Scotch dress for the 12" doll, with red sash. Ideal #9545. Includes a matching tam, undies, shoes, and signature purse (not pictured). $100.00. Janet Mitchell collection.

12" Shirley wearing Ideal #9546, an embroidered pinafore dress similar in style to #9542. The doll is in good condition but has been played with; she has recurled hair and replaced socks and shoes. In this condition, $100.00; dress alone, $40.00.

12" Shirley Temple doll is wearing Ideal outfit #9547, the first version of the *Heidi* dress outfit for the 12" doll. Outfit has a pleated skirt and an embroidered ribbon on the top. Came in a variety of colors and patterns. This doll is wearing a pearl necklace that commonly came in the gift set boxes (did not originally come with this outfit). Complete with signature purse. $200.00. Keith and Loretta McKenzie collection.

Nylon visiting dress for the 12" doll, Ideal #9549. Came in a variety of colors. A signature purse (not pictured) was also included in this set. Mint in box, $80.00 complete. Keith and Loretta McKenzie collection.

Wee Willie Winkie outfit for the 12" doll, Ideal #9560. Outfit was also made for the 15" doll. $75.00. Keith and Loretta McKenzie collection.

Velvet jumper dress for the 12" doll, with two appliqués. Ideal #9551. Came in a variety of colors, with matching signature purse. $45.00 each. Keith and Loretta McKenzie collection.

12" vinyl Shirley Temple doll wearing the *Wee Willie Winkie* outfit. This is the rare red version. $250.00. Outfit alone, $90.00. Iva Mae Jones collection.

Rebecca of Sunnybrook Farm outfit for the 12" doll, Ideal #9550. Consists of a shirt, overalls, and a straw hat. In 1960, a different version of this outfit was released. $75.00. Keith and Loretta McKenzie collection.

12" Shirley wearing Ideal outfit #9561, an ice skater outfit. Outfit includes a long-sleeved shirt with insignia patch, a black skirt with gold elastic waistband, red tights, a matching stocking hat, and white ice skates. $300.00 complete; outfit alone, $125.00. Iva Mae Jones collection.

Mint-in-box 12" Shirley wearing Ideal outfit #9562, a nylon party dress. Outfit includes a straw hat. This doll has unusual original shoes with center-snap closures (more rare than the black plastic slip-on shoes). $250.00. Iva Mae Jones collection.

12" doll is wearing Ideal outfit #9563, a corduroy flared coat and hat set. Set came in a variety of colors, with a signature purse. This doll is pictured with her original script pin; however, the *ple* of *Temple* has broken off and is missing. This often happens to the script pins (it reduces the value from $25.00 to $8.00). $200.00. Keith and Loretta McKenzie collection.

Captain January outfit for the 12" doll, Ideal #9564 (1959 – 1960). Came with pants, shirt, and sailor cap. $80.00. Keith and Loretta McKenzie collection.

Unidentified tagged nylon dress for the 12" doll, from around 1959 or 1960. $35.00. Janet Mitchell collection.

In 1959, Sears continued to sell the gift set in the gold star box; however, other companies released different types of gift set boxes for the 12" doll. The 1959 Ideal catalog advertised this Shirley Temple doll with "TV box," which consisted of a see-through box that resembled a television with a 12" Shirley doll inside wearing a pink satin slip. It also included four additional outfits attached to the back of the box, a signature purse, and glasses. $450.00. Keith and Loretta McKenzie collection.

"SHIRLEY TEMPLE" TV WARDROBE PACKAGE

Popular 12 in. all vinyl Shirley Temple doll in TV window package with carrying handle. Curly rooted Saran hair can be shampooed and curled. Doll is dressed in slip and panties, with complete wardrobe including play outfit, school dress, party dress, purse, raincoat, hat, tote bag, eye glasses and necklace.

N63-9520 .... Each 16.00

Ad from McClurg's Christmas catalog (1959) for the Shirley Temple TV box. Marge Meisinger collection.

The inside of the Shirley Temple TV box gift set, made 1959 through 1961. Keith and Loretta McKenzie collection.

19" Shirley Temple doll is wearing another version of the nylon party dress. This outfit is complete with gloves (the gloves were only produced for a short period of time and are very rare) and script pin. Shown in the original window box. The outside of the box was plain for the 19" Shirley Temple dolls in the window box. This particular doll has discolored legs. The discoloration decreases the value of the doll to $400.00 ($500.00 if mint). Keith and Loretta McKenzie collection.

17" Shirley Temple doll with her original nylon party dress and signature purse (notice that the style differs from that of the purses for the 12" dolls), silver "Shirley Temple" script pin, and hangtag. Shown in her original box. (1959 – 1960.) $325.00. Keith and Loretta McKenzie collection.

15" Shirley Temple doll wearing her original nylon party dress with lace and velvet accents and carrying her original signature purse. She is shown in her original window box. (1959 – 1960.) $275.00. Keith and Loretta McKenzie collection.

Fancy dress with velvet waistband (1959 – 1960), for the 15" and 17" dolls. Resembles the pleated *Curly Top* dress that Shirley wore in the 1930s. Tagged at the waist. $75.00. Keith and Loretta McKenzie collection.

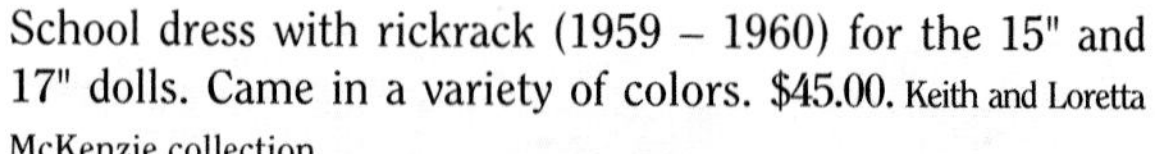

School dress with rickrack (1959 – 1960) for the 15" and 17" dolls. Came in a variety of colors. $45.00. Keith and Loretta McKenzie collection.

17" Shirley Temple doll wearing an original dress (similar in style to outfit #9542 for the 12" doll). With original script pin and hangtag. (1959 – 1960.) Mint in box, $325.00. Iva Mae Jones collection.

This advertisement in the 1959 Ideal doll catalog shows a 19" vinyl Shirley Temple doll in a *Wee Willie Winkie* dress (a rare and sought-after dress for the vinyl doll). Currently valued at $350.00 without box. Marge Meisinger collection.

15" Shirley with mint curls and wearing a yellow nylon dress. (1959 – 1960.) $250.00. Janet Mitchell collection.

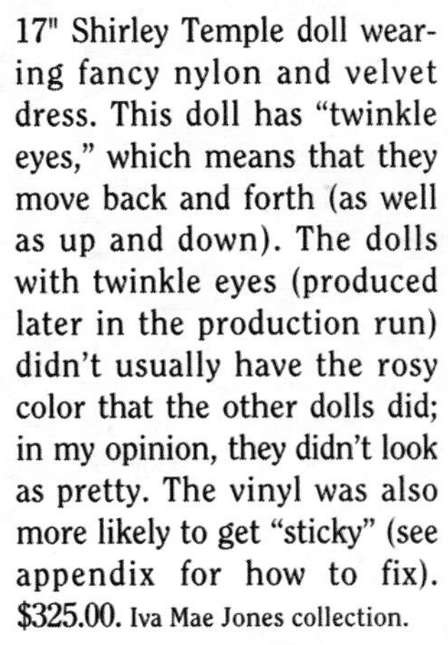

17" Shirley Temple doll wearing fancy nylon and velvet dress. This doll has "twinkle eyes," which means that they move back and forth (as well as up and down). The dolls with twinkle eyes (produced later in the production run) didn't usually have the rosy color that the other dolls did; in my opinion, they didn't look as pretty. The vinyl was also more likely to get "sticky" (see appendix for how to fix). $325.00. Iva Mae Jones collection.

Tag identifying the doll as having "twinkle" eyes. Iva Mae Jones collection.

19" Shirley Temple doll with twinkle eyes and wearing a bright pink nylon dress, in original star box. $400.00. Iva Mae Jones collection.

For a short amount of time in 1959, a Shirley Temple walker doll was produced. This 19" doll was marked "ST-19-R" on the back of the head. It came in a variety of outfits. This one is wearing an unusual pinafore dress. The neck was one piece with the head, and the facial mold was different than that used for the regular Shirley dolls. $600.00. Iva Mae Jones collection.

19" Shirley Temple doll wearing a nylon dress (similar to the 12" doll's dress #9532 from 1958). The curls on this doll's hair have been reset, so she is not worth as much as a doll in completely original condition. $225.00. Iva Mae Jones collection.

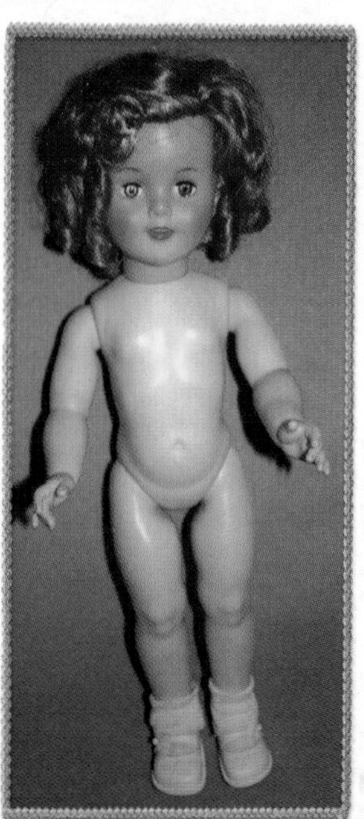

The unusual construction of the Shirley Temple walker doll. Iva Mae Jones collection.

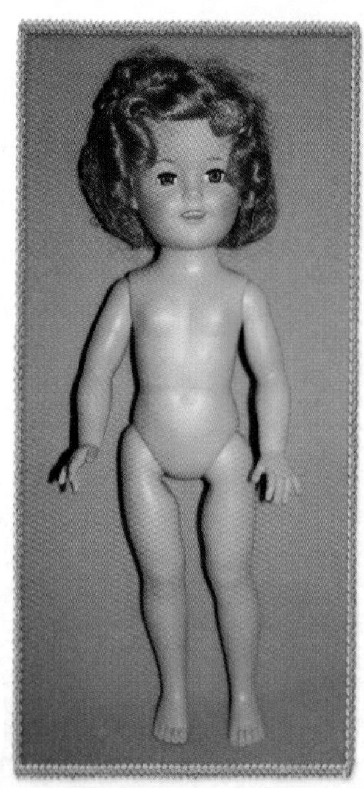

The regular construction of the Shirley Temple body.

The 36" Shirley Temple Playpal doll debuted on March 10, 1959, when Shirley appeared in New York to autograph Shirley dolls. This Shirley Temple doll is the size of a small child and is wearing a nylon party dress. The doll also has twisting wrists, a wristwatch, and a script pin. Marked "IDEALDOLL/ST-35-38-2" on her head and "IDEAL [in a circle] 35-4" on her body. Came in her original box. Mint in box, $2,000.00. Janet Mitchell collection.

The original wristwatch that came with the Shirley Temple Playpal dolls. Very hard to find. $60.00. Janet Mitchell collection.

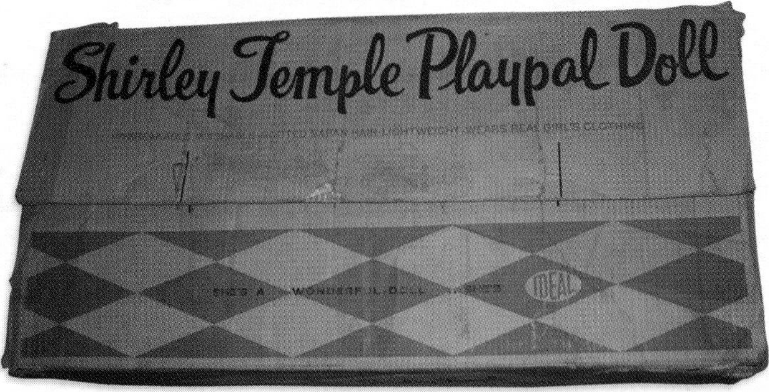

Box for the Shirley Temple Playpal doll. Janet Mitchell collection.

36" Shirley Temple Playpal doll wearing another version of the nylon dress. $1,200.00. Janet Mitchell collection.

36" Shirley Temple Playpal doll wearing a more unusual version of the nylon dress. $1,300.00. Loretta Beilstein collection.

Ad for the 36" Shirley Temple doll in the *Chicago Daily Tribune* newspaper from November 26, 1959. Advertisers also encouraged children to dress their Shirley Playpal dolls in Shirley Temple Cinderella dresses that were being sold at that time. Marge Meisinger collection.

Publicity still of a child wearing a Shirley Temple Cinderella dress dancing with a 36" Shirley Temple Playpal doll. $10.00. Marge Meisinger collection.

Schoolgirl dress for the 12" doll, with rick-rack trim on bodice. Ideal #9712. Includes a signature purse. $35.00. Keith and Loretta McKenzie collection.

Sleeveless school-girl dress for the 12" doll, with attached flower decoration. Ideal #9713. Includes a signature purse (rare version of the purse shown). $75.00. Keith and Loretta McKenzie collection.

12" Shirley Temple doll is wearing Ideal outfit #9714, a felt Scottie dog jumper with matching headband, white shirt, and signature purse. $200.00. Keith and Loretta McKenzie collection.

Velvet dresses (similar in style to outfit #9551) for a 12" doll, Ideal #9715. Shown in pink and blue, the outfits also include signature purses. $50.00 each. Keith and Loretta McKenzie collection.

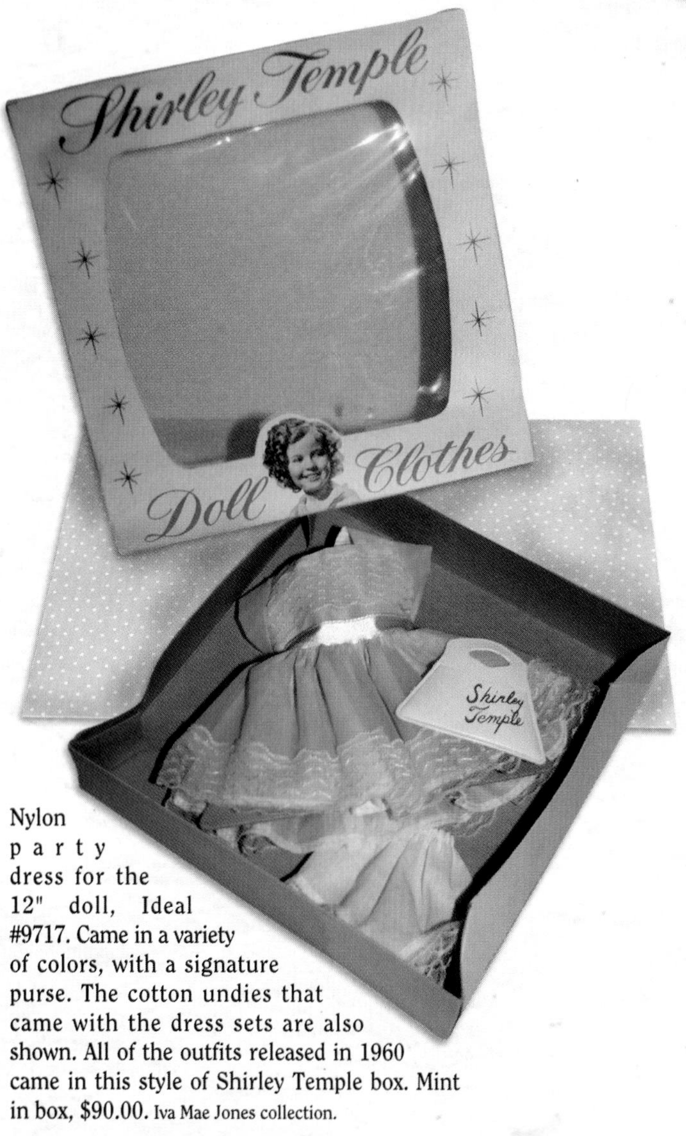

Nylon party dress for the 12" doll, Ideal #9717. Came in a variety of colors, with a signature purse. The cotton undies that came with the dress sets are also shown. All of the outfits released in 1960 came in this style of Shirley Temple box. Mint in box, $90.00. Iva Mae Jones collection.

Pattern print pinafore for the 12" doll, Ideal outfit #9716. Also includes a signature purse. Currently valued at $40.00 (outfit only). Ideal catalog.

Rebecca of Sunnybrook Farm outfit (an updated version of #9550 from 1959), Ideal #9719. Includes a shirt, overalls, and a straw hat. Mint in box, $80.00. Iva Mae Jones collection.

12" Shirley Temple doll wearing Ideal outfit #9718, a cowgirl outfit. Includes a western-style shirt and skirt with fringe decorations, cowboy boots, and a cowboy hat. Very hard to find complete. $265.00. Outfit alone, $125.00. Courtesy Keith and Loretta McKenzie collection.

12" Shirley Temple doll wearing Ideal outfit #9720, a flocked nylon party dress with flower decoration at the waist and a signature purse. Very hard-to-find outfit. $250.00. Keith and Loretta McKenzie collection.

Back of Ideal #9720 dress has a very unusual V-shaped closure. Keith and Loretta McKenzie collection.

Taffeta coat, Ideal #9721. Came with a straw bonnet and signature purse. $70.00. Keith and Loretta McKenzie collection.

12" Shirley Temple doll wearing *Heidi* outfit, Ideal #9722. The modified version of #9547 from 1959. Includes a matching felt headband and a signature purse. A 15" doll also came wearing the same outfit. $175.00. Keith and Loretta McKenzie collection.

Ideal outfit #9724, a sailor dress. Consists of a sailor shirt, pleated skirt, sailor hat, tights, undies, shoes, and signature purse. Mint in box, $100.00. Loretta Beilstein collection.

Flannel Nightgown with cap. Unknown item number; found in many of the ads from 1960. $40.00. Keith and Loretta McKenzie collection.

12" Shirley Temple doll, mint in box, wearing a rare printed organdy dress from around 1959 or 1960 that was not advertised in the catalogs. $300.00. Iva Mae Jones collection.

17

5.97
15-in.

17 SHIRLEY TEMPLE AND HER MIX AND MATCH WARDROBE. Rooted hair, sleeping eyes, famous dimpled cheeks. She wears "Heidi" costume, Tyrolean Jumper with vest, slip and panties, shoes, socks, Shirley Temple pin on her dress. Her wardrobe includes party dress, coat, playclothes outfit—slacks, skirt, blouse.

48 T 4041—15-in. Doll, Wardrobe. Ship. wt. 3 lbs. $9.77

48 T 4305—15-in. Doll Only. Ship. wt. 3 lbs. 5.97

The Wards catalog from 1960 offered a 15" Shirley Temple doll that was dressed as Heidi and came with a wardrobe. Included a party dress, a *Stand Up and Cheer* dress, and a top, pants, and matching skirt set. Currently, this set would be valued at $300.00. Marge Meisinger collection.

The 15" Shirley Temple doll was released wearing a number of different variations of the Heidi outfit throughout the Heidi outfit production run, 1959 – 1962. $200.00 – 300.00 each. Keith and Loretta McKenzie collection.

In 1960, the larger Shirley Temple dolls were produced with movie outfits, including outfits from *Stand Up and Cheer*, *Rebecca of Sunnybrook Farm*, *Captain January*, *Heidi*, and *Wee Willie Winkie*. This is the *Rebecca of Sunnybrook Farm* dress, which came with a matching checked headscarf. $65.00. Keith and Loretta McKenzie collection.

17" Shirley wearing an original "Stand Up and Cheer" dress from 1960, which had been modified from the 1957 design. $225.00. Keith and Loretta McKenzie collection.

17" doll wearing a sailor outfit that is meant to represent one from *Captain January*. Sailor dress with a matching cap. In original box. $325.00. Iva Mae Jones collection.

Mint-in-box 19" doll (1959 – 1960) wearing a fancy velvet and nylon party dress. Complete with her script pin and curler box. $400.00. Iva Mae Jones collection.

17" Shirley wearing an unusual tagged pink cotton dress. $225.00. Iva Mae Jones collection.

19" Shirley Temple doll wearing original tagged floral-patterned taffeta dress. $250.00. Iva Mae Jones collection.

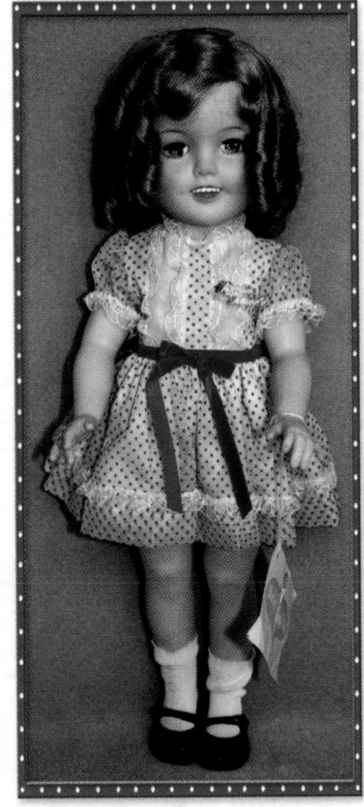

17" Shirley Temple doll with unusual original dotted dress. Notice the distinct ringlet curl set on this doll. $225.00. Loretta Beilstein collection.

19" Shirley Temple doll wearing an unusual original checked dress. $250.00. Loretta Beilstein collection.

This 36" doll is the Shirley Temple Playpal doll that was advertised in the 1960 Sears catalog. The Heidi dress that she is wearing is very similar to those made for smaller dolls during the same time period. This doll doesn't have the jointed wrists that the earlier 36" dolls did. Shirley came with a matching felt hat, a wristwatch (not shown), and socks and shoes, and had a hangtag. $2,200.00. Leslie Tannenbaum collection.

Because the vinyl Shirley Temple dolls were so popular at the time, other companies tried to make their own versions of the Shirley Temple doll. This 19" doll was released as Little Miss Movie Star. She looked very similar to the Shirley doll; however, her blue eyes (instead of the hazel that the Shirley dolls had) were a giveaway that she was not really Shirley. This doll is unmarked. $125.00. Marge Meisinger collection.

This advertisement from the 1960 Sears Christmas catalog shows a 36" Shirley Temple Playpal doll wearing a Heidi dress. Marge Meisinger collection.

36" Shirley Playpal doll wearing a Heidi dress that is not often seen on the larger dolls but is very common on the smaller dolls. This dress was also seen on the Sears Honeymates dolls from 1960. Dress is tagged with a "Shirley Temple" tag. Hat is not original. $2,000.00. Suzi Reed collection.

This is a close-up of Little Miss Movie Star. Notice the differences between this doll's face and the face of the genuine Shirley dolls. Marge Meisinger collection.

This ad for Little Miss Movie Star came in the 1960 Bertschy Furniture Company magazine. This same doll was also advertised in the Niresck 1960 *Book of Gifts* as Curly Head. Notice how the ad never specifically mentions Shirley Temple. Marge Meisinger collection.

This 36" Shirley Temple look-alike very closely resembles the 36" Shirley Temple Playpal doll and is unmarked. Even its nylon dress is very similar to the one that the Shirley Playpal doll wore. $250.00. Suzi Reed collection.

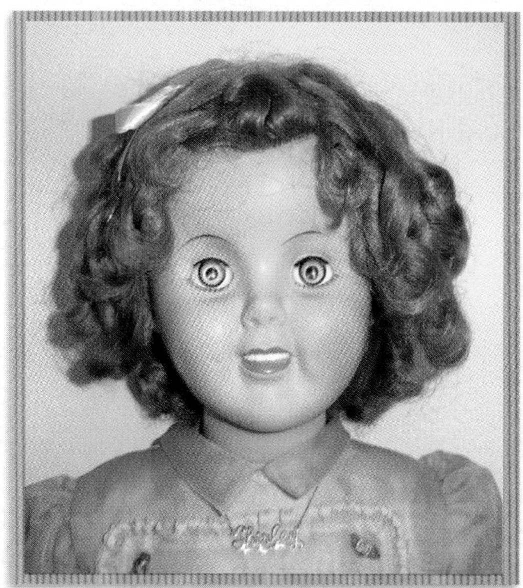

Close-up of the look-alike. This doll looks very similar to the genuine Shirley doll. Suzi Reed collection.

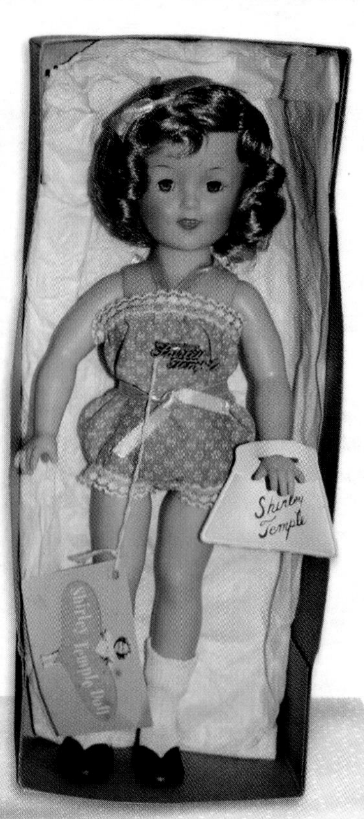

12" Shirley Temple doll in a one-piece playsuit replaced the earlier basic Shirley that came in the pink satin slip. The set also came with script pin, signature purse, and hangtag. It was sold in 1961 and 1962. Mint in box, $225.00. Keith and Loretta McKenzie collection.

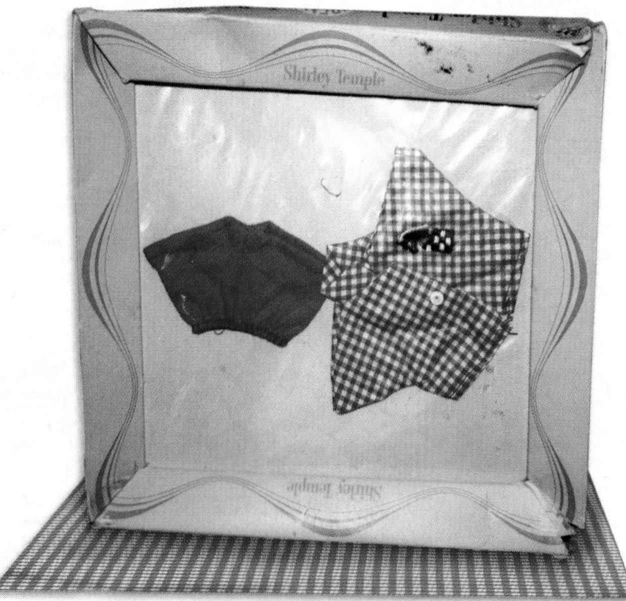

Two-piece play outfit, Ideal #9750. Consists of a checkered shirt with horse head appliqué and matching red shorts. The clothing box changed in 1961. Mint in box, $150.00. Keith and Loretta McKenzie collection.

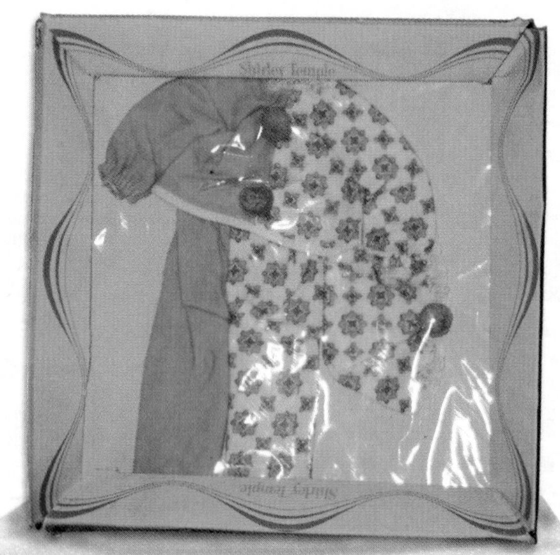

Two-piece clown pajamas set for the 12" doll, Ideal #9755. Consists of flannelette top with pompoms on it, long pants, and a matching stocking cap. Mint in box, $100.00. Keith and Loretta McKenzie collection.

Pique schoolgirl dress with Scottie dog appliqué on skirt, Ideal #9756. Also includes a signature purse. $50.00. Keith and Loretta McKenzie collection.

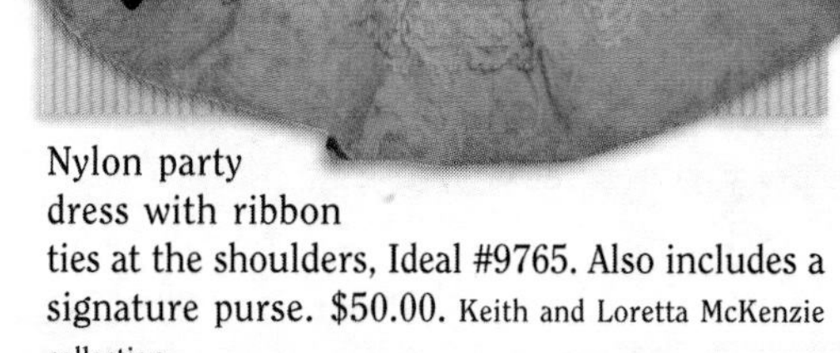

Nylon party dress with ribbon ties at the shoulders, Ideal #9765. Also includes a signature purse. $50.00. Keith and Loretta McKenzie collection.

Pants and shirt set for the 12" doll, Ideal #9760 (similar to #9526 from 1958). Consists of pedal pushers, a patterned shirt, and a straw hat. $60.00. Keith and Loretta McKenzie collection.

Cotton print school dress for the 12" doll, Ideal #9757. Also includes a signature purse. $45.00. Keith and Loretta McKenzie collection.

Felt coat for the 12" doll, with horse appliqué and striped cap. Ideal #9766. Also includes a signature purse. $75.00. Keith and Loretta McKenzie collection.

12" Shirley Temple doll wearing Ideal outfit #9767 (from 1961), a ballerina outfit with net tutu, rhinestone decorations, a flowered headband (hard to find), and ballet shoes (not original; ads from 1961 show this doll wearing the normal black plastic shoes). This is one of the rarest and most sought-after outfits for the vinyl Shirley Temple doll. Very hard to find complete with headband. $325.00. Keith and Loretta McKenzie collection.

12" Shirley Temple doll wearing Ideal outfit #9770, a nylon and velvet party dress with flower decoration at the waist (similar to outfits #9715 and #9551 from previous years). Made in a variety of colors; includes a straw bonnet and signature purse. $225.00. Keith and Loretta McKenzie collection.

A cotton pinafore for the 12" doll, Ideal #9768. Also includes a signature purse. $40.00. Keith and Loretta McKenzie collection.

Cardigan outfit for the 12" doll, Ideal #9771. Includes a sweater, checkered skirt, straw hat, and signature purse. $80.00. Keith and Loretta McKenzie collection.

12" Shirley Temple doll wearing Ideal outfit #9775. Consists of a leatherette coat, felt pants and matching hat, and a scarf. Mint in box, $300.00; outfit alone, $100.00. Iva Mae Jones collection.

15" Shirley Temple doll wearing the Fairyland Heroine version of Little Red Riding Hood's outfit, consisting of patterned long dress, nylon skirt, and red cape. This doll also has her original script pin and hangtag. $300.00. Keith and Loretta McKenzie collection.

In 1961, all of the major mail-order catalogs featured one or more of the Fairyland Heroine Shirley Temple dolls created in honor of Shirley's *Storybook* show, which was on TV at the time. These dolls were packaged in special fairytale boxes. This 15" doll is wearing an Alice from *Alice in Wonderland* outfit, consisting of long blue dress, white nylon apron, and signature purse (not shown). This doll also has a script pin and hangtag. One of the hardest to find in the collection. $400.00. Keith and Loretta McKenzie collection.

15" Shirley Temple doll is wearing the Fairyland Heroine version of Cinderella's outfit, consisting of a long dress with velvet bodice and attached long skirt with lace and nylon overlay and a crown. $250.00. Iva Mae Jones collection.

15" Shirley Temple doll wearing the Fairyland Heroine version of Little Bo Peep's outfit, consisting of a long patchwork dress, matching pantaloons, and a straw hat. This doll also has her original hangtag. A more common Fairyland outfit. $200.00. Keith and Loretta McKenzie collection.

15" Shirley Temple doll wearing an unusual version of the Heidi dress with matching felt hat. May have been a part of the Fairyland Heroine series. Notice the unique box design. All Fairyland Heroines were packaged in this later 1961/1962 style of box. Mint in box, $300.00. Keith and Loretta McKenzie collection.

15" Shirley Temple doll is wearing a party dress with a straw hat. Rare dress. $200.00. Keith and Loretta McKenzie collection.

Mint-in-box 15" Shirley wearing a blue checked summer dress. Box identifies the outfit "Shirley Temple as Junior Prom." Very rare dress. $325.00. Rita Dubas collection.

Extra accessories for the vinyl Shirley Temple doll, including this socks and shoes set, were sold throughout the production run. This set was for a 12" doll. $75.00. Keith and Loretta McKenzie collection.

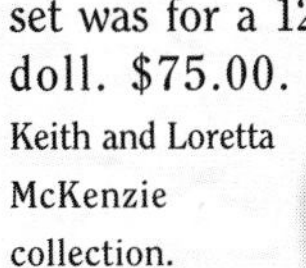

1962

This 15" Shirley Temple doll is wearing a red jumper with green and white trim on the skirt. Outfit includes a matching signature purse, script pin, and hangtag. Rare dress. Doll is packaged in her original window box. $350.00. Keith and Loretta McKenzie collection.

15" Shirley Temple doll wearing a party dress with matador sleeves. Outfit includes a matching signature purse and "Ideal Doll" hangtag. Doll is in truly mint condition. $300.00. Keith and Loretta McKenzie collection.

1963 was the final year that the vinyl Shirley doll was produced. The only doll made that year was the 15". This Ideal ad shows the 15". Has a slightly different facial mold and bangs at the front of her curls. She is wearing a nylon dress that does not seem to have the same quality as the ones shown on dolls released earlier in the production run. Very rare to find. Currently valued at $350.00. Marge Meisinger collection.

17" wearing a nylon dress that is from 1961 or 1962. $150.00. Loretta Beilstein collection.

Unusual container of Shirley Temple curlers. $60.00. Loretta Beilstein collection.

Simplicity pattern for clothes for a 12" doll. The clothes were very similar to the original Shirley clothes. This pattern is shown with clothes made from this pattern by Terry Leslie in the 1960s, for her daughter Loretta McKenzie. $10.00 (for the pattern — doll clothes made by Mom are always priceless). Terry Leslie and Loretta McKenzie collection.

A number of official Shirley Temple doll patterns were released for the Shirley Temple doll. $25.00. Iva Mae Jones collection.

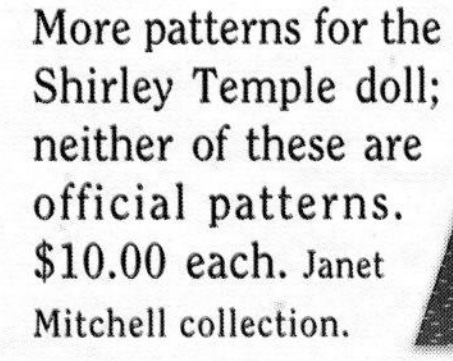

More patterns for the Shirley Temple doll; neither of these are official patterns. $10.00 each. Janet Mitchell collection.

Chapter 8
The 1970s: Shirley Temple Dolls Live On

In addition to being an active wife and mother, Shirley Temple Black was also very involved in her community during the 1960s. She participated in events that promoted education, even hosting a local television show that emphasized the importance of education and responsibility. She also volunteered to take part in local parades and celebrations to give publicity to causes that were important to her. Shirley continued her work with the Junior League, a women's organization committed to the promotion of volunteerism. In 1966, she became chairperson of the Multiple Sclerosis Foundation, an organization close to her heart since her brother George was diagnosed with the disease in 1952, and she participated in many advertisements and interviews regarding awareness of the disease.

Shirley found her true calling in the late 1960s, in politics. In 1967, she ran as a Republican nominee for Congress in California's 11th District. Though she was unsuccessful, this began her full-time work in politics. In 1969, Richard Nixon appointed her as a delegate to the United Nations. She was a natural at diplomacy, and she acknowledged this in an interview at the time: "I'm a friend from their past and they trust me." In 1972, she became an assistant to the chairman of the President's Council for Environmental Quality, a position she held for the next two years. She became the United States ambassador to the Republic of Ghana in 1974. When she left the post in 1976, President Gerald Ford appointed her chief of protocol, a position that involved everything from coordinating celebrations in Washington, D.C., to welcoming visiting heads of state and arranging for their housing and entertainment.

Shirley publicly shared her struggle with breast cancer. After she discovered a lump during a self exam in 1972 and underwent a mastectomy, she spoke openly with journalists about what had occurred, becoming the first public face of the disease. The outpouring of well wishes was overwhelming, and by speaking out publicly, she helped thousands of women become aware of what to look for and how to check themselves for breast cancer.

In late 1972, Montgomery Ward celebrated its 100th anniversary by re-releasing some of its most famous dolls, including the Kewpie doll, the Bye-lo Baby, and the Shirley Temple doll. The vinyl Shirley doll was 15" tall, a re-release of the 15" doll from the 1950s. It sold for $7.99. Though it was produced from the same mold, it did not have the appeal of the 1950s 15" doll. This doll was produced for less than a year, and was then replaced by a new 16" mold designed by Neil Estern, reportedly because Shirley was not happy with the original design quality of the doll. The new doll had a hard plastic body, hard arms and legs, and a vinyl head with rooted saran hair. Her hair was styled in Shirley banana curls in the front and very short curls in the back. The original price was $9.97. This doll was sold through 1975, and four movie outfits were sold separately for her. Other Shirley Temple molds were made as prototypes in 1976 in honor of the bicentennial celebration, and in 1980 when the movie **Little Miss Marker** was remade; however, they were never released to the public.

By this time, Shirley Temple had acquired three generations of fans. Adults and children alike were not only fans of little Shirley from the 1930s, they were also beginning to greatly admire the woman that Shirley Temple Black had become.

1972

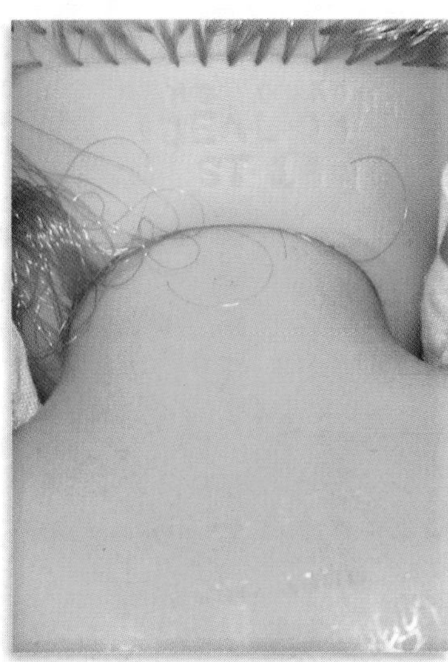

Markings on the back of the commemorative Shirley doll at left.

In 1972, Montgomery Ward re-issued the 15" Shirley that was originally produced between 1958 and 1963. This was a commemorative Shirley doll named Yesterday's Darling, produced in honor of Ward's 100th anniversary. Marked "IDEAL DOLL/ST-15-1" on the back of her head and "IDEAL ST-15/HONG KONG" on her back. Wearing a flocked nylon dress with red velvet bodice, similar to one of the first ones issued on the 1958 vinyl doll. Box is marked "Yesterday's Darling." Mint in box, $150.00.

1973 – 1975

Shirley wasn't completely satisfied with the quality of the Ward's doll released in 1972, so the doll mold was redesigned by Neil Estern and the doll was re-released as a 16" doll marked "1972/IDEAL TOY CORP./ST-14-H-213/Hong Kong" on the head and "IDEAL [in a circle] 1972/2M-5534-2" (or some close variation), on her back. She was the first Shirley doll to have a painted smile instead of separate molded teeth. The doll was first produced wearing a velvet-vested dress similar to the one that the Ward's doll above wore, and was packaged in a plain brown Montgomery Ward shipping box. $100.00 (no box). Iva Mae Jones collection.

The doll was later produced in a *Stand Up and Cheer* dress. Shirley's eyes were stationary and her hair had banana curls in the front and very short curls in the back (oftentimes, it looks like the hair in the back was cut, but it actually came that way). Packaged in a large picture box. Mint in box, $150.00. The doll pieces can still be ordered from the Dollspart Supply Catalog (see appendix).

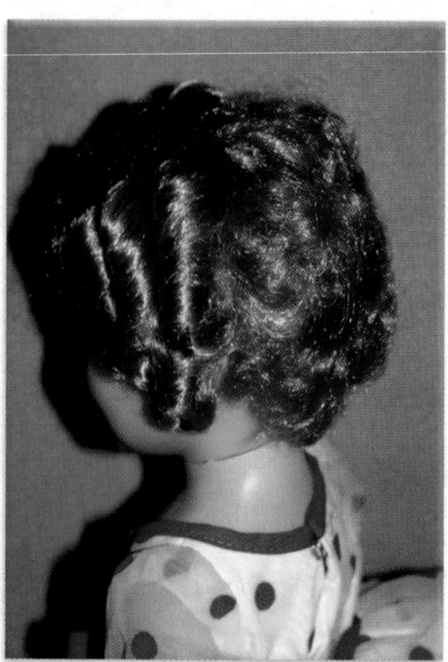

The side of the head, showing the short curls of the back of the hair and the styled ringlets at the front.

This Ideal ad introduced the new Shirley Temple doll to the public. Mary Williams collection.

Four movie outfits were released separately for the new 16" Shirley Temple doll, each in its own picture box. They were the *Rebecca of Sunnybrook Farm* overalls and shirt, the *Heidi* dress, the *Captain January* bellbottom pants and sailor shirt, and the *Little Colonel* dress and pantaloons. $70.00 each; outfits alone, $30.00 each. Janet Mitchell collection.

In 1980, the Shirley movie *Little Miss Marker* was remade. Ideal wanted to release a Shirley Temple doll to correspond with the new film's release, and even had it sculpted by Vincent DeFilippo. However, Shirley did not approve, so it was never actually released to the public. Marge Meisinger collection.

The store display Ideal used to promote this Shirley Temple doll. $250.00. Iva Mae Jones collection.

Vinyl dolls are almost indestructible; they don't crack, break, bubble, or chip like composition dolls do. This makes vinyl Shirley Temple dolls very appealing to Shirley Temple doll collectors. It is much easier to maintain the condition of vinyl dolls simply by keeping them in a cool dry place and avoiding direct sunlight.

Finding a vinyl doll in good condition is also easier. Because of this, only mint vinyl dolls go for high prices. Vinyl Shirley Temple dolls that are in good but played-with condition are usually quite inexpensive. Dolls that have stains, haircuts, and discolorations can be found on eBay, often for less than $30.00.

The low price of the vinyl dolls works to the advantage of people who have dreamed of owning a Shirley Temple doll but have not been able to afford one. For anyone who has always wanted a Shirley Temple doll, a cheap ($40.00 or less) vinyl doll from the 1950s is the doll for you. Vinyl dolls are not too difficult to fix up, and transforming one into the doll of your dreams is a fun project as well. This chapter defines condition and goes through step-by-step methods that can be used to help you make your vinyl Shirley Temple dolls look their best.

Condition Up Close

Condition makes a big difference in the price of vinyl Shirley Temple dolls. Clean vinyl, high facial coloring, no surface scratching, and a shiny perfect curl set are characteristics of the mint doll. In a common original dress, this 15" doll would be worth $300.00 (based on condition). Keith and Loretta McKenzie collection.

This doll has high coloring and the hair is mostly in the original curl set; however, the vinyl is not mint (has a darker look to it), and the hair is not as shiny as that on a mint doll would be. This doll would be considered near mint. This 17" doll is worth $250.00.

The vinyl of this 12" doll has darkened with age and play wear, and the cheek color has faded somewhat as well. The hair has also been reset, and the eyes have clouded a bit. This doll has been played with and is considered to be in good condition. This 12" doll in an original dress is worth $100.00.

15" doll with a blue stain on her forehead, a darker color to her vinyl, messy hair, and eyes that have clouded slightly. Worth $30.00 (naked) on eBay.

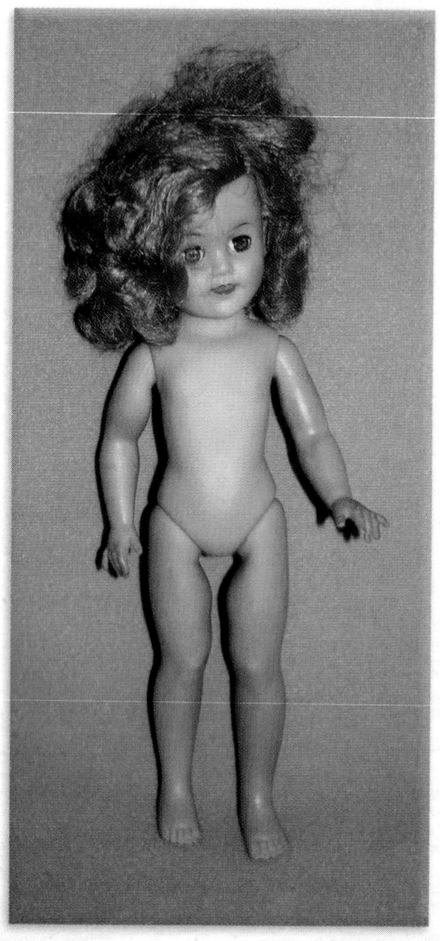

Quick Fix for the Shirley Temple Doll

Quick Fix

The products required to fix up this Shirley Temple doll include Formula 409, children's hair detangler, comb, hairspray, bobby pins, pen, buff puff, Q-tips, paper towels, Oxy acne medicine, clasp lamp, vinegar, blowdryer, red oil paint, replica dress, undies, socks, shoes, and hair ribbon.

This is the 15" doll shown on the preceding page. She is in okay condition, but she can definitely use some help.

First, the doll's hair was wet with water. Then the household cleaner Formula 409 was used to shampoo the hair. After cleaning, the 409 was carefully removed with water.

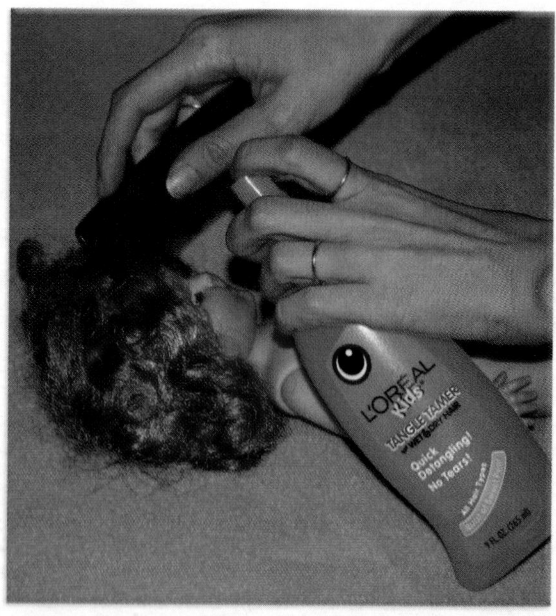

A bit of children's hair detangler was used to help condition the hair and get the knots out. After the knots were combed out, the hair was left to dry for a bit (about two hours).

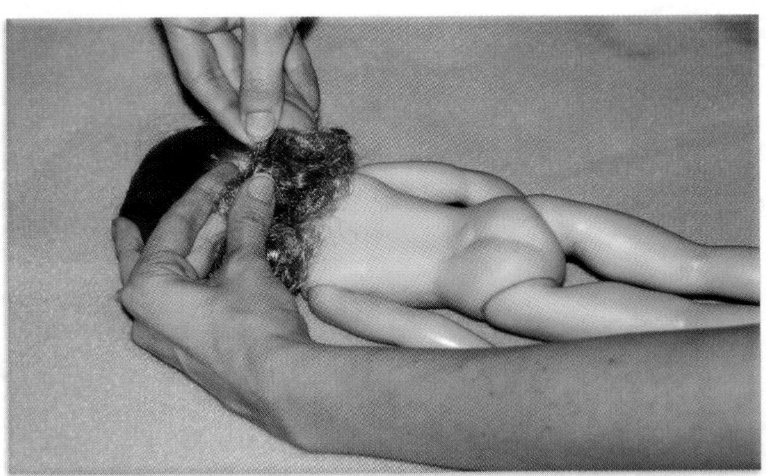

The original vinyl curl set only had curls at the front and sides of the head; the back of the hair was combed smooth at the top and had a curled mass at the bottom. Bobby pins held the hair down properly.

To create the curls, sections of hair were combed, sprayed with maximum-hold hairspray (be careful to avoid spraying the vinyl of the face), and then wrapped around a pen (though it is easier to use curlers for the saran hair). The curl was not wrapped as a long banana curl, but like it was on a roller. The direction of the curls (three on the left, two on the right) was always towards the face (on the left side of the doll, clockwise; on the right side of the doll, counterclockwise). Once wrapped, they were secured with many bobby pins (to get them into the correct position).

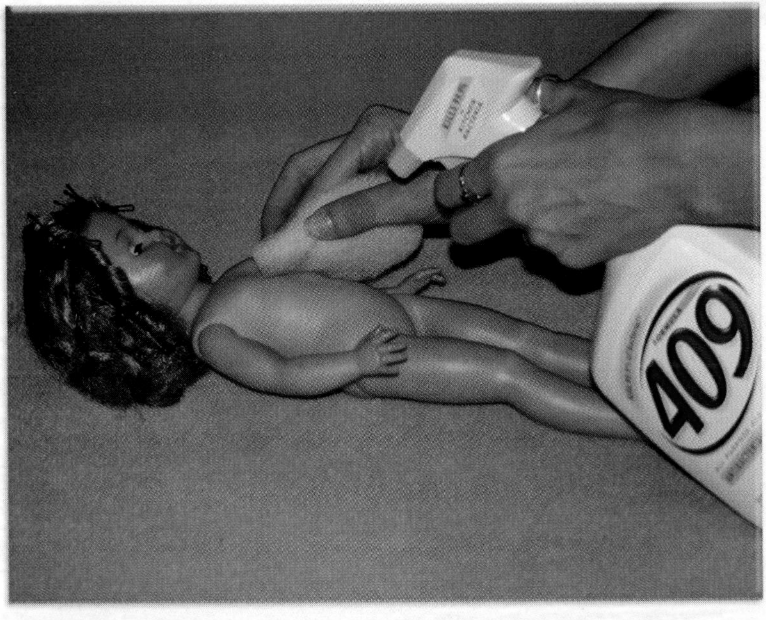

While the curls were drying, the doll was cleaned with 409 on a buff puff. Don't clean the doll with soap and water, because you don't want a lot of water stuck inside her for a long period of time. Once the doll was cleaned, a paper towel and Q-tips got off the excess cleaner.

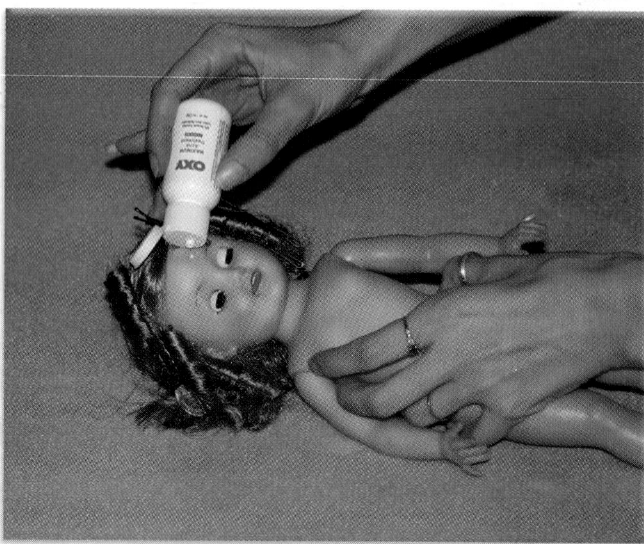

Once the dirt was gone, the doll's face looked much better; however, she still had blue stains on her forehead, upper lip, chin, arm, and leg. Oxy acne medicine (with 10% benzoyl peroxide) was applied to the blue stains on her forehead, chin, arm, and leg.

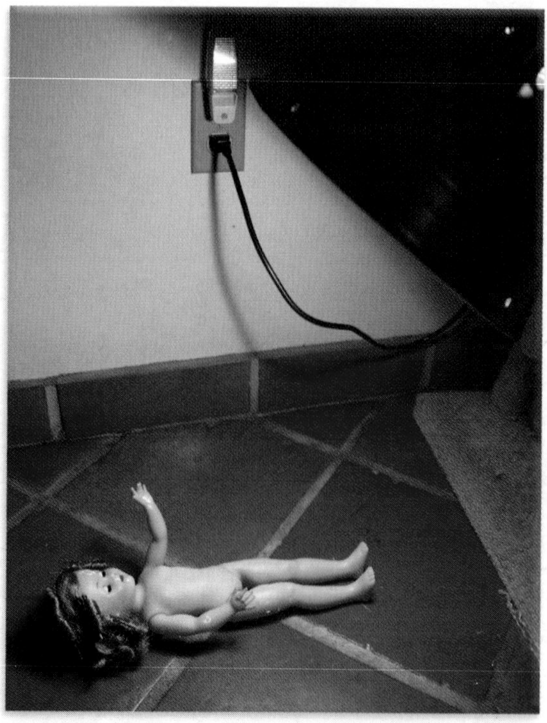

She was then placed under a clasp light for four hour (check every 30 minutes and stop the process once the stain has disappeared). This got the stain out, and the area was cleaned again with 409 on a buff puff.

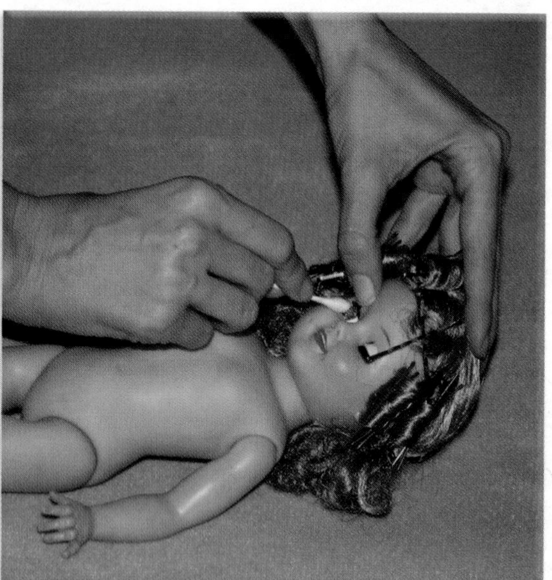

The doll's eyes were cleaned with vinegar on a Q-tip, to get any dirt or mold off the outer part of the eye itself. This really helped clear up this doll's eyes (tip is from A Dolly's World — www.adollysworld.com).

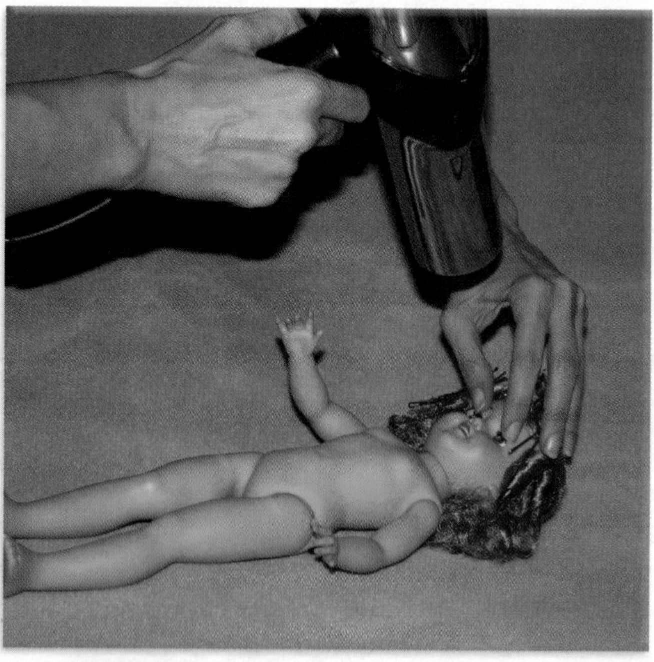

The eyes were then blown with a hair dryer until completely clear. This can take up to 10 minutes, but for this doll, very little was needed. (If they are still cloudy, there are additional things that can be done to clear them; there are more tips at adollysworld.com.)

At this point, she needed a bit more color to her cheeks. A small amount of red oil paint (lipstick can also be used) was applied to her cheeks.

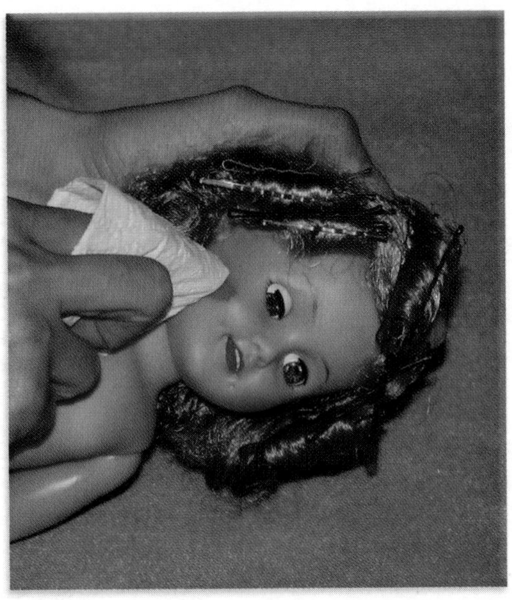

It was then blended in with a tissue. This method also works if a limb is faded; just match the color and then blend.

After drying for two days, her hair was carefully styled (a few hairpins were used to keep it permanently in place). This close-up shows how much better the doll looks now!

A cute $2.00 dress from the local doll show, rayon socks from Dollspart Supply, $1.00 doll shoes from a local doll shop, and a silk ribbon pinned into her hair complete her look. What a beautiful doll she is, and definitely worth more than $30.00!

The demand for Shirley Temple dolls remained strong as Shirley got older. Though children were still interested in the play dolls, the majority of people who bought Shirley Temple dolls were collectors, the Shirley Temple fans who wanted to own reminders of the sweet little girl in the movies that so many of them grew up with. The Shirley Temple dolls began to be catered more to the collector, and were no longer the play toys that they had been previously. In 1982, Ideal created the first collector series of Shirley Temple dolls. Vinyl dolls, 8" and 12", were released in six different movie outfits. These dolls were not designed to be played with and cost an expensive $38.00 for the 12" doll and $24.00 for the 8" doll. Though the dolls were not as pretty as earlier dolls, and the outfits were not as intricately designed as those of earlier dolls, the dolls were nonetheless well received by collectors, who hadn't been able to buy a new Shirley Temple doll for seven years. The next year, the Ideal Toy Company, which had been experiencing declining sales revenues for a number of years, merged with CBS Toys. CBS took over the decisions controlling which dolls were released by Ideal. Because Shirley Temple dolls remained successful for the company, in 1983 a paler version of the 1982 doll was released in six different movie outfits. The first official porcelain Shirley Temple doll was also produced the same year, and it cost a very expensive $399.00. Designed exclusively for the Shirley Temple collector, this doll unfortunately lacked the personality of the earlier Shirley Temple dolls and barely even resembled the child star or the movie outfit that it was meant to portray. It did not sell well, and ended up being the only porcelain Shirley Temple doll released by Ideal. In 1984, for the 50th anniversary of the Shirley Temple doll, Ideal/CBS commissioned Hank Garfinkle to design the Dolls, Dreams, and Love Shirley Temple dolls, a series of child-size vinyl Shirley Temple dolls, which were released during the next two years. Three vinyl 16" Shirley Temple dolls were released in 1984 as well. The last doll of the Dolls, Dreams, and Love series was released in 1986. That year, the 52-year relationship between Shirley Temple and the Ideal Toy Company ended as well.

When the Ideal Toy Company merged with CBS Toys in 1983, the focus of the company shifted away from the dolls and toys that it had been so well-known for. In 1986, CBS closed down the doll and toy divisions of the company. At that time, Shirley Temple had to find another company to manufacture her dolls, which were still in very high demand. She decided on the Danbury Mint, a company focused exclusively on producing high-quality collectibles. That same year, the first official Shirley Temple dolls made by the Danbury Mint were released. The collection included the first in a series of eight porcelain dolls wearing very detailed outfits from her most famous movies.

In 1988, Shirley Temple Black released her autobiography, **Child Star**. It became an instant best seller. The book again renewed interest in Shirley Temple for many of those who grew up with her. It also introduced a fourth generation to the child star. Shirley became quite visible with promotional book signings all over the country, and she was even honored as Grand Marshal of the 100th Rose Bowl Parade. At the same time, the VCR was becoming a household item, and videos were offered of her most famous movies, which Shirley fans could watch again and again. The Danbury Mint quickly took advantage of this renewed interest and began to release the Shirley Temple Portrait Dolls series, the dolls of which were made of the finest porcelain and had hand-painted details, intricately designed outfits, and an assortment of detailed accessories.

The success of the Portrait Dolls encouraged the Danbury Mint to release more high-quality Shirley Temple collector dolls. These included toddler dolls, movie dolls, dolls modeled after the composition dolls of the 1930s, dress-up dolls, dolls inspired by advertising pictures, and even dolls inspired by pictures from Shirley's own family album. Shirley herself had approval over each doll that was released, and they all came with a certificate of authenticity signed by Shirley Temple Black. The demand for Shirley dolls remains strong, and the Danbury Mint continues to produce an ever-expanding high-quality collection of dolls for Shirley Temple fans.

1978

This "Shirley doll" was sold through mail order catalogs in 1978. It is not a Shirley Temple doll and was not approved by Shirley Temple. It was made of bisque (porcelain); however, the quality of the doll itself is quite low. $20.00 (about the same that it originally sold for).

1982

The Shirley Temple Doll Collection Series was released in 1982. Dolls were produced in two sizes, 8" and 12". These dolls came with hazel sleep eyes, rooted saran hair with curls going all around the head, and painted smiles. Dolls came wearing six different outfits, including the *Heidi* outfit (with braided blond hair and wooden shoes), the *Stowaway* Chinese pajamas, the *Stand Up and Cheer* dress, the *Little Colonel* dress, the *Captain January* sailor outfit with sailor cap, and the *Littlest Rebel* dress with pantaloons and eyelet apron. Ideal Doll catalog.

8" Heidi doll, mint in box. This particular doll has light blonde braided hair in honor of Shirley's hairstyle in the "Dutch girl" scene from the movie. The doll was packaged in a pink window box with Shirley's signature on it. $25.00.

This is the 12" *Rebecca of Sunnybrook Farm* doll, mint in box. It was packaged in a blue window box with Shirley's signature on it. Notice the very pale coloring of this doll compared to the ones released in 1982. $35.00.

In 1983, six more dolls were added to the collector series. Clothing included a *Rebecca of Sunnybrook Farm* outfit (overalls and straw hat), a *Dimples* outfit (gray coat and hat), a *Poor Little Rich Girl* outfit (navy blue coat and straw hat), another *Poor Little Rich Girl* outfit (military outfit with matching hat), a *Wee Willie Winkie* outfit (Scotch military outfit), and a *Susannah of the Mounties* outfit (long dress and apron). Dolls were produced in 8" and 12" sizes. They differed from the 1982 dolls because they had very pale coloring, almost white (to resemble porcelain). Ideal Doll catalog.

The first authorized porcelain Shirley Temple doll, released in 1983, was called America's Sweetheart. Personally approved by Shirley Temple Black. 16" tall, wearing a long skirt and apron set that was supposed to resemble an outfit from *The Little Colonel*. Limited edition of 10,000 dolls. Original price, $399.00; current value, $100.00, because many collectors didn't find the face of this doll to be very appealing.

1984 – 1986

Three new collector's edition Shirley Temple dolls were made in 1984. They were 16" tall and were produced with very pale vinyl (similar in coloring to those released in 1983). This one is wearing the *Glad Rags to Riches* outfit. Mint in box, $80.00. Keith and Loretta McKenzie collection.

16" collector's edition Shirley Temple doll, mint in her original box. This doll is wearing the *Stand Up and Cheer* dress. $80.00. Iva Mae Jones collection.

The third in the series came wearing this velvet party dress from *Heidi*. $30.00 (just the dress), $50.00 (doll in dress, without the box). Keith and Loretta McKenzie collection.

In 1984, Ideal had Hank Garfinkle (one of its most respected doll designers) create a series of very large limited-edition vinyl Shirley Temple dolls in honor of the 50th anniversary of the Shirley Temple doll. This was the Dolls, Dreams, and Love series. The first of these was the *Stand Up and Cheer* doll. It was 36" tall and made of vinyl, with sleep eyes. Limited edition of 2,500 dolls. Originally $184.95, now $200.00. *Dolls, Dreams, and Love* catalog.

This Shirley Temple doll was the second in the series. Created by Garfinkle, 1984. 36" tall with sleep eyes. Wearing a fuchsia long dress that is styled after one that Shirley wore in *The Little Colonel*, pantaloons, Buster Brown shoes, and a straw hat. Limited edition of 10,000 dolls. $200.00. *Dolls, Dreams, and Love* catalog.

This vinyl *Captain January* Shirley Temple doll was also created by Garfinkle, and is the last in the Dolls, Dreams, and Love series. It was 30" tall, and the arms were molded so that the doll looked like its hands were on its hips. It was sold as a limited edition of 2,500 dolls. $200.00. Ideal catalog.

28" Shirley Temple doll wearing a bright green satin *Baby Take a Bow* dress. Designed by Garfinkle. This doll was sold in a limited edition of 3,000 dolls. $200.00. *Dolls, Dreams, and Love* catalog.

A vinyl Baby Shirley Temple doll (on the left, shown with an original Shirley baby from the 1930s) was advertised in the 1985 *Dolls, Dreams, and Love* catalog. This one is just not a pretty doll, and was revised before it was sold to the public. *Dolls, Dreams, and Love* catalog.

Different versions of the *Captain January* and *Little Colonel* outfits were advertised in the 1985 *Dolls, Dreams, and Love* catalog as being sold separately, but were never released to the public. *Dolls, Dreams, and Love* catalog.

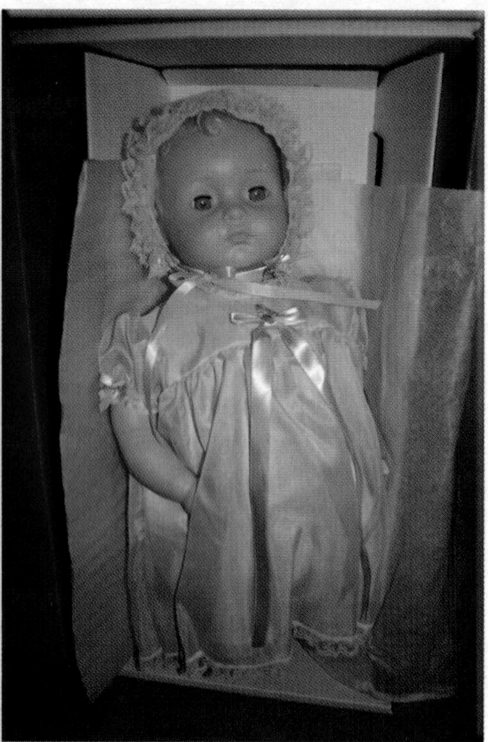

30" vinyl Baby Shirley Temple doll made by Garfinkle. It was part of the Dolls, Dreams, and Love series. The doll has sleep eyes and molded hair. This doll came with a script pin and a certificate of authenticity. $225.00. Iva Mae Jones collection.

Display box that held the baby Shirley Temple doll. Iva Mae Jones collection.

In 1986, the Danbury Mint took over the job of making Shirley Temple collectible dolls. The dolls were designed by Judy Belle. The first dolls released were 14" tall and made of porcelain, with curled wigs and stationary eyes. The first doll wore a dress from the movie *Stand Up and Cheer*. It came meticulously wrapped in a Shirley Temple box, with a certificate of authenticity. A total of eight dolls were released in the series. $50.00.

Other dolls released from 1987 through the 1990s, from left: *The Littlest Rebel*, *Wee Willie Winkie*, and *The Little Colonel* (missing her original straw hat). $50.00 each. Iva Mae Jones collection.

More dolls in the series included, from left, *Poor Little Rich Girl*, *Heidi*, *Rebecca of Sunnybrook Farm* (missing her original gray pail), and *Captain January*. $50.00 each. Iva Mae Jones collection.

In 1990, a new high-quality collector series was released by the Danbury Mint. The dolls were designed by Elke Hutchens. The series was called Shirley Temple Portrait Dolls. From left to right: *Curly Top* bride, complete with bouquet of flowers and gold ring bracelet; *Bright Eyes,* complete with hat, purse, and her own doll; *Dimples,* complete with top hat and cane, and *The Little Princess,* complete with crown and scepter. *The Little Princess* was the first doll released in the series. Dolls were made of porcelain and had stationary eyes, and each came with a certificate of authenticity signed by Shirley Temple Black. These dolls were sold for $234.00 each. Now, $100.00 each.

The next series from the Danbury Mint was The Shirley Temple Toddler Doll Collection, which featured dolls modeled after pictures of Shirley before she became a child star. These dolls were also sculpted by Elke Hutchens. They include (from left to right) Little Miss Shirley; Sunday's Best, complete with dress, coat, hat, and purse; Bathing Beauty, complete with beach ball; and My Friend Corky, complete with Scottie dog. These dolls were approximately 14" tall seated and 17" tall standing. They had stationary eyes and glued-on synthetic wigs full of curls. Released in 1996 and 1997, they originally sold for $129.00 each. Currently, $90.00 each.

Beginning in 1992, four more dolls were released in this series. They included (from top left) *Captain January, Just Around the Corner, Heidi,* and *Little Colonel*. Now, $125.00 each. Danbury Mint catalog.

The Shirley Temple Family Album Doll Collection was offered in 1997. These 17" dolls were sculpted by Elke Hutchens. They were inspired by pictures from Shirley's own album. They included, from left, First Vacation, complete with coat, hat, Hawaiian lei, teddy bear, and suitcase; Birthday Magic, complete with a cake for her to hold; Flower Girl, complete with her own basket of flowers; and Movie Premiere, complete with navy blue coat, white cap, and long-sleeved chiffon dress. $100.00 each.

In 1996, the Danbury Mint released three cheaper vinyl Shirley Temple dolls through Target stores. They included, from left, *The Little Colonel*, *Rebecca of Sunnybrook Farm*, and *Heidi*. Meant to be play dolls. Original price, $24.99 each. Now, mint in box, $30.00 each.

10" porcelain Shirley Temple dolls were made by Elke Hutchens and released beginning in 1998. Clockwise from top left: *Curly Top*; *Littlest Rebel*; *Dimples*; *Baby Take a Bow*; *Stowaway,* with hat and purse; *Heidi,* with flowers; *Wee Willie Winkie* with purse; and *Captain January,* complete with yellow raincoat and hat. They originally sold for (and are currently valued at) $75.00 each.

A higher-quality 16" vinyl Shirley Temple doll, the Shirley Temple Dress Up Doll, was released in 2000 through the Danbury Mint. This one is wearing a duck dress and hat from the movie *Curly Top*; the outfit also includes a purse, panties, socks, and shoes. The doll was free with purchase of the outfits, which sold for $29.95 each. Twenty-five movie outfits were sold with this doll. Shown are 19 of the 25 outfits. Top, left to right: *Captain January*, *The Little Princess*, *Susannah of the Mounties*, (vinyl doll wearing) *Curly Top* duck dress, *Little Princess* birthday dress, and *The Little Colonel*. Middle row, left to right: *The Littlest Rebel*, *Wee Willie Winkie*, *The Blue Bird*, *Just Around the Corner* riding outfit, *Little Miss Broadway*, *Stowaway* Chinese outfit, and *Our Little Girl*. Bottom row, left to right: *Stand Up and Cheer*, *Heidi*, *Baby Take a Bow*, *Dimples*, *Bright Eyes* aviator, and *Stowaway* yellow summer dress. Not shown are a sailor dress from *Poor Little Rich Girl*, silk pajamas from *Poor Little Rich Girl*, a sailor outfit from *Captain January*, a traveling outfit from *Wee Willie Winkie*, a red-dotted dress from *Baby Take a Bow*, and a military outfit from *Rebecca of Sunnybrook Farm*. The complete set also included a red trunk to put them in (not pictured). Complete set, $900.00.

Each costume for the vinyl Dress Up Doll included detailed accessories and was packaged in a white box with the name of the movie on the outside. The boxed outfits came complete with hangers and stands so that they could be displayed properly. This particular boxed outfit was from the movie *Our Little Girl*. It included a pink checked dress with short jacket overlay, white coat with matching hat, panties, socks, shoes, and a certificate of authenticity. $25.00.

The Two of a Kind series was inspired by 1930s advertising pictures of Shirley with the dolls made in her image. First released in 1999. 14" tall (seated) with a 5" tall doll wearing a matching dress. Also included a chair for them to sit on. From left to right: Shirley and her doll (wearing matching Curly Top dresses), Polka Dot Pals, Sailor Pals, and Our Little Girls. $100.00 each.

17" Shirley Temple Red Cross doll was a part of the Danbury Mint's Serving America Doll Collection. Inspired by a public service announcement that Shirley filmed in the 1930s, in which she urged people to give "just one dollar" to the Red Cross. Includes money pail and nurse's hat. Her right hand is sculpted in the "one dollar" pose. Designed by Elke Hutchens and released in 1998. $100.00.

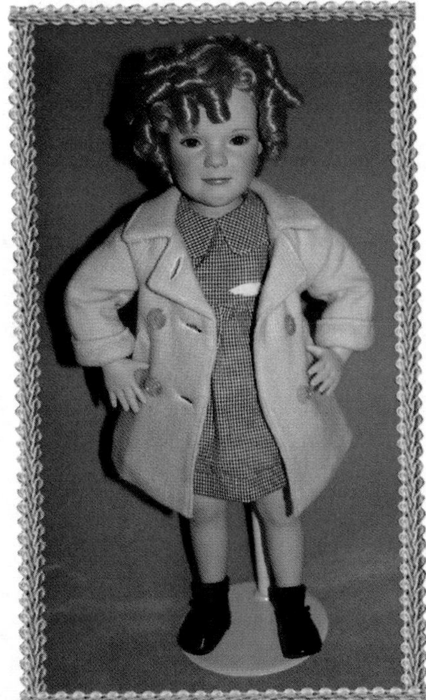

18" doll was named Shirley Temple as...Little Miss Marker. It was released in the late 1990s. This doll is posed in one of Shirley's own favorite movie poses, with her hands on her hips and a pout on her face. She is wearing a (deliberately) torn dress. This doll was sculpted by Elke Hutchens. $100.00.

The Shirley Temple Christmas Doll Collection featured 17" tall porcelain dolls sculpted by Elke Hutchens. They included (from left) The Little Caroler, uniquely scupted with open mouth and complete with real songbook; Gift Bearer, complete with Christmas stocking; Santa's Helper, complete with gift bag; and Good Samaritan Doll, complete with Salvation Army bell and coin bank stand. $100.00 each.

16" doll named Shirley Temple as...Little Bo Peep. She comes with a doll stand that includes molded grass and a lamb, wears a bonnet and windblown skirt (with poseable wire in the bottom of it), and carries a staff. Sculpted by Elke Hutchens in 1999. $125.00.

10" Shirley named Little Lass. Posed dancing in front of a landscape scene. Sculpted by Elke Hutchens, it was released in 1999. $100.00.

17" doll known as "The Little Peacemaker" portrays Shirley Temple during the filming of the movie *Susannah of the Mounties* in 1939, when she was presented with a buckskin dress by the Native Americans in the cast of the movie. Includes beads, feather, and peace pipe. Sculpted by Elke Hutchens in 1999. $125.00.

The Shirley Temple Ballerina Doll, a 16" doll wearing a dancing dress. Inspired by the dream sequence in the movie *The Little Princess* in which Shirley was a ballet dancer. Complete with flowered crown, ballet shoes, and decorative stand. Sculpted by Elke Hutchens in 2000. $125.00.

This lifelike set is called Shirley and Bojangles. It portrays them dancing on a staircase during their famous tap dancing routine in the movie *The Little Colonel*. This beautiful set was sculpted by Elke Hutchens. It was released in 2000 and is a very rare set. $350.00.

Ginny dolls were released by Vogue in honor of each decade of the twentieth century. This vinyl Miss 1930s Ginny doll was sold in the late 1990s and looked quite a bit like Shirley Temple. The dress was almost exactly like Shirley's famous *Curly Top* dress; in fact, it was too similar. The doll had to be discontinued and re-released with a different style dress. $150.00. Keith and Loretta McKenzie collection.

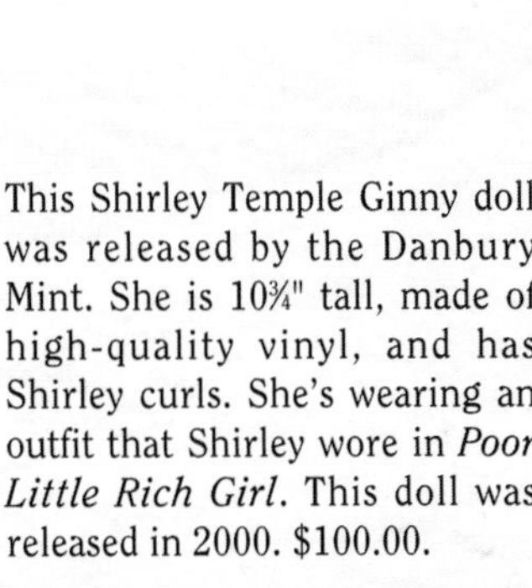

This Shirley Temple Ginny doll was released by the Danbury Mint. She is 10¾" tall, made of high-quality vinyl, and has Shirley curls. She's wearing an outfit that Shirley wore in *Poor Little Rich Girl*. This doll was released in 2000. $100.00.

Vogue's Miss 1930s Ginny doll was re-released in a different dress. $75.00. Janet Mitchell collection.

The Danbury Mint released three dolls in the Shirley Temple Antique Doll series, beginning in 2001. These dolls were meant to resemble the composition dolls from the 1930s. 14" tall and made of porcelain. From left: *The Little Colonel*, *Curly Top*, and *Heidi*.

14" tall (seated) porcelain doll was called Shirley Temple in...Stand Up and Cheer. Came with a white rabbit and signed box for doll and bunny to sit on. It was designed by Susan Wakeen in 2001. $125.00.

The Shirley Temple Antique Doll series dolls also came in their very own boxes, which were very similar to the original boxes from the 1930s.

Shirley Temple as...La Bella Diaperina, a 12" doll wearing an outfit that Shirley wore in the short film *Kid N'Hollywood*. Made by Elke Hutchens in 2001. $80.00.

Shirley Temple is...Littlest Grand Marshall, a 14" doll representing Shirley's appearance at the 1939 Rose Bowl Parade, where she was the grand marshal. Shirley is posed so that she is waving to the crowd. Complete with imitation fur muff, flowers, and large ribbon signifying that she is the grand marshal. Sculpted by Helen Kish in 2001. $100.00.

8" Shirley Temple dolls, released in 2002. Clockwise from left: *The Littlest Rebel, Just Around the Corner, Baby Take a Bow, Curly Top, Poor Little Rich Girl, Poor Little Rich Girl, Stand Up and Cheer*, and *Stowaway*. The series also came with its own display shelf. $50.00 each.

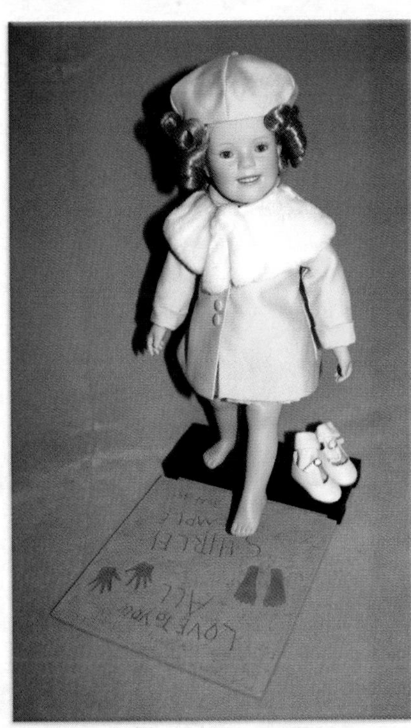

Shirley Makes Her Mark, a 17" doll that portrays Shirley placing her hand- and footprints in cement at the Graumann's Chinese Theatre in 1935. Includes its own cement block with her name, handprints, and footprints, and a small plastic stick for her to write her name with. At the actual event, Shirley wasn't smiling her normally toothy grin, since she had just lost a baby tooth that day and didn't want anyone to catch a photograph of the gap in her smile. Sculpted by Elke Hutchens and released in 2002. $150.00.

This doll is known as Shirley Takes Five. It portrays Shirley relaxing in her own movie-star chair on the set of the movie *Our Little Girl* (circa 1935). Seated height is 13½". This doll was designed by Jeanne Singer in 2002. $125.00.

Elke Hutchens modeled these 15" dolls after a picture of Shirley when she was 18 months old. On the left is Darling Little Shirley, complete with her basket of flowers. On the right is Sweet Dreams Shirley, all ready for bed and with her hairbrush in hand. These dolls were released in 2003. $99.00 each.

This Limited Edition Shirley Temple Collector Doll was released in honor of Shirley Temple's 75th birthday. Only 7,500 of these were produced. The dress was modeled after an outfit that Shirley wore in the movie *The Little Princess*. Outfit includes a velvet dress with organdy sleeves and collar, a navy blue coat with matching velvet hat, an imitation fur collar and muff set, tights, and button-up boots. This doll has her own doll, hazel eyes (most of the collector dolls had brown eyes), and a mohair wig (the other collector dolls all had synthetic wigs). $150.00.

The details of the dress that the limited edition doll is wearing.

This 18" doll is called Cutest Cadet and was made to resemble Shirley during her famous tap dancing scene with Bill Robinson in the 1938 movie *Rebecca of Sunnybrook Farm*. Sculpted by Elke Hutchens in 2004. $125.00.

This 14" (seated) doll is titled Bear Hugs. She is posed hugging the big white teddy bear that came with her. Sculpted by Elke Hutchens in 2004. $125.00.

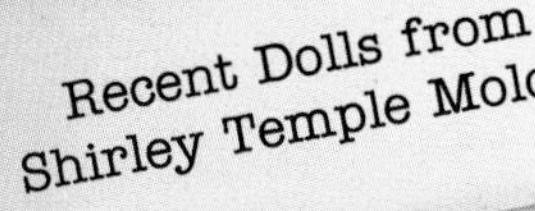

The cute 18" porcelain Shirley Temple doll was custom made from a Shirley Temple mold by Teena's Dolls. $150.00. Iva Mae Jones collection.

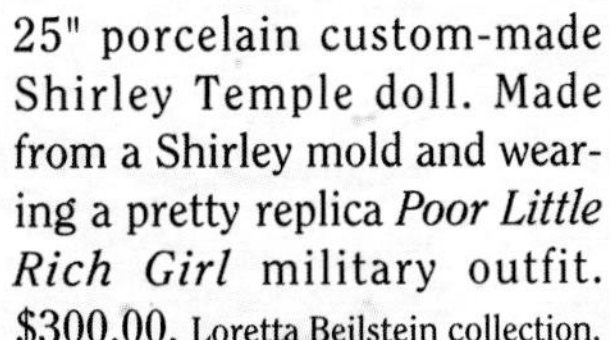

25" porcelain custom-made Shirley Temple doll. Made from a Shirley mold and wearing a pretty replica *Poor Little Rich Girl* military outfit. $300.00. Loretta Beilstein collection.

Not Quite Shirley Temple

Shirley Temple toddler, sculpted by well-known doll artist Dewees Cochran in 1966. Modeled from a picture of Shirley as a toddler. $350.00. Rosemary Dent collection.

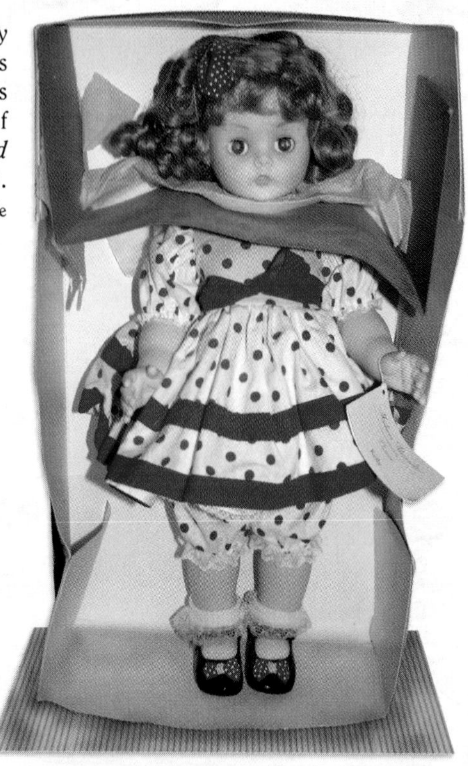

Kelly doll released by Madame Alexander is wearing a dress that is very reminiscent of Shirley's *Stand Up and Cheer* dress. $50.00. Keith and Loretta McKenzie collection.

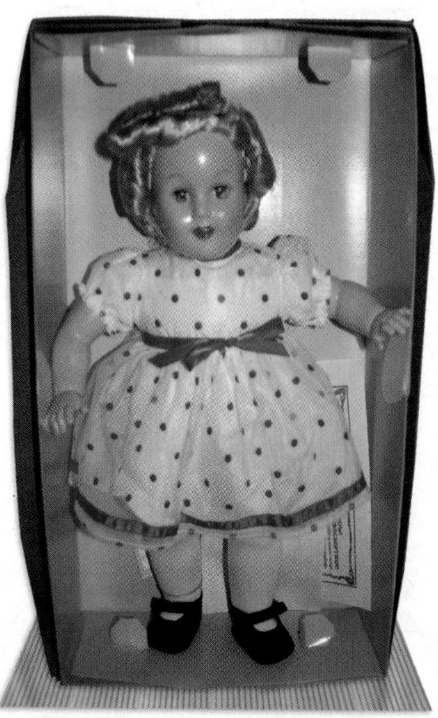

Limited Edition Bright Star doll by Horseman was released in the late 1990s and looks very similar to Shirley. $50.00. Iva Mae Jones collection.

Cute Shirley Temple–looking doll made by Margiana Dolls for the Disney Company. $100.00. Janet Mitchell collection.

As Shirley Temple became more popular, companies quickly began producing many items in her image. This chapter focuses on Shirley Temple paper products. Fox produced movie posters, lobby cards, press books, and movie heralds advertising Shirley's latest movies. The first books were also released by the Fox Film Corporation and included **The Story of My Life** and **A Movie of Me**. Saalfield took over production of the books, expanding the selection to include movie books, paper doll books, coloring books, sewing cards, activity sets, and painting sets. Other companies released sheet music, stationery, trading cards, and school tablets. In the 1950s, when Shirley's television show was running, Saalfield, along with Random House and Gabriel, began to produce even more paper products for Shirley Temple fans. Current paper products include biographies and reissues of popular paper dolls from the 1930s.

The value of a paper collectible varies greatly with rarity and condition. Uncut paper doll sets are more than 50% more valuable than cut paper dolls. Later sheet music, which was originally released in much smaller quantities, is harder to find than earlier sheet music from Shirley's most popular movies. Lobby cards and press books from her most popular movies are worth more than those from her later (less popular) movies.

Magazines, candid photos, postcards, and trading cards are valued based on the Shirley picture itself. The more appealing the picture or artwork, the more valuable it is.

Shirley Temple Dolls and Dresses (#2112), by Saalfield, 1934. Four dolls and a wardrobe of movie and personal outfits. Uncut sets are rare and valuable, worth at least 50% more than cut sets. $150.00 uncut; cut, $50.00 (complete). Janet Mitchell collection.

Six Shirley Temple Dolls with Dresses and Accessories (#280), by Saalfield, 1935. Combination of sets #2112 and #1715. A very rare set. $300.00 uncut. Leslie Tannenbaum collection.

Giveaway paper doll without separate clothes, 1935. $25.00. Loretta Beilstein collection.

Shirley Temple and Her Playhouse (#1780), by Saalfield, 1935. Boxed. $100.00. Leslie Tannenbaum collection.

Shirley Temple Standing Dolls (#1715), by Saalfield, 1935. Doll and clothes have both a front and a back side to them. $150.00 uncut, $40.00 cut (and complete). Leslie Tannenbaum collection.

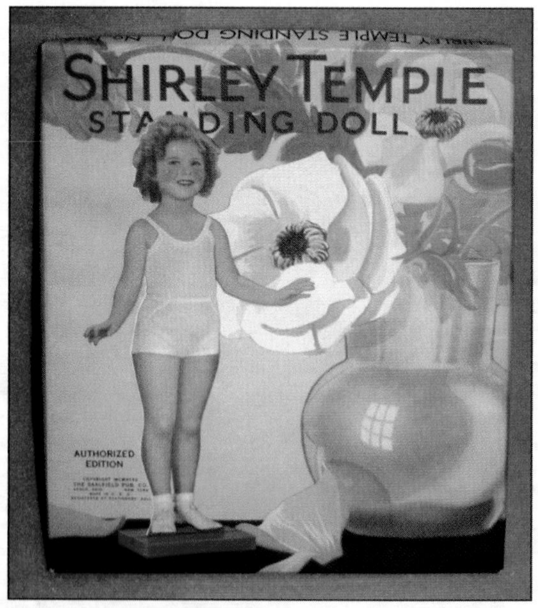

Shirley Temple Standing Doll (#1719), by Saalfield, 1935. Boxed, one doll on the cover with smaller doll and clothes inside. $150.00 uncut. Leslie Tannenbaum collection.

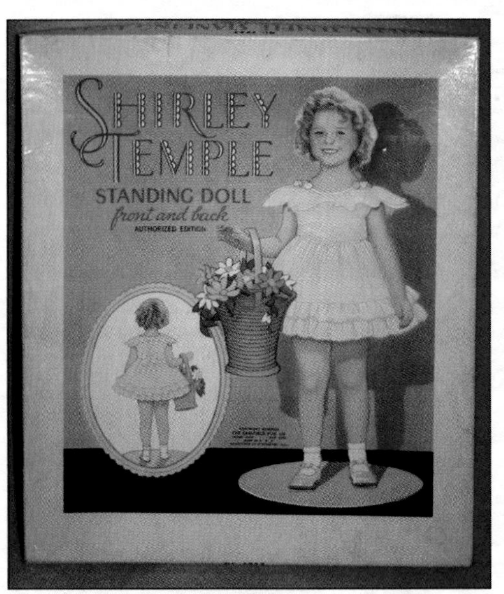

Shirley Temple Standing Doll (#1727), by Saalfield, 1935. Boxed, with two dolls, one on the back and one on the front, and clothes inside. $150.00 uncut. Leslie Tannenbaum collection.

Shirley Temple paper dolls from Spain, 1930s. Only one page of this series is for Shirley. $35.00. Janet Mitchell collection.

Another one-page Shirley Temple paper doll set from Spain. $40.00. Janet Mitchell collection.

Shirley Temple paper dolls from the Netherlands, 1930s. "In deze kast bewaar ik mijn kleertjes," loosely translated, means "In this dresser I keep my clothes." $150.00. Leslie Tannenbaum collection.

Shirley Temple Dolls and Dresses (#1761), by Saalfield, 1937. Two dolls, with an assortment of personal and movie wardrobe outfits. $125.00 uncut. Leslie Tannenbaum collection.

Back cover of paper doll set #1761. Leslie Tannenbaum collection.

Shirley Temple, a Life-like Paper Doll Cut-out (#1765), by Saalfield, 1936. 34" paper doll that came in two pieces (to be put together), a smaller 13" doll, and a wardrobe for the dolls. $300.00 uncut, $120.00 cut. Leslie Tannenbaum collection.

Shirley Temple paper doll book from Spain, 1930s. "Recortables Ediciones" roughly translates to "Cut-out Edition." $100.00. Janet Mitchell collection.

Shirley Temple Dolls and Dresses, Her Movie Wardrobe (#1773), by Saalfield, 1938. Doll with a wardrobe of Shirley's most famous movie outfits. $200.00 uncut. Janet Mitchell collection.

Shirley Temple in Masquerade Costumes (#1787), by Saalfield, 1940. Shirley paper doll with unusual dress-up costumes for the doll. This particular set is missing the cover and has the dolls (loose) and the inside clothes (uncut). $80.00 (as shown); completely uncut, $175.00. Janet Mitchell collection.

Shirley Temple Movie Wardrobe set was reproduced by the H. Sharkman Company in 2001. $10.00. Loretta McKenzie collection.

Shirley Temple Masquerade Costumes set was reproduced by B. Shackman and Company in 1998. $15.00. Janet Mitchell collection.

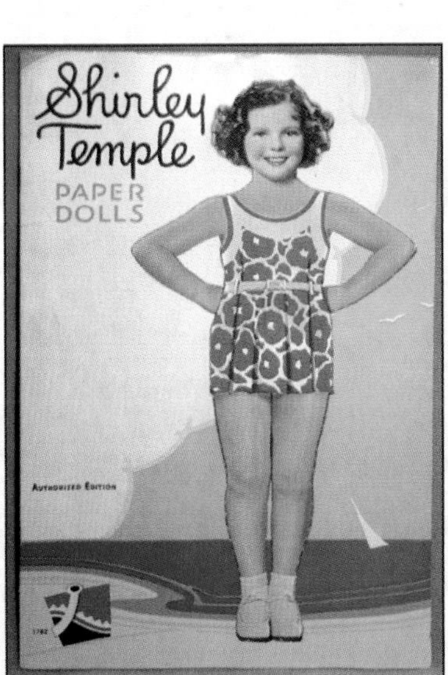

Shirley Temple Paper Dolls (#1782), by Saalfield, 1939. Two paper dolls with movie and personal wardrobes. $175.00 uncut. Leslie Tannenbaum collection.

The New Shirley Temple in Paper Dolls (#2425), by Saalfield, 1942. Two teenage Shirley Temple dolls with movie and personal wardrobes. The movie wardrobe outfits are from *Kathleen*. $150.00 uncut. Leslie Tannenbaum collection.

Shirley Temple Paper Dolls (#4435), by Saalfield, 1958. First Shirley Temple paper doll set produced in the 1950s. Folder contains two paper dolls, and dresses in the 1950s style that don't resemble any that Shirley wore in the 1930s. This set was reissued with slight modifications over the next four years. $30.00. Janet Mitchell collection.

Shirley Temple (#5160), by Saalfield, 1959. Folded doll with outfits and accessories. Reissued over the years and modified slightly. $35.00. Loretta Beilstein collection.

Shirley Temple, an 18" Standing Doll (#4470), by Saalfield, 1959. Folder contained a large two-piece doll with outfits and accessories. Reissued over the years. $25.00. Iva Mae Jones collection.

Shirley Temple Dolls and Dresses, 1959, by Saalfield. Released as either a folder or paper doll book. On the left is the paper doll book, #1053; on the right is the doll folder, #4440. The folder cost 29¢ whereas the paper doll book cost only 10¢. Reissued over the years. $20.00 and $30.00 respectively. Janet Mitchell collection.

Shirley Temple Paper Dolls, 1960, by Saalfield, came as a paper doll book and as a stand-up set. On the left is the paper doll book, #1725, and on the right is the stand-up set, which also came with a pair of scissors. $30.00 and $50.00 respectively. Janet Mitchell collection.

Shirley Temple Snap-on Paper Doll (#299), by Gabriel, 1959. Doll, doll snaps, and an assortment of clothes. A rare set. $80.00. Leslie Tannenbaum collection.

Another version of #299, with different clothes. $80.00. Leslie Tannenbaum collection.

Shirley Temple Magnetic Doll (#301), by Gabriel, 1961. Boxed set with a paper doll and wardrobe that attaches magnetically. $50.00 (boxed). Leslie Tannenbaum collection.

Shirley Temple Snap-On Paper Dolls (#300), by Gabriel, 1958. Boxed set with a paper doll and modern clothes that could be attached with small plastic snap accessories. The doll and accessories were the same as those in set #299. $40.00. Leslie Tannenbaum collection.

Shirley Temple Magnetic Doll with Jewelry (#303), by Gabriel, 1961. Boxed set (similar to #301) with metallic "jewelry" to accessorize the doll. $60.00. Leslie Tannenbaum collection.

Shirley Temple Stand-up Paper Doll with Authentic Life-like Hair (#304), by Gabriel, 1958. 24" tall paper doll with mohair attached to the head and a modern wardrobe that could be attached with snap-on accessories. $85.00. Loretta Beilstein collection.

Dover Publications reproduced some of the earlier paper doll series in the mid-1980s. Still sold today. From left: Original Shirley Temple Paper Dolls in Full Color (reissue of #2112), Classic Shirley Temple Paper Dolls in Full Color (reissue of #1765), and Authentic Shirley Temple Paper Dolls and Dresses (reissue of #1761). $5.00 each. Loretta Beilstein collection.

Shirley Temple Paper Doll, life size (#305), by Gabriel, 1960. Boxed set with a huge 40" tall doll and a movie wardrobe that snaps on. $125.00. Loretta Beilstein collection.

Shirley Temple Paper Doll, 1976, by Whitman. $15.00. Iva Mae Jones collection.

Shirley Temple Paper Doll Book (#1986), by Whitman, 1976. $10.00. Janet Mitchell collection.

Sheet Music

"Baby Take a Bow" (with Shirley on the cover), from *Stand Up and Cheer,* by Movietone Music Corporation, 1934. $20.00. Leslie Tannenbaum collection.

The songs "Baby Take a Bow" and "Stand Up and Cheer" were also released without Shirley pictured on the cover, by Movietone, 1934. $10.00. Janet Mitchell collection.

From *Little Miss Marker*: "Laugh You Son-of-a-Gun," by Famous Music Corporation, 1934. Also released (but not pictured): "I'm a Black Sheep Who's Blue." $10.00 each. Iva Mae Jones collection.

From *Now and Forever*: "Now and Forever," by Famous Music Corp., 1934. Also released (but not pictured): "The World Owes Me a Living." $20.00 each. Leslie Tannenbaum collection.

From *Bright Eyes*: "On the Good Ship Lollipop," by Movietone Music Corp., 1934. Two versions were released. On the left is the common version (pink and blue); on the right is a special Christmas version (red and green), which is much rarer. $10.00 and $40.00 respectively. Janet Mitchell collection.

From *Baby Take a Bow*: "On Account-a I Love You," by Movietone Music Corp., 1934. $20.00. Janet Mitchell collection.

Re-release of "On the Good Ship Lollipop," by Movietone Music Corp., 1950s. $10.00. This particular one is signed, so it is worth $50.00. Leslie Tannenbaum collection.

From *The Little Colonel*, from left: "Little Colonel" (included is "Love's Young Dream") and "Love's Young Dream" (very rare to find alone), both by Movietone Music Corp., 1935. $15.00 and $40.00 respectively. Janet Mitchell collection.

From *Our Little Girl*: "Our Little Girl," by Movietone Music Corp., 1935. Shirley also sang "Lullaby to a Doll" in the movie, but it was not released as sheet music. $20.00. Leslie Tannenbaum collection.

From *Curly Top*: "Animal Crackers in my Soup," by Sam Fox Publishing Company, 1935. Also released (but not pictured): "When I Grow Up," "The Simple Things in Life," "Curly Top," "It's All So New to Me." $10.00 each. Iva Mae Jones collection.

From *The Littlest Rebel*: "Polly-Wolly-Doodle," by Movietone Music Corp., 1936. Also released (but not pictured): "Believe Me, if All Those Endearing Young Charms." $15.00 each. Iva Mae Jones collection.

From *Captain January*: "At the Codfish Ball," by Movietone Music Corp., 1936. Also released (but not pictured): "Early Bird," "The Right Somebody to Love." $15.00 each. Iva Mae Jones collection.

From *Poor Little Rich Girl*: "When I'm with You," by Robbins Music Corp., 1936. Also released (but not pictured): "You Gotta Eat Your Spinach, Baby," "But Definitely," "Oh, My Goodness," "Military Man," and "Ride a Cock-Horse to Banbury Cross." $10.00 each. Janet Mitchell collection.

From *Dimples*: "Hey! What Did the Blue Jay Say?" by Leo Feist Inc., 1936. Also released (but not pictured): "Picture Me without You" and "He Was a Dandy." $15.00 each. Iva Mae Jones collection.

From *Stowaway*: "Goodnight My Love," by Robbins Music Corp., 1936. Also released (but not pictured): "One Never Knows, Does One?" and "You Gotta S-M-I-L-E to be H-A-Double-P-Y." $15.00 each. Iva Mae Jones collection.

From *Stowaway*: "That's What I Want for Christmas," released especially for Christmas 1936. $20.00. Iva Mae Jones collection.

From *Heidi*: "In Our Little Wooden Shoes," by Sam Fox Publishing Co., 1937. $20.00. Janet Mitchell collection.

Rebecca of Sunnybrook Farm sheet music included "An Old Straw Hat," "Come and Get Your Happiness," "Alone With You," "Crackly Grain Flakes," and "Happy Endings" (cut from final version, but sheet music was released). Shown in the variety of different covers that were released. Clockwise from upper left: "The Toy Trumpet," "An Old Straw Hat" (rare cover), "Come and Get Your Happiness" (rare cover), and "An Old Straw Hat" (from England). $15.00 – 30.00 each. Janet Mitchell collection.

From *Little Miss Broadway*: "Be Optimistic," by Robbins Music Corp., 1938. Also released (but not pictured): "How Can I Thank You," "If All the World Were Paper," "We Should Be Together," and "Little Miss Broadway." More rare are "Thank You For the Use of the Hall," "Swing Me an Old Fashioned Song," and "Hop Skip Jump & Slide" (cut from the final version of the film, but the sheet music was released). $20.00 – 50.00 (depending on rarity). Leslie Tannenbaum collection.

From *Just Around the Corner*: "This is a Happy Little Ditty," by Robbins Music Corp., 1938. Also released (but not pictured): "I Love to Walk in the Rain," "I'll Always Be Lucky With You," "Brass Buttons and Epaulets," "I'm Not Myself Today," and "Just Around the Corner." $25.00 – 50.00 each (depending on rarity). Leslie Tannenbaum collection.

From *The Blue Bird*: "Someday You'll Find Your Bluebird," by Robbins Music Corp., 1940. $30.00. Janet Mitchell collection.

From *I'll Be Seeing You*: "I'll Be Seeing You," by Williamson Music Inc., 1944. $30.00. Janet Mitchell collection.

From *Young People*: "I Wouldn't Take a Million," by Robbins Music Corp., 1940. Also released (but not pictured): "Young People," "Tra-la-la-la." Her next picture, *Kathleen*, released one piece of sheet music (not pictured): "Around the Corner," which is very hard to find. $20.00 – 50.00 (depending on rarity) for *Young People* sheet music, $50.00 for *Kathleen* sheet music. Loretta Beilstein collection.

From *Since You Went Away*, from left: "Together" and "Since You Went Away," by Crawford Music Corp., 1944. "Since You Went Away" is very hard to find. $10.00 and $30.00 respectively. Janet Mitchell collection.

From *Honeymoon*: "I Love Geraniums," by Edward H. Morris and Co. Inc., 1946. Also released (but not pictured): "Ven Aqui." $25.00. Dorothy Dagne collection.

From *The Bachelor and the Bobbysoxer*: "The Bachelor and the Bobbysoxer," by Paull-Pioneer Music Corp., 1947. $25.00. Dorothy Dagne collection.

From *The Shirley Temple Storybook*: "Dreams Are Made for Children," by Fullerton Music Inc., 1950s. Also released (but not pictured): "The Enchanted Melody." $20.00 each. Leslie Tannenbaum collection.

Special Releases

"Curly Top's Birthday," by Movietone, 1937, was dedicated to Shirley in honor of her birthday. Very rare. $50.00. Leslie Tannenbaum collection.

"Hollywood Dance Folio No. 16," by Robbins Movie Corp., included the most famous movie sheet music for the year 1937. $15.00. Loretta Beilstein collection.

From left: *Sing with Shirley Temple (Shirley Temple Song Album)*, 1935, by Movietone; *Shirley Temple Song Album No. 2*, 1936, by Movietone; and *Shirley Temple Song Album*, 1957, by Movietone. Not pictured: *Shirley Temple's Favorite Songs*, 1937, by Robbins Music Corp. $25.00 each. Loretta Beilstein collection.

Books

A Movie of Me, by Fox Film Corp., 1934. This was a flip book; as you flipped through it, Shirley appeared to move (as if in a movie). Reproduced in early 2000. $40.00 original, $5.00 reproduction. Iva Mae Jones collection.

The Story of My Life, a softcover book by the Fox Film Corp., 1934. $50.00. Leslie Tannenbaum collection.

Big Little Books, 4½" x 5¼" each, produced during the 1930s by Saalfield. Clockwise from upper left: *The Story of Shirley Temple,* 1934, hardcover (#1089); *Shirley Temple in The Littlest Rebel,* 1935, hardcover (#1115); *My Life and Times,* 1936, hardcover (#1116); *Shirley Temple and Lionel Barrymore in The Little Colonel,* 1935, hardcover (#1095). Softcover editions were also produced. Big Little Books have also been found in a number of different languages from different countries. $15.00 each. Leslie Tannenbaum collection.

From left: *Shirley Temple's Favorite Poems* (#1720), a hardcover book by Saalfield, 1936; *Shirley Temple* (#1737) a hardcover biography by Jerome Beatty, Saalfield, 1935 (later reissued with updated information); and *The Little Colonel*, a hardcover book released by Johnston Bust & Co., 1935, the original story by Anne Fellows Johnston with pictures of Shirley from the movie interspersed. $20.00 – 40.00 each. Leslie Tannenbaum collection.

Hardcover *Shirley Temple in Heidi* book by Saalfield, from the 1930s. $20.00. Janet Mitchell collection.

Shirley Temple at Play (#1712), a softcover book by Saalfield, 1935. $20.00. Iva Mae Jones collection.

Shirley Temple scrapbooks were blank, softcover books in which the owners could place their Shirley Temple clippings and articles. By Saalfield. From left: scrapbook from 1935 (#1714), reissue from 1936 with a different cover (#1722), and reissue from 1937 (#1763). $20.00 each if empty, $100.00 and up if full of Shirley newspaper clippings — oftentimes these full scrapbooks can be the most exciting things to collect because of the amount of information about Shirley that they contain. Janet Mitchell collection.

Another scrapbook with Shirley Temple on the cover, not by Saalfield. Very similar to the composition books of the time. $20.00. Janet Mitchell collection.

Shirley Temple Story Book (#1736), a hardcover book by Saalfield, 1935. Also came as a boxed set called Shirley Temple, Her Books (#1749), with *Shirley Temple* (#1737) by Jerome Beatty. $20.00.

Shirley Temple Little Star (#1762), a softcover book by Saalfield, 1936. $50.00. Janet Mitchell collection.

Softcovers by Saalfield, from left: *How I Raised Shirley Temple* (#945), from 1935, was a republication of an article written by Shirley's mother for *Silver Screen Magazine*, and *Shirley Temple through the Day* (#1716) from 1936. $20.00 – 30.00 each. Loretta Beilstein collection.

Shirley Temple, 5 Books about Me (#1730), a boxed set of five softcover books by Saalfield, 1936. Includes *Shirley Temple, Little Playmate*; *Shirley Temple in Starring Roles*; *Shirley Temple — Just a Little Girl*; *Shirley Temple on the Movie Lot*; and *Shirley Temple, Twinkletoes*. $125.00 for the boxed set; each book sells for $15.00. Iva Mae Jones collection.

Shirley Temple's Book of Fairy Tales (#1748), a thick hardcover book by Saalfield, 1936. *Fairy Tales* had been published previously; this one had cute Shirley pictures interspersed throughout. $30.00. Janet Mitchell collection.

All softcover, by Saalfield. Clockwise from left: *Shirley Temple in The Poor Little Rich Girl* (#1723), 1936; *Shirley Temple in "Dimples"* (#1760), 1936; *Shirley Temple in "Stowaway"* (#1767), 1936; and *Shirley Temple in "Wee Willie Winkie"* (#1769), 1937. $20.00 – 30.00 each. Janet Mitchell collection.

Softcover, by Saalfield. From left: *Shirley Temple in Heidi*, in black and white (#337, very rare) and in color (#1771), 1937. $50.00 and $30.00 respectively. Janet Mitchell collection.

All softcover by Saalfield (except for #1774, which is hardcover). Clockwise from upper left: *Now I Am Eight* (even though, at the time, she was actually nine; #1766), 1937; *Shirley Temple, the Real Little Girl, and Her Own Honolulu Diary* (#1775), 1938; *Shirley Temple, Her Life in Pictures* (#1774), 1938; and *Shirley Temple in Little Miss Broadway* (#1778), 1938. $20.00 – 30.00 each. Janet Mitchell collection.

Two softcover books by Saalfield, 1939. From left: *Shirley Temple in The Little Princess* (#1783) and *Shirley Temple in Susannah of the Mounties* (#1785). $25.00 – 35.00 each. Janet Mitchell collection.

Coloring Books/Activity Sets from the 1930s

Shirley Temple Coloring Book (#1735), a hardcover coloring book by Saalfield, 1935. Produced for libraries. Other library sets (not pictured) from the same year are *Shirley Temple Drawing Book* (#1725) and Shirley Temple Coloring Box (#1731). $100.00 and up each. Leslie Tannenbaum collection.

Shirley Temple Pastime Book (#1726), a hardcover book by Saalfield, 1935. $30.00. Iva Mae Jones collection.

All softcover books by Saalfield. Clockwise from upper left: *This is My Crayon Book, Shirley Temple* (#1711), 1935; *Shirley Temple, My Book to Color* (#1768), 1937; *Shirley Temple Christmas Book* (#1770), an activity book from 1937; and *Shirley Temple, a Great Big Book to Color* (#1717), 1936. Another Saalfield coloring book (not pictured) is *Shirley Temple Coloring Book* (#1772), 1937. $20.00 – 50.00. Loretta Beilstein collection.

Another version of *This is My Crayon Book, Shirley Temple* (#287), Saalfield, 1935. In this version, Shirley's head is not cut out. Very rare. $50.00. Janet Mitchell collection.

Shirley Temple's Birthday Book, softcover, by the Dell Publishing Company, 1935, in honor of Shirley's birthday. Contains a paper doll and dresses, puzzles, cutouts, games, and pictures to color. $40.00. Janet Mitchell collection.

Shirley Temple Coloring Set (#1738), Saalfield, 1935. Boxed set with a coloring book, crayons, and watercolors. $100.00. Loretta Beilstein collection.

Shirley Temple Drawing Set (#1738), Saalfield, 1935. Boxed set with a coloring book, crayons, and watercolors. $100.00. Loretta Beilstein collection.

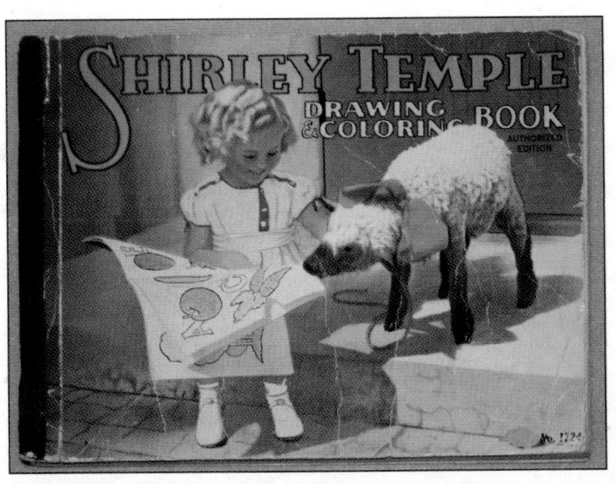

Shirley Temple Drawing and Coloring Book (#1724), a hardcover book by Saalfield, 1935. $50.00. Janet Mitchell collection.

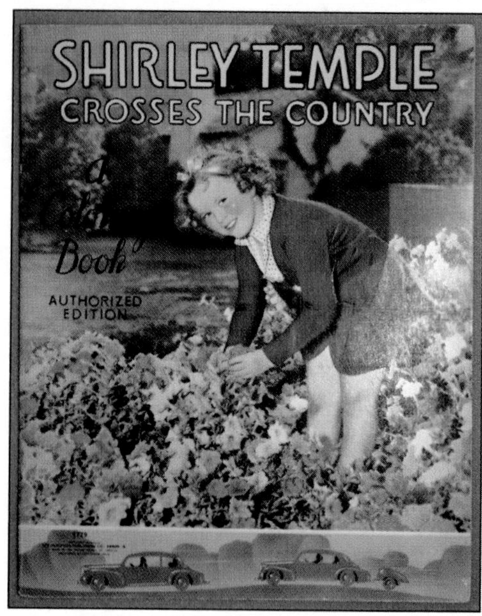

Shirley Temple Crosses the Country (#1779), a softcover coloring book by Saalfield, 1939. $40.00. Leslie Tannenbaum collection.

Shirley Temple's Sewing Cards (#1721), a boxed set of punched-out cards that strings could be woven through. By Saalfield, 1936. $100.00. Loretta Beilstein collection.

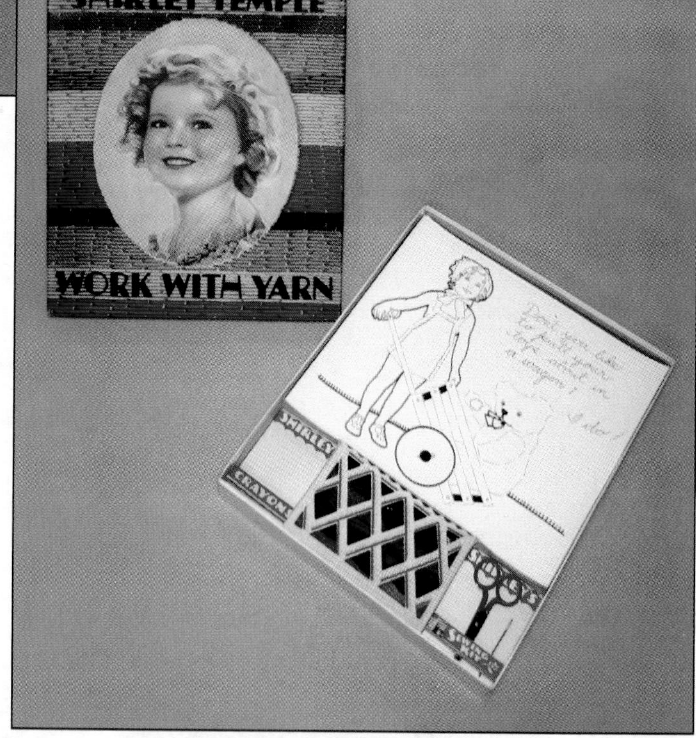

Shirley Temple Work with Yarn (#1750), a boxed set by Saalfield, 1936. $100.00. Janet Mitchell collection.

Softcover by Saalfield, from left: *Shirley Temple's Blue Bird Coloring Book* (#1788), 1940, and *Shirley Temple — The Little Princess Coloring Book* (#1784), 1939. $30.00 each. Leslie Tannenbaum collection.

4 Books Shirley Temple Pastime Box (#1732), Saalfield, 1937. Boxed set of four books: *Shirley Temple Favorite Coloring Book, Shirley Temple Favorite Puzzles, Shirley Temple Favorite Games,* and *Shirley Temple Favorite Sewing Cards.* $100.00. Janet Mitchell collection.

Shirley Temple Coloring Box (#1728), Saalfield, 1935. Boxed set with a coloring book (had same cover picture as the box) and crayons. Only the coloring book itself is pictured here. Library version of this set has the same cover in red (#1731). $75.00 and up complete, $25.00 as pictured. Janet Mitchell collection.

International Books from the 1930s

Petite Princesse, a hardcover French version of *The Little Princess*. $50.00. Leslie Tannenbaum collection.

There were many Shirley Temple books sold in Europe during the 1930s, including *Shirley Temple's Annual,* a thick hardcover book by Daily Herald Ltd. London that was produced in different volumes during the 1930s. *Shirley Temple's Annual*s from 1935 (on left) and from 1936 (on right). $50.00 each. Leslie Tannenbaum collection.

Shirley Temple Dipinge, an Italian coloring book. $40.00. Leslie Tannenbaum collection.

A French Shirley Temple scrapbook. $35.00 blank. Leslie Tannenbaum collection.

Spanish Shirley Temple book *Nuestra Hijita* which means "Our Little Daughter" (probably a translation of the movie *Our Little Girl*). $50.00. Loretta Beilstein collection.

Books from the 1940s

Shirley Temple and the Spirit of Dragonwood (#2311) and *Shirley Temple and the Screaming Specter* (#2330) are hardcover mystery novels by Kathryn Heisenfelt, Whitman, 1945. $25.00 each. Janet Mitchell collection.

My Young Life, a hardcover autobiography written by a teenage Shirley, released by Garden City Publishing Company, 1945. Another book released at this time (not pictured) was *Honeymoon* (#103), a softcover book released by Bart House, 1946. $40.00. Janet Mitchell collection.

Shirley Temple 21st Birthday Album, a softcover book by Dell, April 1949. $20.00. Loretta Beilstein collection.

Books from the 1950s and 1960s

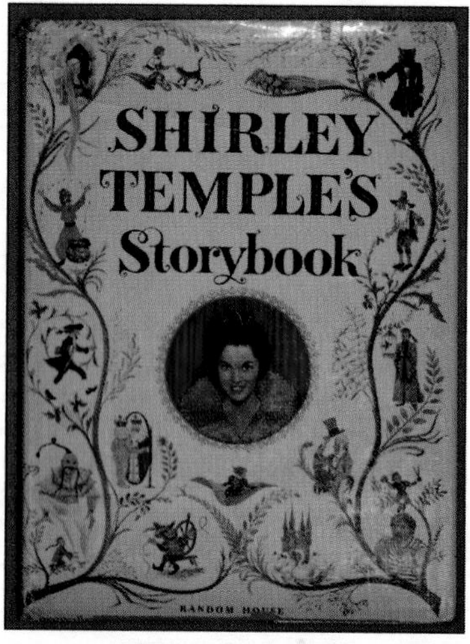

Shirley Temple's Storybook, a hardcover book by Random House, 1958. $40.00 with dust jacket, $20.00 without dust jacket. Iva Mae Jones collection.

Hardcover Shirley Temple Edition books by Random House, 1959. Clockwise from upper left: *The Littlest Rebel* (X-2), *Captain January and The Little Colonel* (X-5); consisted of two stories in one book, *Heidi* (X-1), *Susannah of the Mounties* (X-4), and *Rebecca of Sunnybrook Farm* (X-3). $15.00 each. Leslie Tannenbaum collection.

Hardcover by Random House, from left: *The Shirley Temple Treasury*, 1959, which included *Heidi, The Little Colonel, Rebecca of Sunnybrook Farm*, and *Captain January*, and *Shirley Temple's Fairyland*, 1958. $20.00 – 40.00 each. Leslie Tannenbaum collection.

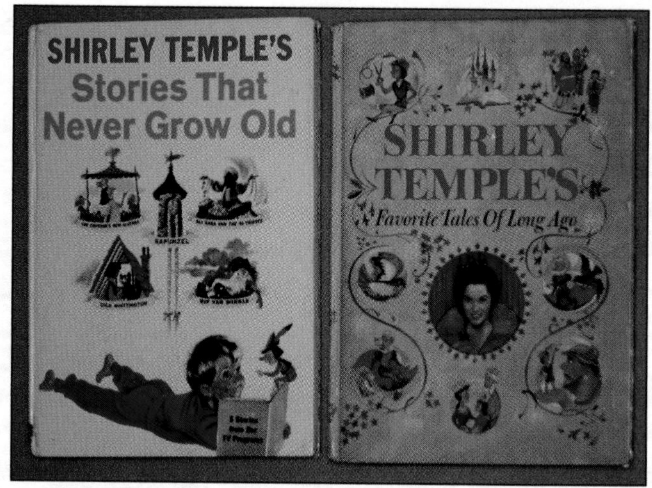

Hardcover by Random House, from left: *Shirley Temple's Stories that Never Grow Old*, 1958, and *Shirley Temple's Favorite Tales of Long Ago*, 1959. $20.00 – 40.00 each. Loretta Beilstein collection.

Shirley Temple's Bedtime Book, a hardcover book by Random House, early 1960s. $30.00. Leslie Tannenbaum collection.

Shirley Temple scrapbook of blank pages has a picture of Shirley Temple and her family on the cover, late 1950s. $20.00. Loretta Beilstein collection.

Shirley Temple's Storytime Favorites, a hardcover book by Random House, 1962. $40.00. Loretta Beilstein collection.

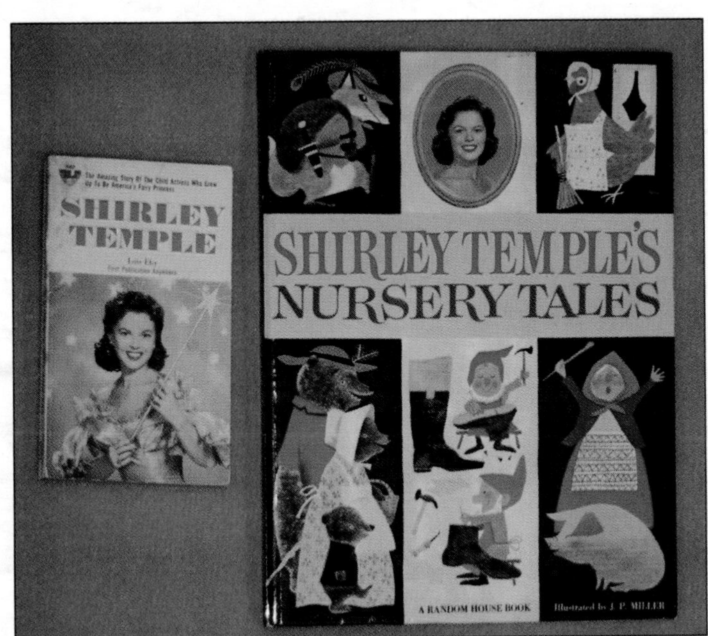

Shirley Temple, by Lois Ely, was a softcover book released by Monarch Books, 1962, and *Shirley Temple's Nursery Tales*, was a hardcover book featuring the stories of *Sleeping Beauty*, *Beauty and the Beast*, *Rumpelstiltskin*, and *The Wild Swan*, by Random House, 1961. $20.00 – 30.00 each. Janet Mitchell collection.

Coloring Books/Activity Sets from the 1950s

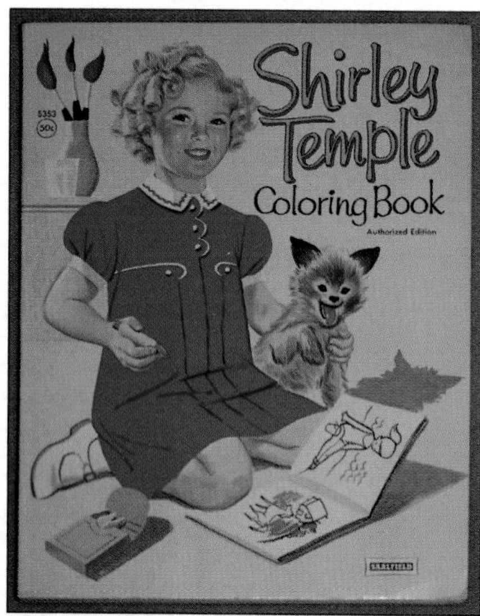

Shirley Temple Coloring Book (#5353), Saalfield, 1959. Other Shirley Temple coloring books (with different covers) included #4884, #5653, #4624, #4589, and #4584, all from 1959, as well as #1554 from 1958. $15.00. Iva Mae Jones collection.

Shirley Temple Coloring Book (#4584), Saalfield, 1959. $15.00. Janet Mitchell collection.

Coloring books from Saalfield, from left: *Shirley Temple Coloring Book* (#4624), 1959, and *The Favorite Pictures of Shirley Temple: A Book to Color* (#1654), 1958. $15.00 each. Loretta Beilstein collection.

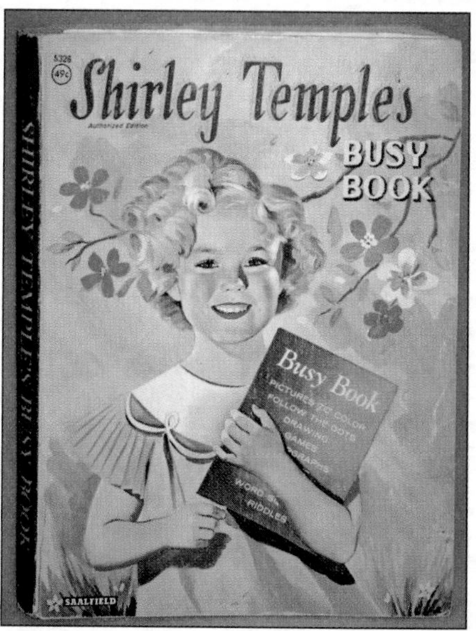

Shirley Temple's Busy Book (#5326), Saalfield, 1958. Large softcover book with activities, games, and coloring pages. $25.00. Leslie Tannenbaum collection.

Shirley Temple's Magnetic TV Theater, 1959, by Amsco. With a stage and accessories. $100.00 and up. Iva Mae Jones collection.

Shirley Temple's Treasure Board (#8806), by Saalfield, 1959. $25.00. Loretta Beilstein collection.

Shirley Temple Play Kit (#9859), by Saalfield, 1958. Also produced as #6030 and #6032. $80.00 and up. Janet Mitchell collection.

Inside of #9859. 9" and 6½" dolls with mainly modern outfits that could be laced on to the dolls. Also, a coloring book, crayons, and other activities. Janet Mitchell collection.

Another Shirley Temple Play Kit (#9869), by Saalfield, 1961. $80.00 and up. Janet Mitchell collection.

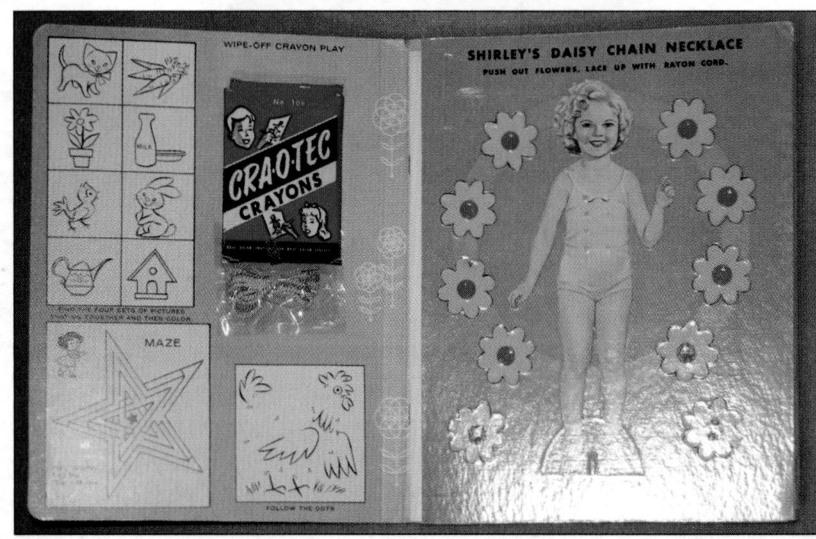

Opening the inside page of #9869 reveals a paper doll with clothes and a Shirley Temple coloring book. Janet Mitchell collection.

Biographies, clockwise from top: *Shirley Temple Black: Actor and Diplomat*, by Jean F. Blashfield, 2000; *Shirley Temple,* by Jeanine Bassinger, 1975; *Shirley Temple, Child Star*, by John Barkston, 2003; and *The Shirley Temple Story*, by Lester and Irene David, 1983. *The Boy Who Looked Like Shirley Temple,* by Bill Mahan, is a fiction book that actually has nothing to do with Shirley Temple. $5.00 – 10.00 each. Loretta Beilstein collection.

Child Star, 1988, Shirley Temple Black's autobiography. Also released as a limited edition leather-bound signed volume (not pictured). $5.00 and $100.00 respectively.

Uncorrected page proof copy of *Child Star*. $200.00. Leslie Tannenbaum collection.

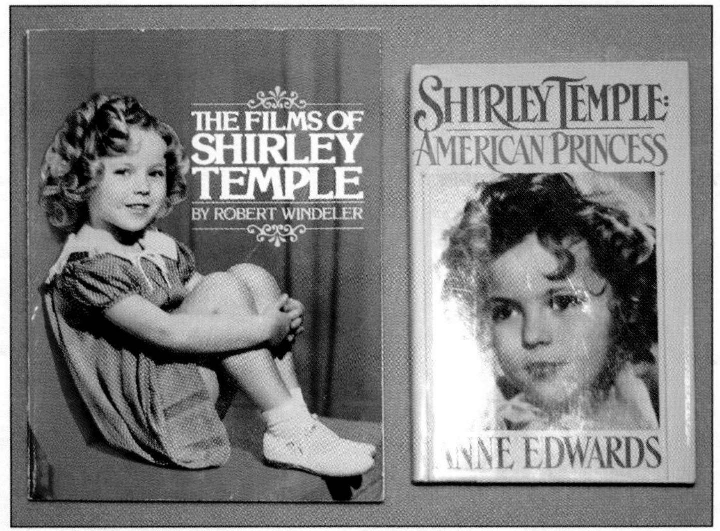

From left: *The Films of Shirley Temple,* 1978, by Robert Windeler and *Shirley Temple: American Princess* by Anne Edwards, 1989. $10.00 each.

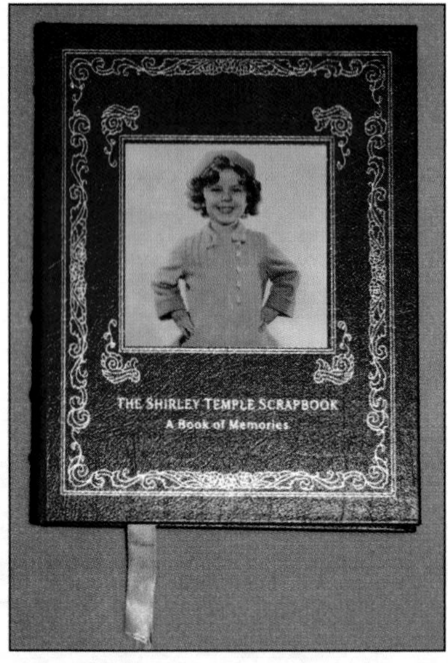

The Shirley Temple Scrapbook, a Book of Memories, by Lorraine Burdick, 2002. This is the special leather-bound limited edition, signed by Shirley Temple Black. *The Shirley Temple Scrapbook* was also available in paperback, first released in 1975 and then re-released in 2001. $150.00.

The inside of the limited-edition Shirley Temple Scrapbook is signed by Shirley Temple Black, and the book comes with a certificate of authenticity, signed by Shirley and witnessed by Charles Black (her husband).

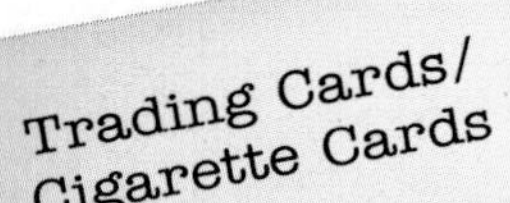

Cuban trading cards produced with Shirley's image on them during the 1930s. $5.00 each. Loretta Beilstein collection.

More Dutch gum cards. $8.00 – $10.00 each. Loretta Beilstein collection.

A series of Dutch gum cards were produced with Shirley's image on them during the 1930s. $8.00 – 10.00 each. Loretta Beilstein collection.

A series of German Shirley Temple tobacco cards from 1936. $8.00 – 10.00 each. Loretta Beilstein collection.

This Shirley Temple card (front and back shown) came in a package of cigarettes from the 1930s. $5.00 – 8.00 each. Loretta Beilstein collection.

Another series of German tobacco cards from the 1930s. $8.00 – 10.00 each.
Loretta Beilstein collection.

More Shirley Temple trading cards from the 1930s. $5.00 – 8.00 each.
Loretta Beilstein collection.

American trading cards from the 1930s featuring Shirley Temple. $5.00 – 8.00 each. Loretta Beilstein collection.

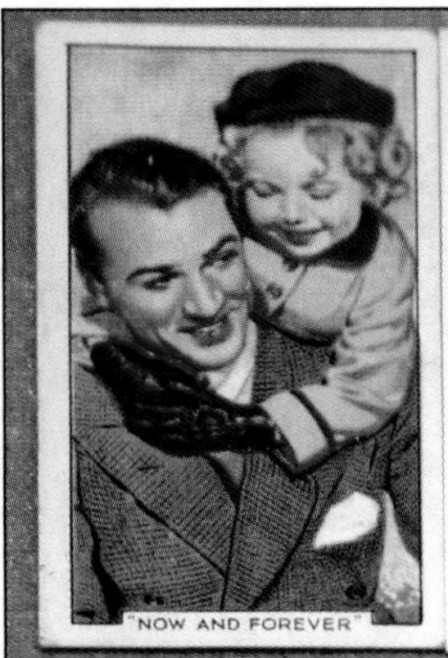

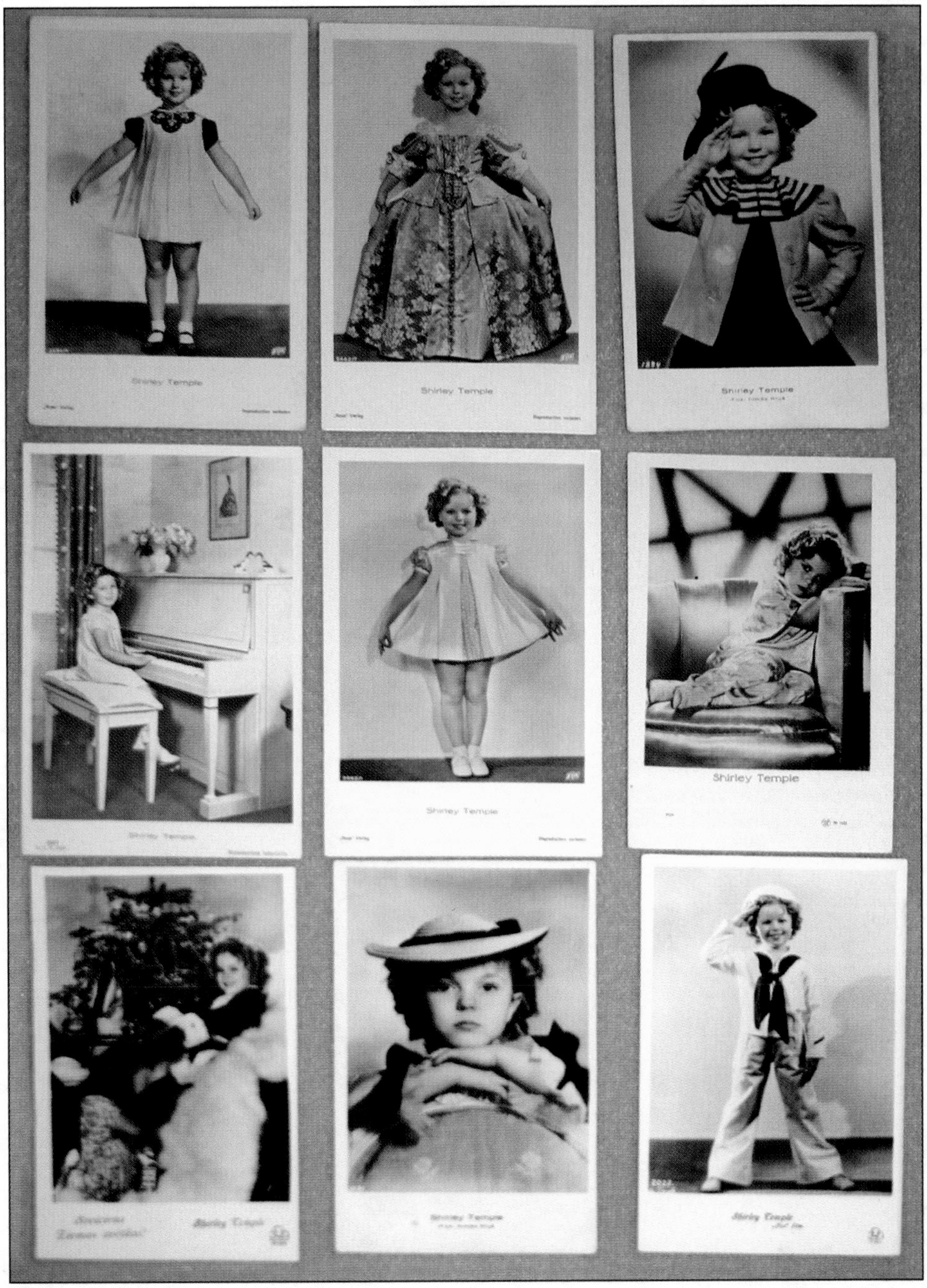
Shirley Temple

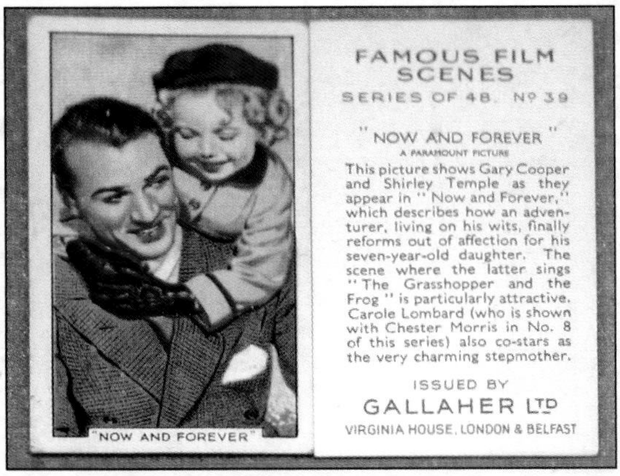
"NOW AND FOREVER"
FAMOUS FILM SCENES
SERIES OF 48. Nº 39
"NOW AND FOREVER"
A PARAMOUNT PICTURE
This picture shows Gary Cooper and Shirley Temple as they appear in "Now and Forever," which describes how an adventurer, living on his wits, finally reforms out of affection for his seven-year-old daughter. The scene where the latter sings "The Grasshopper and the Frog" is particularly attractive. Carole Lombard (who is shown with Chester Morris in No. 8 of this series) also co-stars as the very charming stepmother.
ISSUED BY
GALLAHER LTD
VIRGINIA HOUSE, LONDON & BELFAST

British Shirley Temple cigarette card from the 1930s (front and back shown). $5.00 – 8.00. Loretta Beilstein collection.

Postcards

Unique Shirley Temple caricature postcard from overseas, 1930s. $15.00. Loretta Beilstein collection.

Shirley Temple postcards from the 1930s. Shirley Temple was a common postcard subject in America and abroad. $10.00 – 15.00 each. Loretta Beilstein collection.

Six similar postcards from England and New Zealand. Each shows a picture of Shirley and names the city that the sender got it from and has a small area in the front that can be opened to reveal a map of that region. $20.00 each. Leslie Tannenbaum collection.

Jig Star card game, 1930s, that when arranged properly revealed a picture of Shirley Temple and pictures of other celebrities. $25.00. Loretta Beilstein collection.

Five different examples of Shirley Temple playing cards made in the 1930s. Sets in boxes, $65.00 and up each; loose sets, $30.00 each. Iva Mae Jones collection.

Lobby Cards/Movie Posters/ Movie Heralds/Souvenir Programs

Movie poster for a series of short films that Shirley appeared in, 1934. $150.00. Janet Mitchell collection.

Lobby card for *Little Miss Marker*, 1934. $200.00. Leslie Tannenbaum collection.

BROWNIE THEATRE

Excellent Photoplays at Popular Prices
10c and 15c, Including Tax

SUNDAY, APRIL 24

She Made Tough Mugs Believe in Fairies!

Little MISS MARKER

with
ADOLPHE MENJOU
DOROTHY DELL
CHARLES BICKFORD
SHIRLEY TEMPLE

Showed dames and wise guys how dumb they were about love!

"Jungle Jim" Chapter No. 7
Musical "Violets in Spring"

MONDAY, APRIL 25

Hopalong Cassidy talks with six-guns . . . the only language western desperadoes understand . . . for justice and romance.

Clarence E. Mulford's "THREE ON THE TRAIL"

WILLIAM BOYD
JIMMY ELLISON
ONSLOW STEVENS

Novelty "Killer Dog"
Comedy "Bored of Education"
"Jungle Jim" Chapter No. 7

Small three-fold movie herald from Brownie theatre announcing when Shirley's latest movie, *Little Miss Marker,* was showing. $15.00. Janet Mitchell collection.

Early four-card lobby set advertising the short film series that featured Shirley Temple (who didn't play major characters in the films), 1934. This set came out right after Shirley became popular. $400.00 (set). Leslie Tannenbaum collection.

Lobby ad for *Bright Eyes*. $300.00.
Loretta Beilstein collection.

Large (about 5" x 7") color movie herald announcing when Shirley's latest movie, *Bright Eyes,* was to be shown. $30.00. Janet Mitchell collection.

Small three-fold movie herald from Manring Theatre announcing when Shirley's latest movie was to be shown. $15.00. Janet Mitchell collection.

Movie theatre display advertising *The Little Colonel*, 1934. $200.00. Loretta Beilstein collection.

Large movie herald announcing when Shirley's latest movie, *The Little Colonel,* was to be shown. $30.00. Janet Mitchell collection.

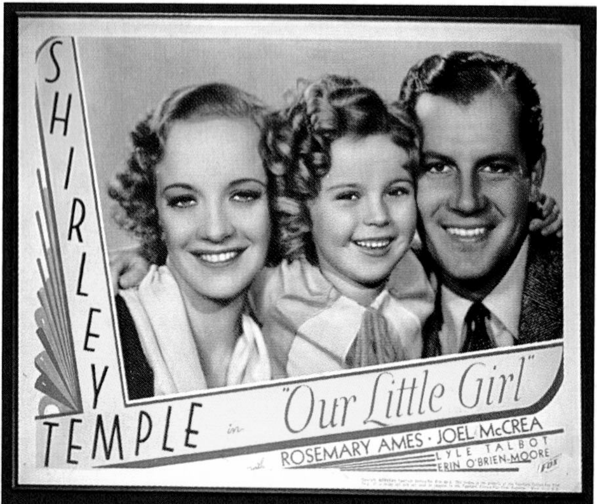

Lobby card for *Our Little Girl*. $200.00.
Leslie Tannenbaum collection.

A different lobby card for *Our Little Girl*. $200.00.
Leslie Tannenbaum collection.

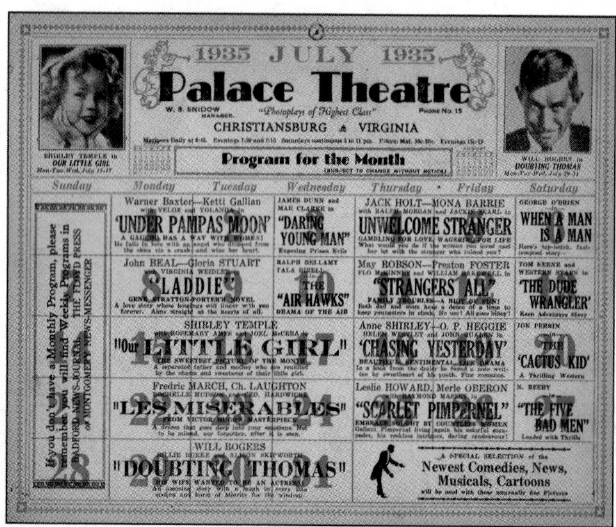

Movie calendar that advertised when Shirley's latest movie, *Our Little Girl*, was to be shown. $30.00. Janet Mitchell collection.

Lobby card for *Curly Top*, 1935. $200.00.
Leslie Tannenbaum collection.

Lobby card ad for *The Littlest Rebel*. $200.00.
Leslie Tannenbaum collection.

Large movie herald announcing when Shirley's latest movie, *Captain January*, was showing. $30.00. Janet Mitchell collection.

BROWNIE THEATRE

Excellent Photoplays at Popular Prices
10c and 15c, Including Tax

SUNDAY and MONDAY, MAY 23 and 24

She's the sweetheart of the sailor-folk, the lighthouse keeper's idol!

SHIRLEY TEMPLE
CAPTAIN JANUARY
GUY KIBBEE
SLIM SUMMERVILLE

You'll laugh and cheer and shed a tear as she charms their storm-swept hearts!

COMEDY "STYLISH STOUTS"
BUCK JONES in "PHANTOM RIDER" No. 13

TUESDAY, MAY 25

"O'Malley of the Mounted"
With GEORGE O'BRIEN
CARTOON "SOUTHERN HORSEPITALITY"
COMIC "COLLEGE CAPERS"

WEDNESDAY, MAY 26

CASH NIGHT
$15.00 CASH GIVEN FREE TO HOLDER OF LUCKY REGISTRATION NUMBER
Amount Carried Over From Previous Wednesday (If Any) Will Be Added to Above

"Join the Marines"
With PAUL KELLY
SELECTED SHORT SUBJECTS
Remember—Prices Always 10c and 15c

402—National Program & Printing Co.

Small three fold movie herald from Brownie Theatre announcing when Shirley's latest movie, *Captain January*, was to be shown. $15.00. Janet Mitchell collection.

Another lobby card for *The Littlest Rebel*. There were multiple lobby cards produced for popular movies. $200.00. Leslie Tannenbaum collection.

Lobby card for *Dimples*, 1936. $200.00.
Leslie Tannenbaum collection.

Large movie herald announcing when Shirley's latest movie, *Dimples*, was to be shown. $30.00. Janet Mitchell collection.

Lobby card for *Stowaway*, 1936. $200.00.
Leslie Tannenbaum collection.

Large picture show souvenir from *Dimples*. $40.00.
Janet Mitchell collection.

Lobby card for *Wee Willie Winkie*, 1937. $200.00.
Leslie Tannenbaum collection.

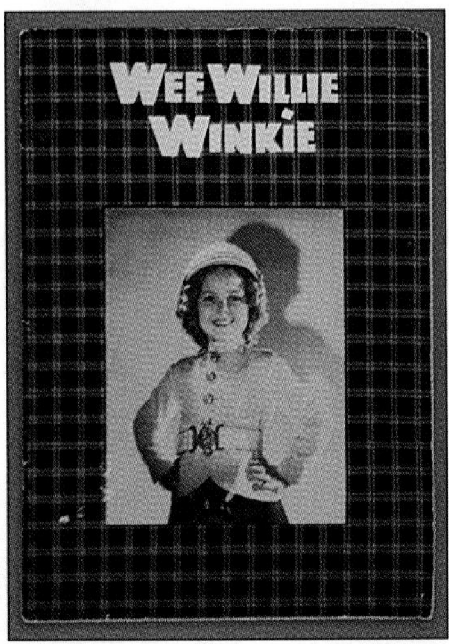

Wee Willie Winkie, a softcover souvenir program that was given out at the movie. It tells the story of *Wee Willie Winkie*. 1937. $30.00. Loretta Beilstein collection.

Lobby card for *Heidi*, 1937. $200.00. Leslie Tannenbaum collection.

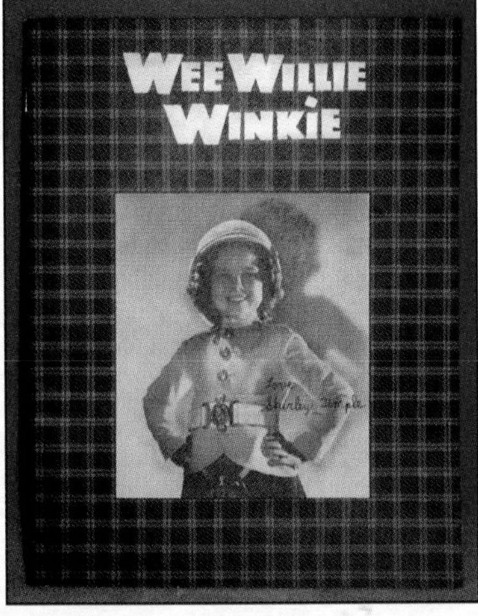

This version of the *Wee Willie Winkie* book has Shirley's signature (preprinted) on the cover. $40.00. Leslie Tannenbaum collection.

Lobby card for *Little Miss Broadway*, 1938. As Shirley grew older, her movies became less popular, and the lobby cards became less valuable. $150.00. Leslie Tannenbaum collection.

Rare program given out at the press preview of the movie *Rebecca of Sunnybrook Farm* has also been autographed on the cover by Shirley Temple. $400.00 and up; if not signed, $150.00 and up. Leslie Tannenbaum collection.

Large (about 5" x 7") *Miss Annie Rooney* movie herald. $30.00. Janet Mitchell collection.

Large color ad for *The Little Princess*. $20.00. Iva Mae Jones collection.

Inside of the *Miss Annie Rooney* movie herald. Janet Mitchell collection.

Huge (3' x 5') movie theatre painting from France, advertising Shirley movies. It describes Shirley as "The Biggest Little Star." $1,000.00 and up. Iva Mae Jones collection.

Lobby card for *The Blue Bird*, 1940. One shown from a set of eight. $300.00 complete set, $40.00 each. Leslie Tannenbaum collection.

That Hagen Girl movie poster. $80.00. Loretta Beilstein collection.

Kiss and Tell movie poster. The movie posters from Shirley's teenage years are not as valuable, because Shirley's later movies were not as popular as her earlier ones. $80.00. Loretta Beilstein collection.

Souvenir program from *Since You Went Away*. $30.00. Janet Mitchell collection.

Mr. Belvedere Goes to College movie poster. $80.00. Loretta Beilstein collection.

Adventures in Baltimore lobby card. $50.00. Loretta Beilstein collection.

Press book for *The Little Colonel*. $250.00 and up. Leslie Tannenbaum collection.

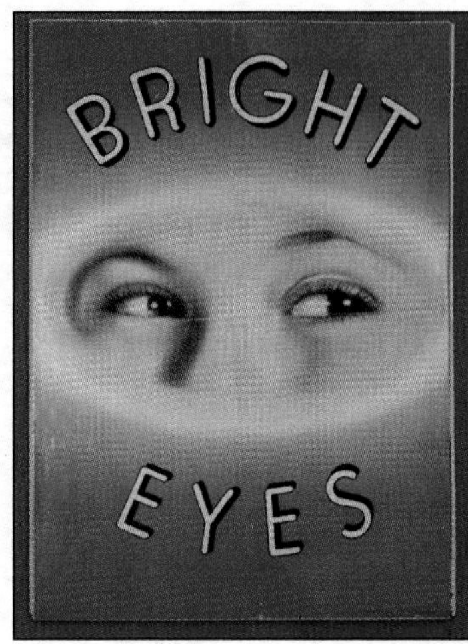

Movie companies promoted the advertising material that went with a particular movie in press books. These books contained listings of all of the advertising material available for movies. They could be very thin for smaller movies with little promotional material; they could be very large for movies that had lots of advertising material associated with them. This press book is for *Bright Eyes*. At that time, Shirley had just become very popular, and it has many pages detailing all of the commercial items that tied in to the movie. This type of information can be very valuable for collectors; it can help them identify all the items that were related to a particular movie. Very large (about 14" x 21"). $250.00 and up. Leslie Tannenbaum collection.

Press book for *Captain January*. $250.00 and up. Leslie Tannenbaum collection.

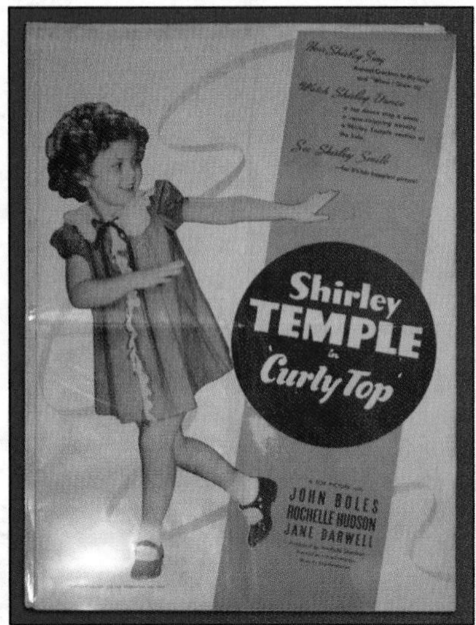

Press book for *Curly Top*. $250.00 and up. Leslie Tannenbaum collection.

The back of the *Captain January* press book showed all the different movie posters created for the film. Leslie Tannenbaum collection.

Press book for *Stowaway*. $250.00 and up. Leslie Tannenbaum collection.

Press book for *Dimples*. $250.00 and up. Leslie Tannenbaum collection.

Authentic SHIRLEY TEMPLE LICENSEES

Firm	Address	Product
GENERAL MILLS		Sperry Flour, "Drifted Snow" Flour.
H. & J. BLOCK	501 7th Ave., N. Y. C.	Coats and Snow Suits
BROWN DURRELL CO.	200 Madison Ave., N. Y. C.	Bathing Suits (Forest Brand)
GLENSDER TEXTILE CO.	417 5th Ave., N. Y. C.	Scarfs, Handkerchiefs.
GREEN SHOE MFG. CO.	960 Harrison Ave., Boston, Mass.	Shoes.
IDEAL NOVELTY & TOY CO.	200 5th Ave., N. Y. C.	Dolls, Doll Carriages, Doll Trunks.
KAUFMAN BROS. UNDERWEAR CO., INC.	131 W. 35th St., N. Y. C.	Underwear, Sleeping Garments, Bathrobes.
KERK GUILD, INC.	347 Fifth Ave., N. Y. C.	Soap Novelties.
KRAMER BROS.	16 E. 34th St., N. Y. C.	Hosiery and Socks.
L. LEWIS & SON	928 Broadway, N. Y. C.	Hats and Berets.
McKEM, INC.	1350 Broadway, N. Y. C.	Swim Suits (Shawmut Brand)
PYRAMID LEATHER GOODS CO.	6 West 32nd St., N. Y. C.	Handbags.
RESTFUL FOOTWEAR CO.	341 Wilkinson Ave., Jersey City, N. J.	Slippers and Sandals.
THE RIBBON MILLS CORP.	102 Madison Ave., N. Y. C.	Hair Ribbons, Head Band Ribbon Bows, Ribbon Garters.
ROSENAU BROS.	25th & Westmoreland Sts., Phila., Pa.	Shirley Temple Cinderella Dresses.
SAALSFIELD PUBLISHING CO.	Akron, Ohio.	Books, Stationery, Cut-Out Paper Dolls.
SHERMAN BROS.	205 W. 39th St., N. Y. C.	Raincoats, Rainwear Sets.
MONOCRAFT PRODUCTS, INC.	6 West 32nd St., N. Y. C.	Children's Jewelry.
NOLAN GLOVE CO.	425 Fourth Ave., N. Y. C.	Gloves.
F. A. WHITNEY CARRIAGE CO.	Leominster, Mass.	Doll Carriages.
DAVID KAHN, INC.	North Bergen, N. J.	Pen and Pencil Sets.
GEM BABY WEAR CO., INC.	18-20 W. 4th St., N. Y. C.	Bathrobes.

The press books also specified who produced the genuine Shirley Temple products that were sold at that time. Loretta Beilstein collection.

Press book for *Wee Willie Winkie*. $250.00 and up. Leslie Tannenbaum collection.

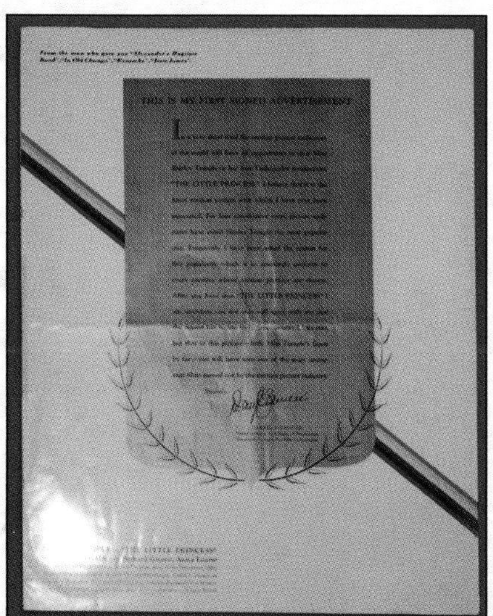

Press book for *The Little Princess*. Letter from Darryl Zanuck on the cover that promotes Shirley's first Technicolor production. $200.00 and up. Leslie Tannenbaum collection.

Press book for *The Blue Bird*. This one is much smaller (fewer pages also) than the earlier ones, probably because at the time, Shirley's popularity was waning. Also notice how Shirley's name and image are not displayed prominently on the front page. $125.00 and up. Leslie Tannenbaum collection.

The back of the press book for *The Blue Bird* showed the different movie posters created for the film. Again, Shirley's name is not above the title in any of them, and the artwork does not show a close-up of her face in the promotion. Leslie Tannenbaum collection.

The back of the press book for *The Little Princess* showed all the different movie posters created for the film. Leslie Tannenbaum collection.

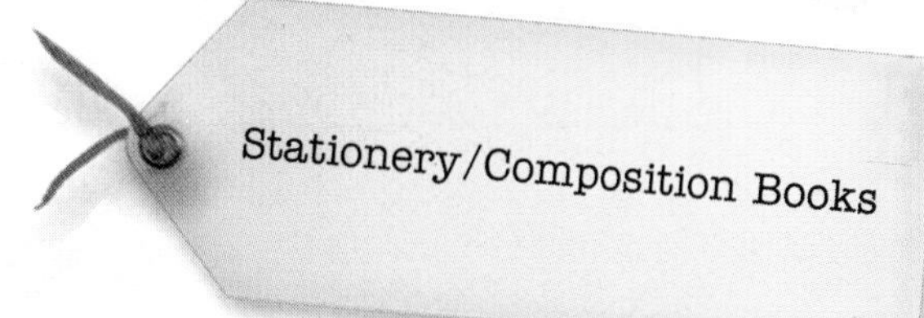

Stationery was released with Shirley's image on the cover throughout the 1930s, by W.T. & S. Corp. Came with Shirley's picture on the box (the stationery inside did not have her image on it). $50.00. Leslie Tannenbaum collection.

Shirley Temple loose-leaf filler paper. Shirley's image was on the first page; the other sheets were blank. $10.00 each (just the cover sheets). Loretta Beilstein collection.

Composition books were produced by the Western Publishing Company. Shirley's image was on the cover of each (lined paper was inside). $40.00 each. Janet Mitchell collection.

Shirley Temple school tablets with lined paper inside. $40.00 each. Janet Mitchell collection.

Shirley Temple composition pad from the 1950s. $20.00. Janet Mitchell collection.

Shirley Temple tablet with pencil and cardboard backing from the 1930s. $80.00. Leslie Tannenbaum collection.

Personality Photos

Still Photographs for all occasions

These 8" by 10" Personality stills, are available in the complete set at the Fox Exchange. These can be used to add further interest to your window displays or interior displays. They are the same as the regular stills furnished the Exhibitor on all pictures.

Prices for Complete Set of 15, $1.50

During the 1930s, Shirley Temple photos were given away with all sorts of things, including dolls, movie tickets, and magazine contests. This ad shows many of the photos available at that time. Marge Meisinger collection.

Hand-colored giveaway photo commonly included as a free gift with the early composition dolls. $20.00.

Many recent reproductions of photos are available; usually they are printed on photo paper or thick card stock. This one is an 8" x 10". $5.00.

Original hand-colored giveaway photo of Shirley with a dog, from the 1930s. $20.00.

Original hand-colored giveaway photo of Shirley wearing the duck dress from *Curly Top,* 1930s. $20.00.

Common giveaway photo of Shirley with a Shirley baby and doll carriage, often given away with the composition dolls between 1936 and 1939. $20.00.

Original giveaway photo of Shirley from the 1930s. $20.00.

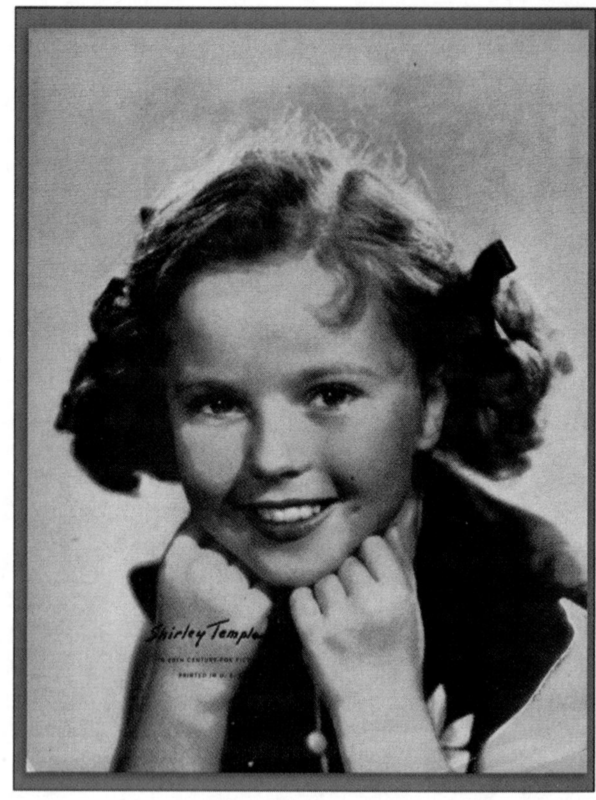

Giveaway photo of Shirley with her hair in pigtails, from *Rebecca of Sunnybrook Farm*. $20.00.

Cute publicity photo of Shirley from the 1930s. In this photo, her smile seems so genuine. $25.00. Keith and Loretta McKenzie collection.

Publicity still from the movie *The Blue Bird*, when it was re-released in the 1950s. $20.00. Keith and Loretta McKenzie collection.

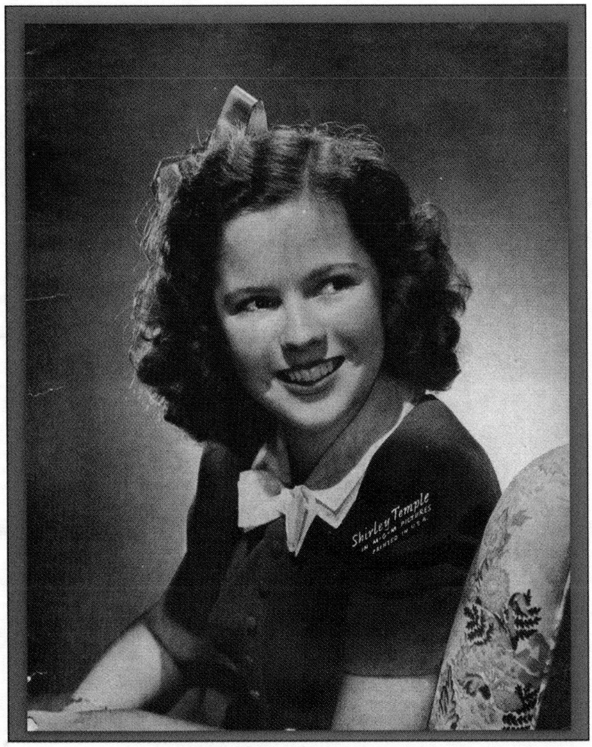

Small 7" x 9" MGM giveaway photo of Shirley Temple in the movie *Kathleen*, 1941. Printed on a thinner paper. $10.00.

Publicity photo of Shirley with her stand-in, Mary-Lou Isleib, in 1936. $25.00. Keith and Loretta McKenzie collection.

Magazines

Clockwise from upper left: *Popular Songs,* Sept. 1935; *Photoplay,* March 1936; *Movie Mirror,* May 1936; and *Hollywood,* June 1936. $35.00 each. Keith and Loretta McKenzie collection.

During the 1930s, there were hundreds of magazines that had Shirley Temple on the covers or had articles about her. (See chapter 16 to find out how to get a complete listing of all the magazines that featured Shirley Temple.) This is one of the nicest, *Photoplay* from January 1935. A Shirley magazine increases in value for two reasons: cover artwork and the article inside (if there is one; often there was just a cover photo). $40.00 (for the complete magazine). Keith and Loretta McKenzie collection.

From left: *Popular Songs,* Nov. 1936, and *Movie Classic,* Feb. 1936. $25.00 – 35.00 each. Keith and Loretta McKenzie collection.

1939 *Tournament of Roses* magazine shows a picture of Shirley on the cover (she was the Grand Marshal of the Rose Bowl parade that year). She was Grand Marshal three times: 1939, 1989, and 1999. $50.00. Keith and Loretta McKenzie collection.

Two *Gentlewoman* magazines, from left: October 1934 and February 1937. $25.00. Loretta Beilstein collection.

Another magazine from the 1939 Rose Bowl parade, with the original envelope. $50.00. Loretta Beilstein collection.

Two French magazines featuring Shirley Temple on the covers. $30.00 each. Loretta Beilstein collection.

Some magazine covers from the 1940s. From left: *Movie Life,* August 1945; *Modern Screen,* April 1947; and *Movie Life,* May 1949. $15.00 each.

Candid Photos

A candid of Shirley with Doc Bishop (her publicist). $100.00 and up. Leslie Tannenbaum collection.

Candid photo of Shirley with a look-a-like fan, August 1936. $125.00 and up. Leslie Tannenbaum collection.

Candid photo of Shirley on a merry-go-round. $100.00 and up. Leslie Tannenbaum collection.

Another candid of Shirley and Doc Bishop. $100.00 and up. Leslie Tannenbaum collection.

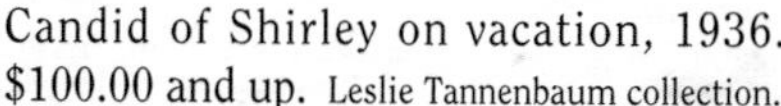

Candid of Shirley on vacation, 1936. $100.00 and up. Leslie Tannenbaum collection.

Candid pictures are valuable because each is unique. The nicer the picture, the higher the value. This picture is of Shirley Temple with Darrylin Zanuck (Darryl Zanuck's daughter) on the set of *The Littlest Rebel*, 1935. Notice that both of them are wearing outfits from the movie. This photo, an 8" x 10", was bought directly from Darrylin Zanuck. $200.00 and up. Leslie Tannenbaum collection.

Candid photo of Shirley, hoisted on the shoulders of bodyguards, waving to fans. $125.00 and up. Leslie Tannenbaum collection.

Close-up candid photo of Shirley, 1936. $125.00 and up. Leslie Tannenbaum collection.

Candid shot of Shirley, Darryl Zanuck, and his daughter, Darrylin, 1935. 8" x 10". $200.00 and up. Leslie Tannenbaum collection.

Miscellaneous Paper Products

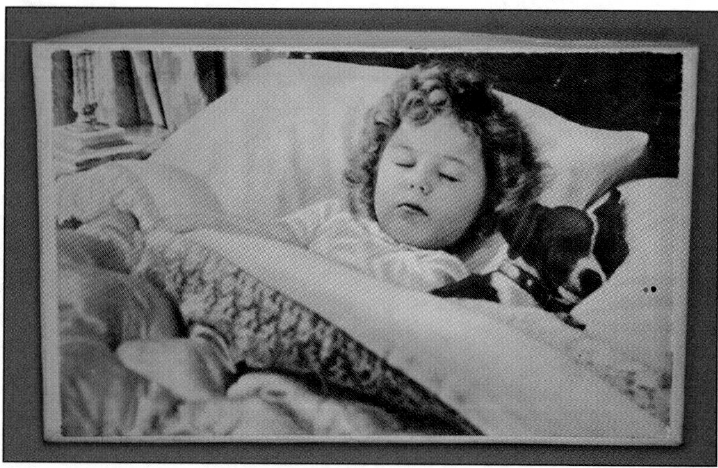

Chocolate box with Shirley Temple on the cover. $30.00. Iva Mae Jones collection.

Shirley Temple giveaway photo that came with a box of chocolate. $15.00. Loretta Beilstein collection.

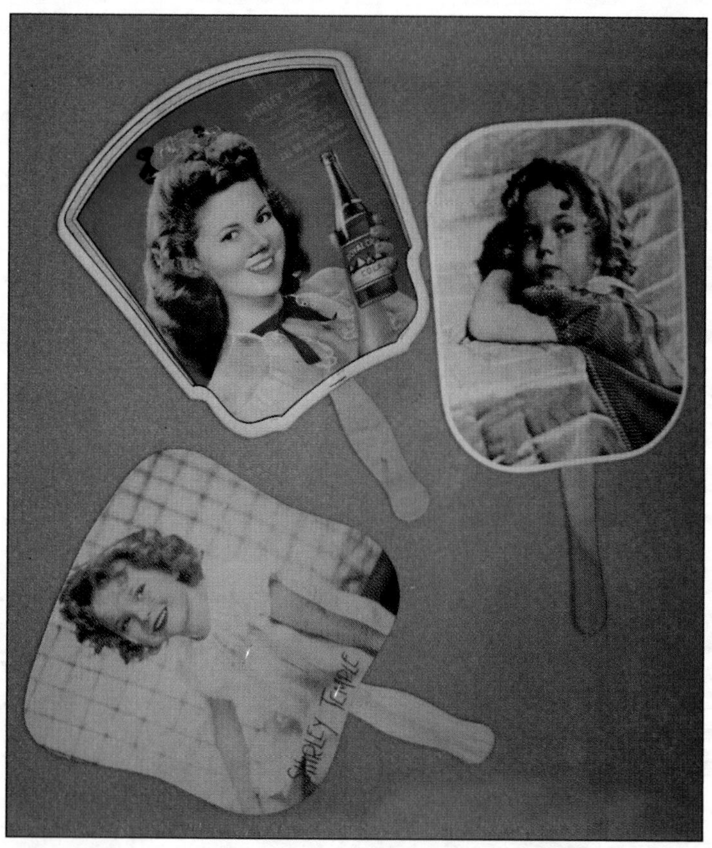

Recent Shirley Temple fans. The color one of a teenage Shirley Temple is commonly sold as original. It is a reproduction. (The original had writing in the lower left corner describing the next movie that Shirley was starring in; the reproduction has that writing in the upper right corner.) $5.00 – 10.00 each. Loretta Beilstein collection.

Shirley Temple paper fan from Italy, 1930s. $60.00 and up. Leslie Tannenbaum collection.

Japanese Shirley Temple "googly eyed" fan from the 1930s. $60.00 and up. Loretta Beilstein collection.

1990 Shirley Temple calendar. $10.00.

Door hanger; girl is called Miss Curly Locks. Not genuine Shirley, but certainly meant to resemble her in *The Little Colonel*. $20.00. Loretta Beilstein collection.

Advertising calendar featuring Shirley Temple, from the 1930s. A very rare find. $75.00 and up. Loretta Beilstein collection.

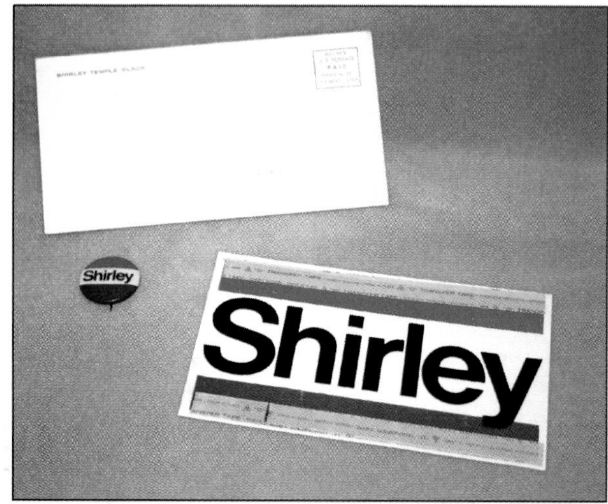

In 1968, Shirley Temple Black ran for the Republican congressional nomination in California. Though she didn't win, this began her work in politics. The sticker, envelope, and pin were from the campaign. $40.00. Leslie Tannenbaum collection.

Advertisement for 4' tall Shirley Temple Standees, sold to merchants in the 1930s, to advertise Shirley Temple memorabilia for sale. Currently, these are worth $300.00 and up each. Loretta Beilstein collection.

Ad for a Shirley Temple window Standee. Currently valued at $125.00 and up. Loretta Beilstein collection.

Tiny photobooks by Ross consisted of six to ten different photos of Shirley Temple. $30.00 each. Leslie Tannenbaum collection.

Campaign handout from Shirley's run for Congress, 1968. $15.00. Suzi Reed collection.

Another type of advertising hanger. $125.00 and up. Iva Mae Jones collection.

Advertisement for the double-sided Shirley Temple "star hanger" from the 1930s. Loretta Beilstein collection.

Original star hanger. $125.00 and up. Loretta Beilstein collection.

Limited edition commemorative poster by Nostalgia Collectibles, from 1977, signed at the bottom by Shirley Temple. $150.00. Iva Mae Jones collection.

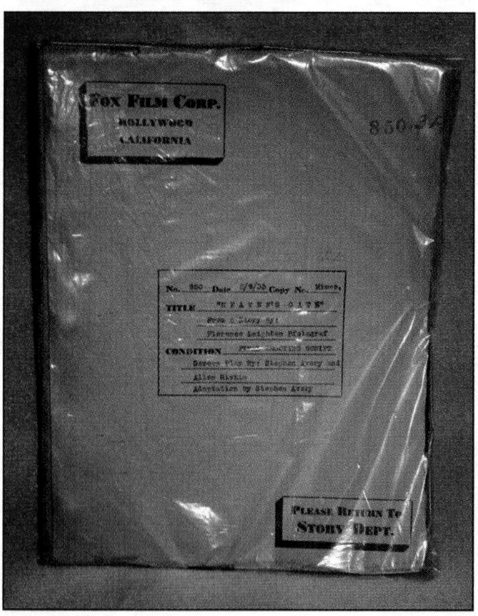

Original script for the movie *Our Little Girl*, which during production was called *Heaven's Gate*. A very rare find. $500.00 and up. Leslie Tannenbaum collection.

Cuban cigar bands. These were actually wrapped around Cuban cigars. 1930s. $15.00 each. Iva Mae Jones collection.

Paper Shirley Temple mask thought to be from the 1934 Chicago World's Fair. $50.00. Leslie Tannenbaum collection.

In the 1930s, there were a series of 12 Wheaties boxes that had Shirley pictures on the backs of them. These are the first six in the series. $10.00 each when cut. Janet Mitchell collection.

The last six Wheaties backs. $10.00 each. Janet Mitchell collection.

The third box in the series, shown with most of the original Wheaties box attached. $25.00. Janet Mitchell collection.

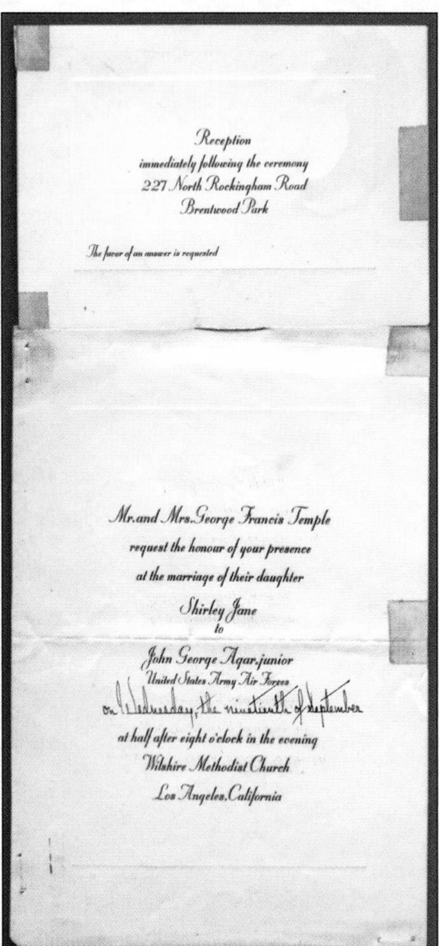

Reception
immediately following the ceremony
227 North Rockingham Road
Brentwood Park

The favor of an answer is requested

Mr. and Mrs. George Francis Temple
request the honour of your presence
at the marriage of their daughter
Shirley Jane
to
John George Agar, junior
United States Army Air Forces
on Wednesday, the nineteenth of September
at half after eight o'clock in the evening
Wilshire Methodist Church
Los Angeles, California

Wedding invitation from Shirley's marriage to John Agar, 1945. $150.00 and up. Leslie Tannenbaum collection.

The Shirley Temple doll was so popular in the 1930s that one was even present in this famous Coca-Cola Santa advertisement from 1936. Janet Mitchell collection.

Shirley Temple was a commonly used theme on birthday cards and Valentine's Day cards from the 1930s. $10.00 each. Janet Mitchell collection.

Little girls not only wanted their own Shirley Temple dolls, but they also wanted to look as much like Shirley Temple as possible. Many curled their hair in rag curls every night, and they also wanted to wear what Shirley was wearing. Soon, stores and catalogs were filled with everything Shirley Temple.

Dresses in the latest Shirley Temple fashions were produced for toddlers by Nannette and for little girls by Cinderella. Made of the finest quality fabrics, such dresses were must-haves for any Shirley Temple fan. Shirley Temple coats and snowsuits were made by H & J Block, swimsuits by Shawmut and Forest Mills, raincoats by Sherbrooke, slips and undies by Kaufman Bros., socks by Trimfit, slippers by Restful, and shoes by Green. Each item came with a Shirley Temple tag identifying it as a genuine Shirley Temple product. There were also Shirley Temple hats, gloves, purses, muffs, scarves, and even Shirley Temple hair bows. Children's jewelry with Shirley's image on it, including rings, pins, charms, and necklaces, was also sold. In most cases, advertisements for these products showed a smiling Shirley wearing the outfit or accessory. The luckiest little Shirley Temple fans could be dressed head to toe in genuine Shirley Temple products.

When a grown-up Shirley appeared on TV in the 1950s, Nannette and Cinderella began to produce Shirley Temple dresses again, this time for everyone from toddlers to teens. The clothes resembled styles of the day instead of Shirley's styles from the 1930s. Though not of the same quality as the earlier dresses, they were still very nice and quite popular. In addition to the reintroduction of Shirley Temple dresses, Shirley Temple high-end jewelry, play jewelry, and "glamour" play products for children were manufactured by Gabriel.

In the 1980s, the Japanese company "Shirley Temple" launched its own line of new high-end Shirley Temple dresses, which have no relation to the original Shirley Temple dresses from the 1930s.

Real Shirley Temple Dresses

This dress was worn by Shirley Temple in the 1930s. A very rare and valuable find. $1,500.00 and up. Leslie Tannenbaum collection.

Tag on the inside of the dress, marked "20th Century Fox" and "Shirley Temple." Leslie Tannenbaum collection.

1930s Nannette Toddler Dresses

Each Nannette dress came with an ornate picture tag of Shirley. The paper tags themselves have even become collectibles. $30.00. Loretta Beilstein collection.

1935 newspaper advertisement for the Nannette Shirley Temple toddler dresses. Marge Meisinger collection.

Our Shirley Temple Dresses Will Be Modeled By One of Streator's Smart Little Tots

SHIRLEY TEMPLE
"SHEERS"
FOR LITTLE MISS
1 TO 3

All the little cherubs who plan to grow up as charming as Shirley Temple will want these dainty summer frocks just like hers! Of fine dimity, sheer voile, or crisp organdie, beautifully made—the Nannette way—so they positively thrive on soapsuds.

$1.95

SHIRLEY TEMPLE
TWENTIETH CENTURY—FOX FILM STAR
FROCKS
BY NANNETTE

a nannette toddler
SHIRLEY TEMPLE
BRAND

Nannette (a division of Rosenau Brothers) made toddler dresses for the smallest Shirley Temple fans (sizes 1 to 3). Silk Nannette Shirley Temple toddler dress in the original box. $300.00. Leslie Tannenbaum collection.

Tag in the back of the dress on the left. Loretta Beilstein collection.

Fragile green silk Nannette Shirley Temple toddler dress. Original price varied from $1.95 to $3.95, a high price in the 1930s. Current price for each dress usually varies based on condition of dress, intricacy of the design, and how closely the dress resembles one that Shirley Temple wore in a movie. $75.00. Loretta Beilstein collection.

Tag in the back of the dress on the right.
Loretta Beilstein collection.

Silk Shirley Temple toddler dress with pleating and intricate smocking. Because silk is so fragile, oftentimes these dresses are now found with tears or stains. As pictured (with stains), $40.00; mint condition, $100.00. Loretta Beilstein collection.

Tag in the back of the dress on the left.
Loretta Beilstein collection.

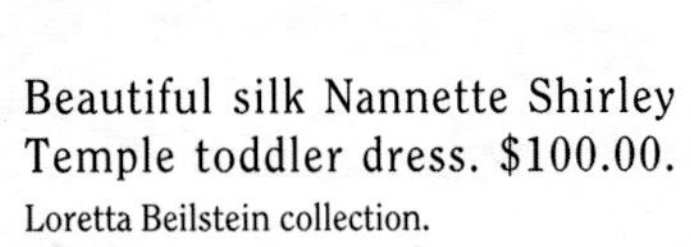

Beautiful silk Nannette Shirley Temple toddler dress. $100.00.
Loretta Beilstein collection.

Organdy Nannette Shirley Temple dress. $75.00. Loretta Beilstein collection.

Yellow silk Nannette Shirley Temple toddler party dress. $100.00. Loretta Beilstein collection.

Cotton Nannette Shirley Temple dress. $100.00. Loretta Beilstein collection.

Printed organdy Nannette Shirley Temple dress. $75.00. Courtesy Loretta Beilstein collection.

Tag in the back of the dress on the right. Loretta Beilstein collection.

Dark blue velvet Nannette Shirley Temple toddler dress. $50.00. Loretta Beilstein collection.

Christmas picture tag for the Nannette toddler dresses. $35.00. Loretta Beilstein collection.

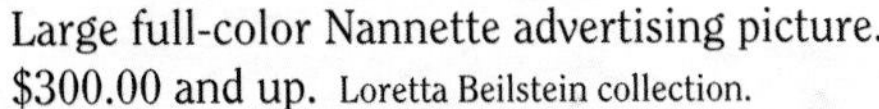

Large full-color Nannette advertising picture. $300.00 and up. Loretta Beilstein collection.

1950s Nannette Dresses

Blue nylon Nannette Shirley Temple party dress. $50.00. Loretta Beilstein collection.

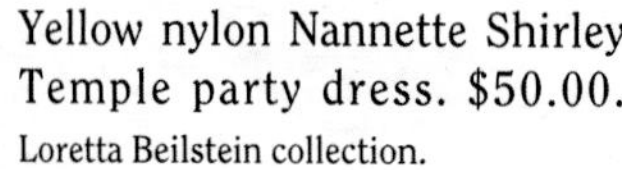

Yellow nylon Nannette Shirley Temple party dress. $50.00. Loretta Beilstein collection.

Yellow cotton Nannette Shirley Temple party dress. $50.00. Loretta Beilstein collection.

Cloth tag in the back of the Nannette Shirley Temple dress. All of the Nannette dresses from the 1950s were labeled with this tag. Loretta Beilstein collection.

White cotton Nannette Shirley Temple party dress, from the 1950s. $50.00. Loretta Beilstein collection.

Cotton Nannette Shirley Temple dress with embroidery at the bottom. $50.00. Loretta Beilstein collection.

Green cotton Nannette Shirley Temple school dress, from the 1950s. $50.00. Loretta Beilstein collection.

1930s Cinderella Dresses

In the 1930s, Cinderella (a division of Rosenau Brothers) made Shirley Temple dresses for girls (sizes 3 to 12). Each dress came with an ornate picture tag of Shirley, usually showing Shirley dressed in an identical Shirley Temple dress. The paper tags themselves have even become collectibles. $35.00. Loretta Beilstein collection.

Cotton Shirley Temple sailor shirt by Cinderella. Resembles one that Shirley wore in the movie *Captain January*. Originally came with matching pants. Shirt, $75.00; complete outfit, $400.00. Iva Mae Jones collection.

Cotton Cinderella Shirley Temple dress. Closely resembles the military dress that Shirley wore in *The Little Colonel*, which adds significantly to its value. $300.00. Loretta Beilstein collection.

Cotton Cinderella Shirley Temple dress. Closely resembles one that Shirley wore in the movie *Poor Little Rich Girl*, which adds to its value (though not as much as it would a more recognizable dress). $150.00. Iva Mae Jones collection.

Cotton Cinderella Shirley Temple dress that resembles one that Shirley wore in *Little Miss Broadway*. $100.00. Keith and Loretta McKenzie collection.

Cotton Cinderella Shirley Temple dress. Closely resembles one that Shirley wore in the movie *Rebecca of Sunnybrook Farm*, which adds to its value. $250.00. Iva Mae Jones collection.

Silk Cinderella Shirley Temple dress. $75.00. Loretta Beilstein collection.

Organdy Cinderella Shirley Temple party dress, mint condition. $100.00. Iva Mae Jones collection.

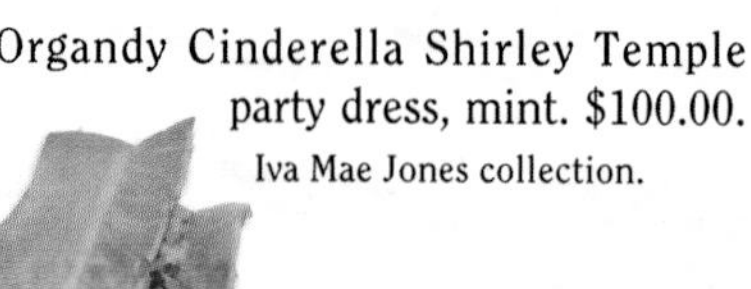

Organdy Cinderella Shirley Temple party dress, mint. $100.00. Iva Mae Jones collection.

Unusual peach Cinderella Shirley Temple party dress. $100.00. Loretta Beilstein collection.

Red cotton Cinderella Shirley Temple school dress with matching bloomers. $75.00. Keith and Loretta McKenzie collection.

Taffetta Cinderella Shirley Temple dress with matching purse. Small amount of staining on taffeta. $150.00; if mint, $300.00. Loretta Beilstein collection.

Beautiful silk Cinderella Shirley Temple dress. $100.00. Loretta Beilstein collection.

Tag in the back of the dress on the left. Loretta Beilstein collection.

Organdy Cinderella Shirley Temple party dress with embroidered flowers on it (missing silk ribbon at waist). $100.00. Loretta Beilstein collection.

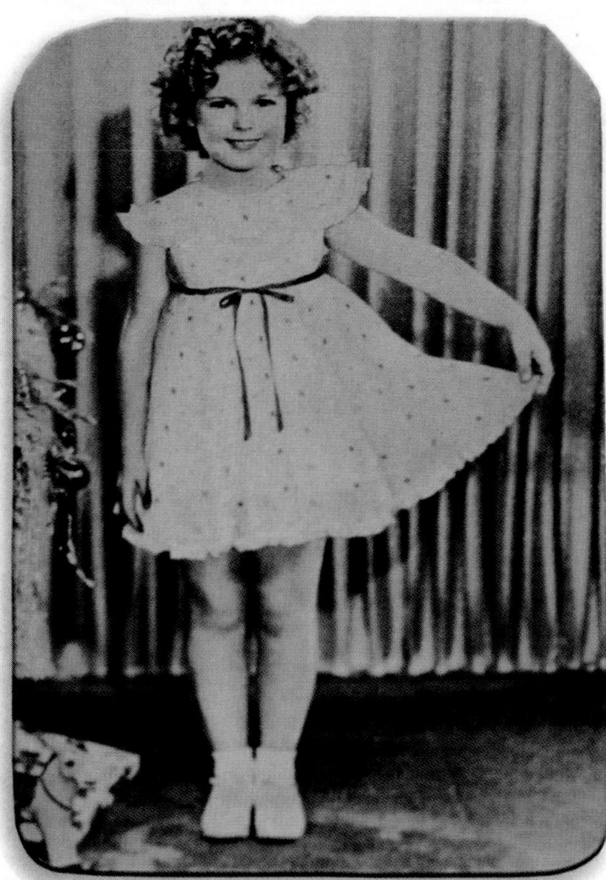
Paper tag for this dress shows Shirley Temple wearing the same outfit. Most dresses came with a tag of Shirley modeling the dress. $15.00. Loretta Beilstein collection.

Cotton Cinderella Shirley Temple bolero-style dress. $75.00.
Loretta Beilstein collection.

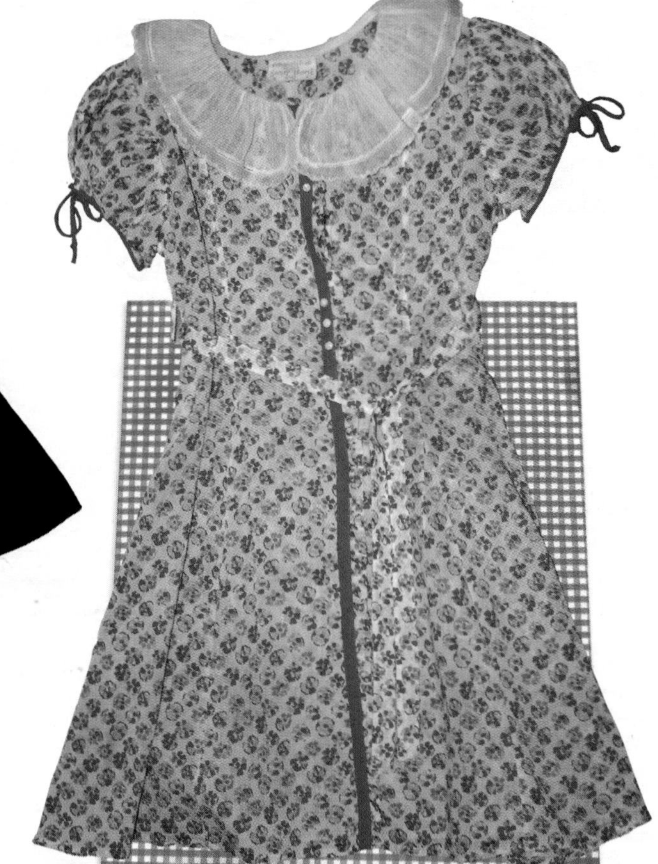

Cotton Cinderella Shirley Temple school dress for an older girl. $50.00. Loretta Beilstein collection.

Blue cotton Cinderella Shirley Temple dress. $75.00.
Loretta Beilstein collection.

Tag in the back of dress to the left.
Loretta Beilstein collection.

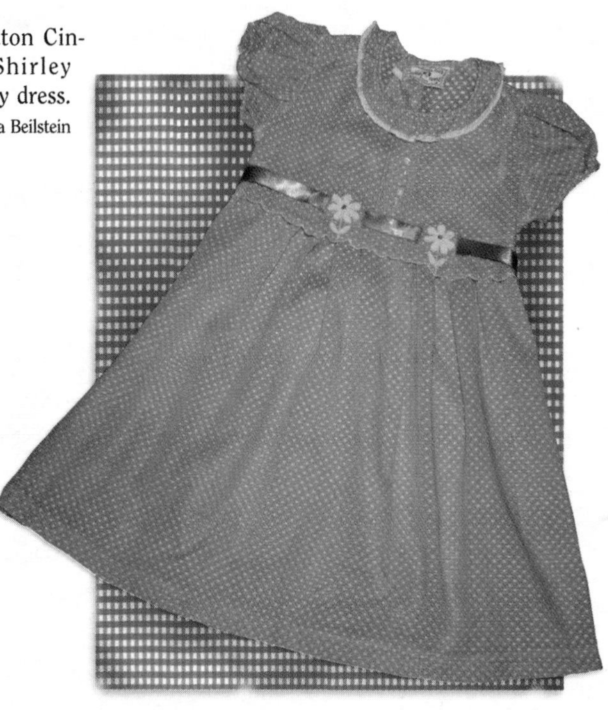

Flocked cotton Cinderella Shirley Temple party dress. $80.00. Loretta Beilstein

Organdy Cinderella Shirley Temple dress with matching organdy bonnet. It is being modeled by a 3' tall vinyl Shirley Temple doll (see chapter 7 for more information about this doll). Dress and bonnet, $200.00. Loretta Beilstein collection.

Cotton Cinderella Shirley Temple play dress. $60.00. Loretta Beilstein collection.

Delicate silk Cinderella Shirley Temple dress with smocking at the waist. $80.00. Loretta Beilstein collection.

Cotton Cinderella Shirley Temple bolero-style school dress. $60.00. Loretta Beilstein collection.

Blue/yellow cotton Cinderella Shirley Temple play dress with detailed embroidery at the bottom. $50.00. Loretta Beilstein collection.

Aqua cotton Cinderella Shirley Temple school dress. $75.00. Loretta Beilstein collection.

Taffeta Cinderella Shirley Temple party dress with matching jacket. $100.00. Loretta Beilstein collection.

Gorgeous peach taffeta Cinderella Shirley Temple fancy dress. $100.00. Loretta Beilstein collection.

Fancy cotton Cinderella Shirley Temple dress with pleated skirt. $100.00. Loretta Beilstein collection.

Pink cotton Cinderella Shirley Temple party dress. $75.00. Loretta Beilstein collection.

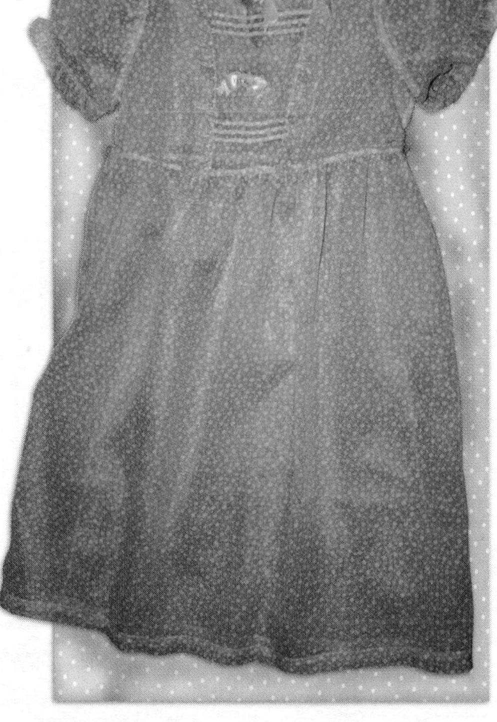

Peach printed organdy Cinderella Shirley Temple party dress for an older girl. $75.00. Loretta Beilstein collection.

Tag in the back of dress above. Loretta Beilstein collection.

Fancy paper tag for a Cinderella Shirley Temple dress. $25.00. Loretta Beilstein collection.

Fancy paper tag for a Cinderella Shirley Temple dress. $30.00. Loretta Beilstein collection.

Fancy paper tag for a Cinderella Shirley Temple dress. $40.00. Loretta Beilstein collection.

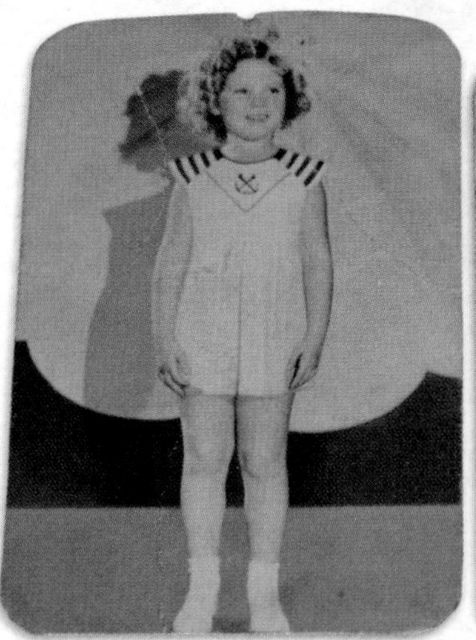

Paper tag for a Cinderella Shirley Temple dress. $10.00. Loretta Beilstein collection.

Large color cardboard ad for Cinderella Frocks. $200.00. Loretta Beilstein collection.

Color ad for Cinderella Shirley Temple dresses in the 1936 Cinderella catalog. Loretta Beilstein collection.

1950s Cinderella Dresses

Paper tag that was attached to all Cinderella Shirley Temple dresses made in the 1950s (front and back shown). $10.00. Loretta Beilstein collection.

Pink nylon Cinderella Shirley Temple party dress. $50.00. Loretta Beilstein collection.

Cotton Cinderella Shirley Temple dress with embroidered sleeves. $50.00. Loretta Beilstein collection.

Pink cotton Cinderella Shirley Temple party dress with netting underskirt. $50.00. Loretta Beilstein collection.

Cloth tag in the back of the Cinderella Shirley Temple dress below. All of the Cinderella dresses from the 1950s were labeled with this tag. Loretta Beilstein collection.

Blue nylon Cinderella Shirley Temple party dress that closely resembles the styles that the 1950s Shirley dolls wore. $50.00. Loretta Beilstein collection.

Unusual velvet and taffeta Cinderella Shirley Temple dress, definitely in 1950s style. $50.00. Loretta Beilstein collection.

Cotton Cinderella Shirley Temple shirt. $20.00. Loretta Beilstein collection.

Pink nylon Cinderella Shirley Temple dress. $50.00. Loretta Beilstein collection.

Blue cotton Cinderella Shirley Temple school dress. $30.00. Loretta Beilstein collection.

Matching Cinderella Shirley Temple dresses (probably for sisters). $150.00 for the pair. Loretta Beilstein collection.

1980s Shirley Temple Dresses

Dress from the Shirley Temple company in Japan. $75.00. Loretta Beilstein collection.

Dress from the Shirley Temple company in Japan. This company produced dresses in the 1980s and is still around today, producing a variety of things with the Shirley Temple label. $75.00. Loretta Beilstein collection.

Close-up of the Shirley Temple tag. Loretta Beilstein collection.

Dress from the Shirley Temple company in Japan. $75.00. Loretta Beilstein collection.

Dress from the Shirley Temple company in Japan. $75.00. Loretta Beilstein collection.

Accessories from the 1930s

Rare silk Shirley Temple undies by Kaufman Bros. Underwear Company. $110.00. Loretta Beilstein collection.

Tag in the back of the undies. Loretta Beilstein collection.

Color advertisement for a Shirley Temple coat made by H. & J. Block. $20.00. An authentic Shirley Temple coat would be worth $200.00 – 300.00. Loretta Beilstein collection.

Front and back of a paper tag for the Shirley Temple undies. Sometimes there was a picture of Shirley in her bedwear on the front and no picture on the back. $10.00. Loretta Beilstein collection.

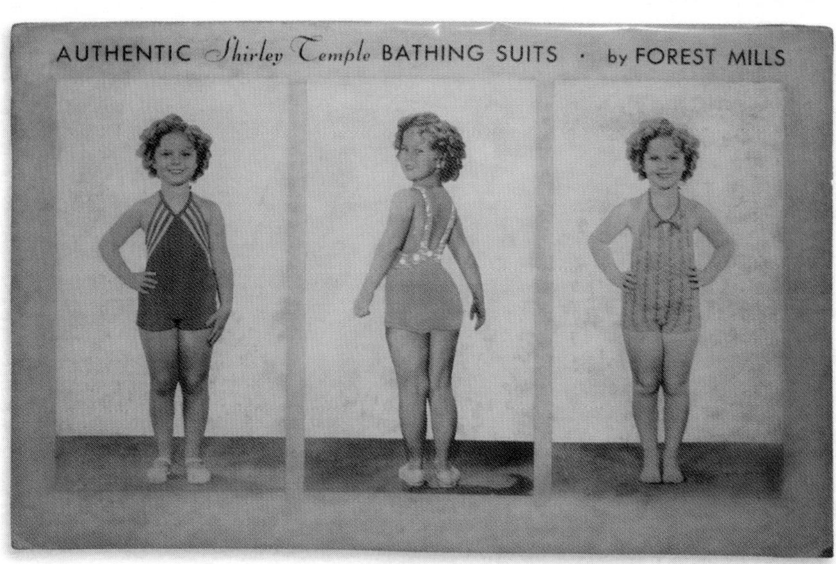

Ad for Shirley Temple swimsuits made by Forest Mills. Shawmut also made genuine Shirley Temple swimsuits. $60.00. Leslie Tannenbaum collection.

Another ad for a Shirley Temple coat. $20.00. Loretta Beilstein collection.

An ad for a Shirley Temple snowsuit made by H. & J. Block. $20.00. Loretta Beilstein collection.

Ad for a Shirley Temple raincoat made by Sherbrooke. $10.00. Loretta Beilstein collection.

Shirley Temple socks (came in a group of two pairs) by Trimfit, complete with box. $400.00 and up. One pair, $100.00 and up. Loretta Beilstein collection.

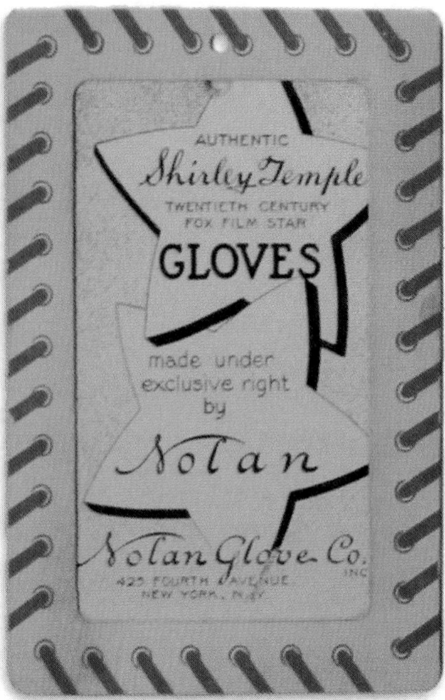

Paper tag for Shirley Temple gloves (had a picture of Shirley on the front). $20.00. Loretta Beilstein collection.

Paper tag at the toe of the socks.
Loretta Beilstein collection.

Large color advertisement for Shirley Temple socks. $20.00. Loretta Beilstein collection.

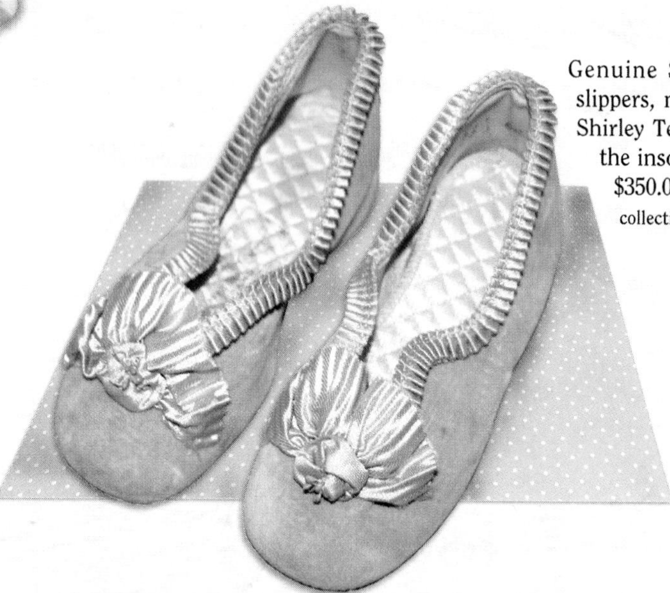

Genuine Shirley Temple slippers, marked "Original Shirley Temple Brand" on the insoles of the shoes. $350.00. Leslie Tannenbaum collection.

Insole of the Shirley Temple slipper, identifying the brand. Leslie Tannenbaum collection.

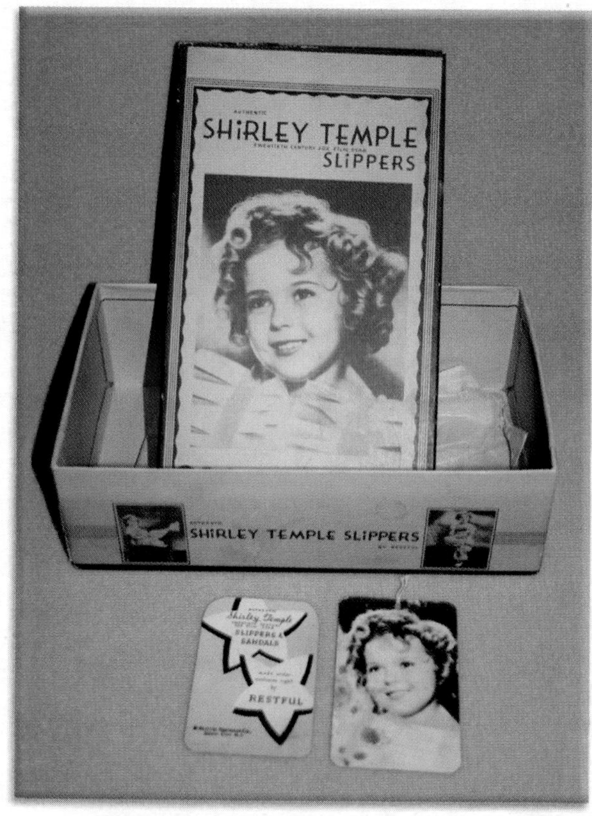

Box and paper tag for Shirley Temple slippers by Restful Footwear. $60.00. Loretta Beilstein collection.

New Shirley Temple shoes in the original box. Shoes are marked "The Authentic Shirley Temple Shoe" on the soles and insoles. These are so rare because shoes were generally used and then thrown away. And even if the shoes were not thrown out, they would not be identifiable unless barely worn (because the "Shirley Temple" marking would have worn off). $600.00. Loretta Beilstein collection.

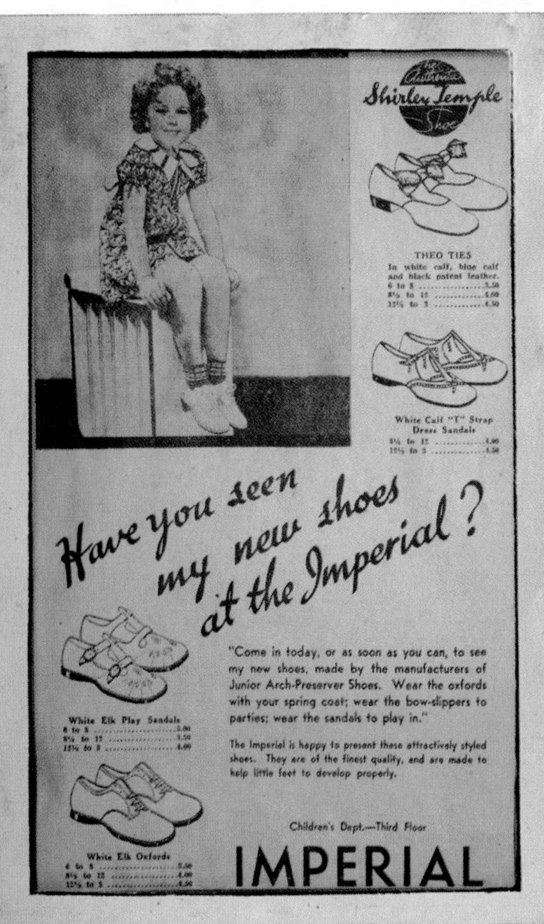

Advertisement for the Shirley Temple shoes.
Loretta Beilstein collection.

Felt Shirley Temple hat by L. Lewis & Sons. $75.00.
Leslie Tannenbaum collection.

Ad for Shirley Temple hat sets.
Marge Meisinger collection.

Rayon tag on the inside of the Shirley Temple hat. Leslie Tannenbaum collection.

Black taffeta Shirley Temple bonnet by Lewis, with original hangtag. $125.00. Leslie Tannenbaum collection.

Tag inside the rare 1950s Shirley Temple hat on the right. Leslie Tannenbaum collection.

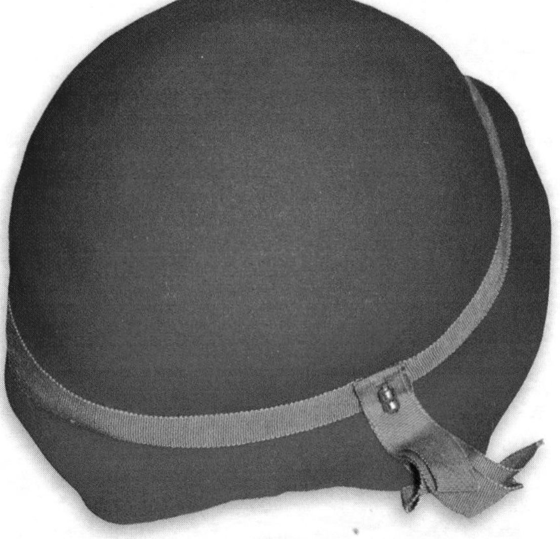

Stylish felt Shirley Temple hat by Richard Englander. This style of hat was one of the few Shirley accessories produced in the 1950s and are very rare. $150.00. Leslie Tannenbaum collection.

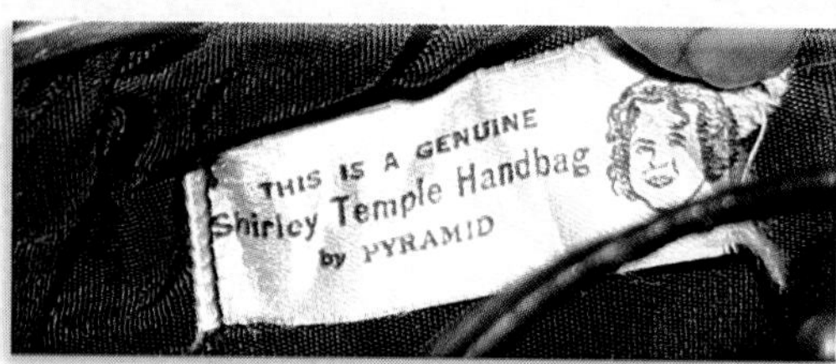

Rayon tag on the inside of the purse on the right. Loretta Beilstein collection.

Plaid Shirley Temple Purse by Pyramid, from the 1930s. $80.00. Loretta Beilstein collection.

Ad for a Shirley Temple purse from the 1930s. The one shown in the ad was modeled after an outfit that Shirley wore in the movie *Curly Top*. Currently, that purse is valued at $200.00 and up. Marge Meisinger collection.

Black Shirley Temple purse by Pyramid, with a gold pin on it that says "Shirley Temple's Pet Rowdy." This pin was also sold separately. $100.00. Leslie Tannenbaum collection.

Another Shirley Temple purse by Pyramid, with the original hangtag. $130.00. Keith and Loretta McKenzie collection.

Red velvet Shirley Temple purse by Pyramid, with elephant appliqué and the original hangtag. $130.00. Leslie Tannenbaum collection.

Boxed Shirley Temple silk hair-bow barrette with cameo by The Ribbon Mills Corp. $120.00. Leslie Tannenbaum collection.

Two types of Shirley Temple silk hair bows with Shirley Temple cameo by the Ribbon Mills Corp. $85.00 and up each. Leslie Tannenbaum collection.

Rare velvet Shirley Temple muff. $200.00. Leslie Tannenbaum collection.

More variations of the original Shirley Temple hair-bow ribbon, this time without cameos in the centers. $60.00 and up each. Leslie Tannenbaum collection.

Shirley Temple headband and plastic barrette on card backing. Headband, loose, $25.00; barrette, $50.00. Leslie Tannenbaum collection.

Original hair ribbon Shirley Temple cut-out display, with Shirley Temple hair ribbon attached. $600.00. Leslie Tannenbaum collection.

Original Shirley Temple handkerchiefs. $150.00. Janet Mitchell collection.

"Original Shirley Temple Handkerchief" sticker used to mark hankies. Janet Mitchell collection.

Boxed hankerchiefs by Madame Alexander (who bought the copyright for *The Little Colonel* trademark while Shirley was filming *The Little Colonel*), using *The Little Colonel* trademark. These are not Shirley Temple, but are clearly meant to resemble Shirley from the movie. $75.00. Leslie Tannenbaum collection.

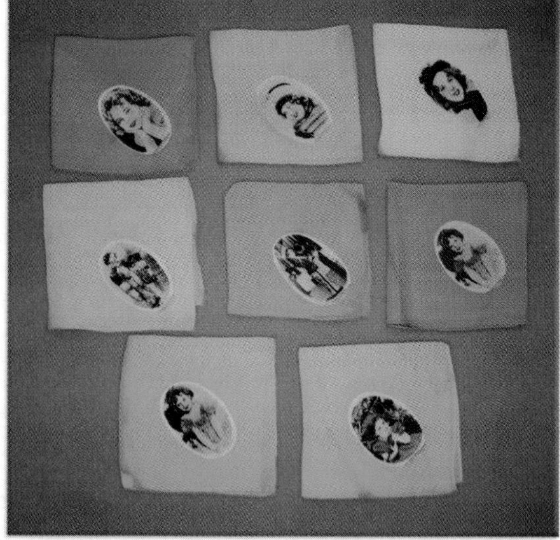

Silk hankerchiefs from Japan with Shirley's picture on them. $20.00 each. Janet Mitchell collection.

Close-up of the Shirley Temple scarf tag. Leslie Tannenbaum collection.

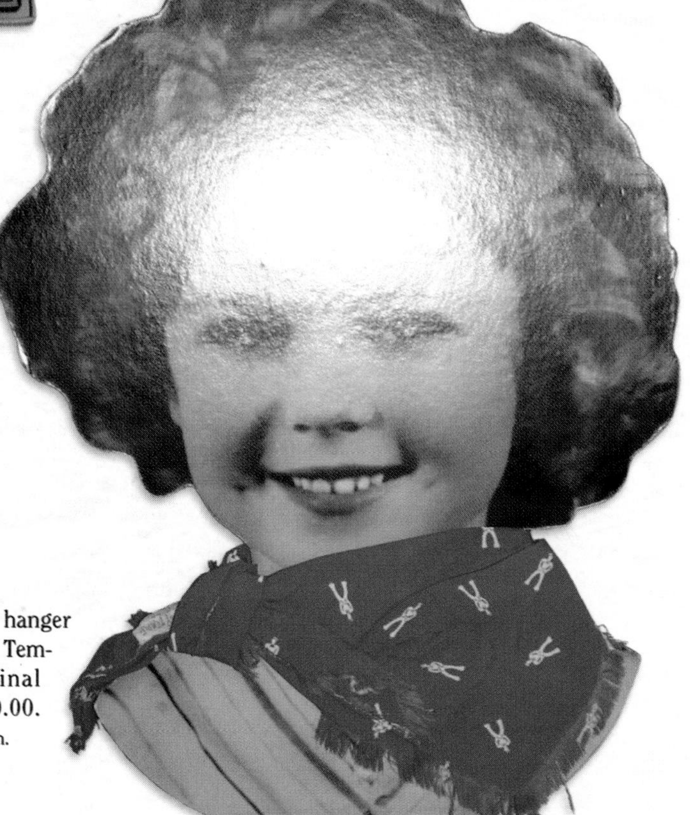

Large Shirley Temple hanger advertising the Shirley Temple scarf (with original scarf attached). $600.00. Leslie Tannenbaum collection.

Jewelry from the 1930s

Booklet advertising the Shirley Temple "dangles." Included 12 color pages describing the variety of charms available. $25.00. Loretta Beilstein collection.

Original pin. $25.00.
Leslie Tannenbaum collection.

The last page of the *"Dangles" for Bracelets* booklet showed the different pins that were available on which to display the charms. Loretta Beilstein collection.

Assortment of jewelry. Top row, from left: heart, fan mail, and teddy bear (all in the original packaging). Middle row, on the original charm bracelet, from left: heart, camera, Shirley, toy automobile, Shirley and Corky, and fan mail. Bottom row, from left: Shirley pin, charm from Shirley necklace, doll house charm (in original packaging), and ballerina charm. Charms not shown: Shirley drinking milk, teddy bear, Shirley in school, Corky (her dog), and monkey. The charms alone are worth $20.00 – $30.00 each (depending on rarity). In the original packaging, $50.00 each; as a complete set (with all charms), $300.00 – 400.00. Pin, $25.00. Janet Mitchell collection.

The charms were originally painted gold, but most gently faded to silver over the course of time. From left to right: Shirley, heart, and Shirley drinking milk that have all faded to silver. $60.00 (set). Loretta Beilstein collection.

A Shirley Temple head charm on a necklace and bracelet set came in this Shirley Temple box. Box only, $20.00; necklace and bracelet in box, $125.00. Leslie Tannenbaum collection.

Shirley Temple ring. Marked "Sterling" on the inside of the ring. $40.00. Monique Cabrera collection.

A recent reproduction of the Shirley Temple charm cannot compare in detail and quality when displayed side-by-side with the original. On the left is the reproduction; on the right, the original. Reproduction, $5.00; original, $20.00. Monique Cabrera collection.

Assortment of original celluloid pins. These are very fragile and rare. $50.00 and up each. Leslie Tannenbaum collection.

On the left is an original pin from the 1930s, and on the right is a reproduction. Notice the difference in quality — the original has enamel coloring, and the reproduction is painted. Original, $40.00; reproduction, $5.00. Leslie Tannenbaum collection.

"Shirley Temple's Pet Rowdy" pin. It can also be found on the Shirley Temple purse from the same era. $25.00. Iva Mae Jones collection.

Unusual *Little Colonel* tin watch (marked "Made in Japan" on the back) that was most likely a party favor from the 1930s. Shirley is on the watch face. $30.00. Loretta Beilstein collection.

Cracker Jack–style Shirley Temple pin that is believed to be from the 1930s (Lorraine Burdick describes a similar one as being from Czechoslovakia) and a Shirley Temple locket. $30.00 each. Iva Mae Jones collection.

1950s Jewelry/Makeup/Embroidery Sets

Advertisement for Shirley Temple jewelry. Most of these sets are very valuable, because there were not many produced. Except for the watch, these items are not recognizable as Shirley Temple products unless in the original box. Marge Meisinger collection.

High-quality Shirley Temple necklace and bracelet in original signature box. $300.00. (Courtesy Leslie Tannenbaum collection)

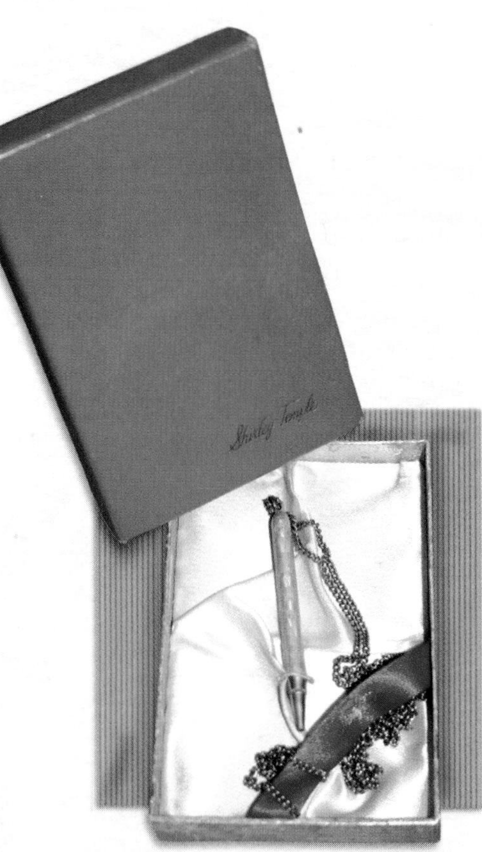

High-quality Shirley Temple necklace with pen attached, in signature box. $300.00. Leslie Tannenbaum collection.

High-quality Shirley Temple jewelry items were sold in signature boxes. Shirley Temple fairy tale charm bracelet, in original signature box. $300.00. Leslie Tannenbaum collection.

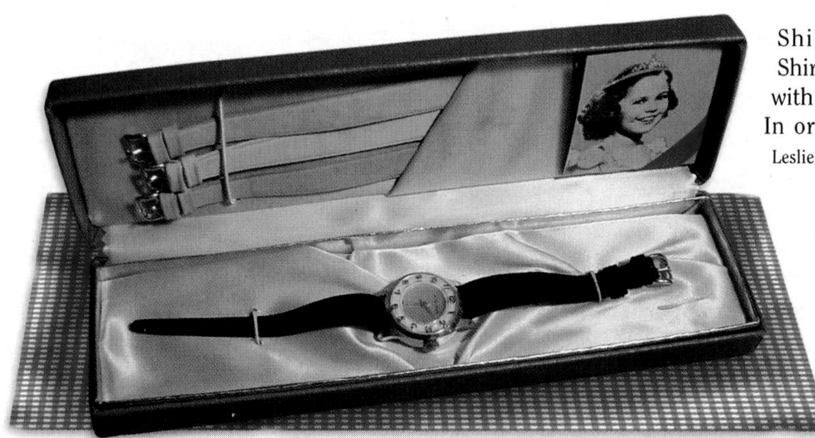

Shirley Temple watch, with Shirley's signature on the face and with interchangeable watch bands. In original signature box. $300.00. Leslie Tannenbaum collection.

Shirley Temple locket necklace, bracelet, and ring on original card. Carded jewelry was sold in dime stores at the time and has nowhere near the quality of the signature boxed items. However, it is rare and sought after by collectors. It is also unrecognizable as being Shirley Temple jewelry if not on its original card. $200.00 and up. Leslie Tannenbaum collection.

Shirley Temple necklace, bracelet, and ring set on original card. $200.00 and up. Leslie Tannenbaum collection.

Shirley Temple necklace with imitation pearl and on original card. $150.00 and up. Leslie Tannenbaum collection.

Shirley Temple Snap-On Jewelry Set by Gabriel, late 1950s, #302. A very rare set. $100.00 and up. Leslie Tannenbaum collection.

Shirley Temple imitation pearl necklace and bracelet on original card. $200.00 and up. Leslie Tannenbaum collection.

Hard-to-find version of Shirley Temple Pretty Play by Gabriel, #340. $75.00. Loretta Beilstein collection.

Shirley Temple Hair Styler by Gabriel, #339. $50.00.
Loretta Beilstein collection.

Shirley Temple tiara on original card. This is similar to one that Shirley wore in the movie *Little Miss Broadway*. $250.00 and up. Leslie Tannenbaum collection.

A different (more common) version of Shirley Temple Pretty Play by Gabriel, #340. Other beauty sets from Gabriel are listed in chapter 16. $50.00. Leslie Tannenbaum collection.

1950s – 1960s Embroidery Sets

Shirley Temple Luncheon Embroidery Set, 1960, #311. $75.00. Loretta Beilstein collection.

Shirley Temple Movie Favorites Embroidery Set, 1960, #301. $100.00. Janet Mitchell collection.

Shirley Temple Movie Favorites Embroidery Set, 1959, #310. $50.00. Iva Mae Jones collection.

Reproductions

Reproduction Shirley Temple watch. $15.00. Iva Mae Jones collection.

Reproduction Shirley Temple ring. $5.00. Loretta Beilstein collection.

Shirley Temple's name and image have been attached to everything from tea sets to matchboxes, soap to cookie tins. The following collectibles don't fall into any particular category. Included are common items from the 1930s, such as the cobalt blue glassware and salt figurines, and less common pieces, such as Shirley Temple pen sets and doll carriages. Items from the 1950s include a Shirley Temple tea set, Shirley Temple records, and a Shirley Temple ironing set. Recent items from Nostalgia Collectibles and the Danbury Mint are also grouped into the miscellaneous category. This includes plates, figurines, a calendar, and a charm bracelet. Many of these Shirley collectibles are common; others are much more rare. With so many pieces of Shirley memorabilia around, there is always an opportunity to find a wonderful Shirley collectible that no one else has noticed. Prices given are what these items have sold for in the past, but with such unusual items, prices are variable and timing is key. Keep searching and one day you too will find a great one-of-a-kind Shirley Temple deal.

Cobalt Blue Glassware

Advertisement for the occasion dish, 1935. Janet Mitchell collection.

Three types of cobalt blue glassware were produced with Shirley Temple's image on them. The "occasion dish" (bowl) was released by Wheaties as a promotion for the movie *Our Little Girl,* 1935. On the left is the original bowl, and on the right is a reproduction made in the 1970s. Original, $40.00; reproduction, $15.00. Janet Mitchell collection.

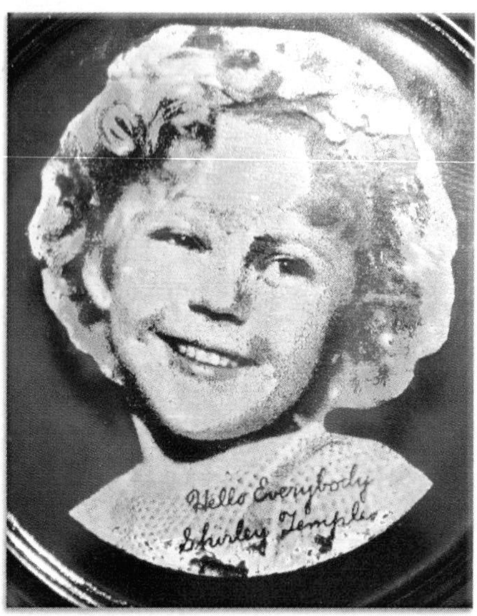

Close-up of the Shirley image on the original bowl. Notice the detail that is visible on the facial features. Janet Mitchell collection.

Close-up of the Shirley image on the reproduction bowl. Notice how the facial features seem less detailed; the glassware also has more air bubbles in it. Janet Mitchell collection.

Advertisement for the Shirley Temple mug, 1935. Janet Mitchell collection.

The mug was a free giveaway with the purchase of a package of Bisquick during the promotion of *The Littlest Rebel,* late 1935 – early 1936. On the left is the original mug, and on the right is a reproduction made in the 1970s. Original, $40.00; reproduction, $15.00. Janet Mitchell collection.

Shirley Temple reproduction glassware. $50.00 set.
Loretta Beilstein collection.

Advertisement for the Shirley Temple pitcher, 1936. Courtesy Janet Mitchell collection.

The pitcher was a free giveaway with the purchase of two boxes of Wheaties during the promotion of *Captain January,* 1936. On the left is the original pitcher, and on the right is a reproduction made in the 1970s. Another very rare original wider cobalt blue pitcher has been found as well (not pictured). Original, $30.00; reproduction, $15.00. Janet Mitchell collection.

Reproduction glassware was produced from the 1970s through the 1990s. It came in a variety of colors. These are not as valuable as the originals. $15.00 each. Loretta Beilstein collection.

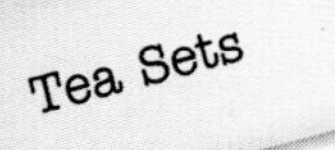

Shirley Temple tea set, late 1950s – early 1960s. This pink and white tea set was produced by Ideal. $300.00 boxed, $10.00 – 20.00 per piece. Iva Mae Jones collection.

"SHIRLEY TEMPLE" CAMEO TEA SETS
Metal and Plastic Pieces

Delicate **peach tinted** plastic cups, teapot and creamer with a cameo of Shirley Temple. Included in this set are metal plates and saucers lithographed with Shirley Temple monograms and **silver-colored** plastic tableware. Set in beautifully decorated window box.

14-Pc. Sets...Service for 2...$2.00 Retail
Y33-4571—1 doz. sets O.S. 16 lbs.
Doz. sets 32.00

21-Pc. Sets...Service for 3...$3.00 Retail
Y33-4572—½ doz. sets O.S. 24 lbs.
Doz. sets 48.00

Advertisement for the Shirley Temple tea set. Marge Meisinger collection.

Unusual variation of the Shirley Temple tea set, with flowers on the plates instead of Shirley's initials. $400.00. Leslie Tannenbaum collection.

Each of these plastic cups has a Shirley Temple cameo on it that is similar to the one on the tea set pitcher from the 1950s; however, the origin of these cups is unknown. $20.00 each. Leslie Tannenbaum collection.

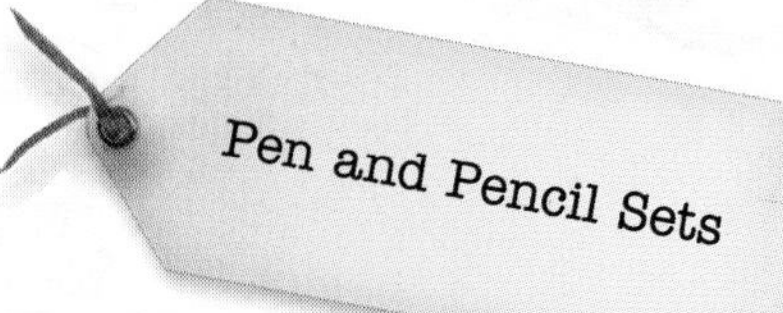

Shirley Temple pencil set, 1930s, came with pencils and two drawers to hold rulers, maps, etc. $200.00 and up (complete). Leslie Tannenbaum collection.

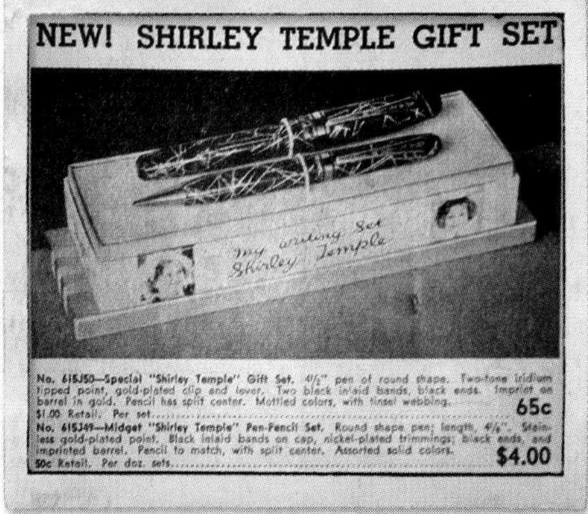

NEW! SHIRLEY TEMPLE GIFT SET

No. 615J50—Special "Shirley Temple" Gift Set. 4½" pen of round shape. Two-tone iridium tipped point, gold-plated clip and lever. Two black inlaid bands, black ends. Imprint on barrel in gold. Pencil has split center. Mottled colors, with tinsel webbing. $1.00 Retail. Per set........ 65c

No. 615J49—Midget "Shirley Temple" Pen-Pencil Set. Round shape pen; length, 4⅛". Stainless gold-plated point. Black inlaid bands on cap, nickel-plated trimmings; black ends, and imprinted barrel. Pencil to match, with split center. Assorted solid colors. 50c Retail. Per doz. sets........ $4.00

Ad from a 1930s newspaper for the Shirley Temple pen and pencil set. Marge Meisinger collection.

Shirley Temple pen and pencil set, 1930s, by Eversharp had "Shirley Temple" stamped on the barrels of the pen and pencil and/or on the gold clips. It came in its own carrying box. $75.00. Iva Mae Jones collection.

Shirley Temple My Writing Set from the 1930s. Shirley Temple pens with original box. The pen clips said "Shirley Temple" on them. $150.00 in the box, $80.00 and up just the pens. Leslie Tannenbaum collection.

Another Shirley Temple My Writing Set from the 1930s. The pens have "Shirley Temple" stamped on the barrels. $150.00. Janet Mitchell collection.

Soap

Shirley Temple soap was released by Kerk Guild Inc. in the 1930s. Two 5" Shirley soap figurines. Boxed set, $75.00. Iva Mae Jones collection.

Circular Shirley Temple soap by Kerk Guild (came as part of a set). $30.00. Janet Mitchell collection.

Shirley Temple soap from the 1960s. $20.00. Janet Mitchell collection.

Unusual single 5" Shirley Temple soap made by Kerk Guild Inc. in the 1930s, a very rare piece. $150.00. Leslie Tannenbaum collection.

Plaster and Figurines

Large plaster Shirley Temple disk from the 1930s. Rare item. $500.00 and up. Leslie Tannenbaum collection.

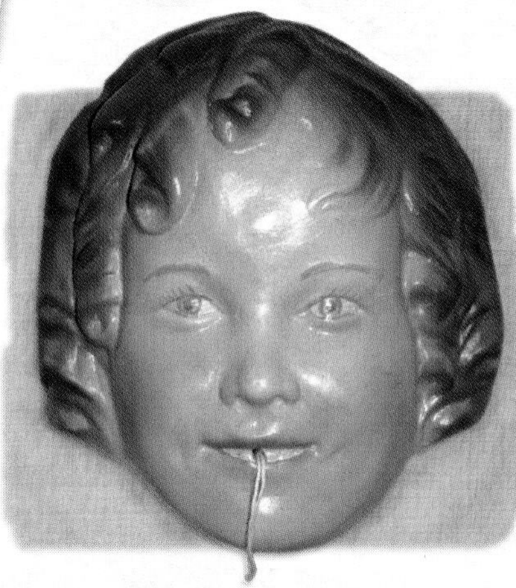

Shirley Temple string holder from the 1930s, made of painted plaster. $200.00. Leslie Tannenbaum collection.

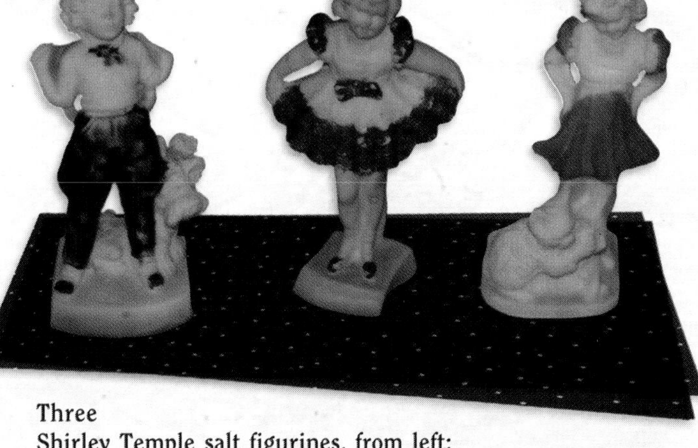

Three
Shirley Temple salt figurines, from left:
with a Scottie dog, in *Baby Take a Bow* pose, and with a kitty. The figurines have flocking on them, which has come off (somewhat) over time. The kitty figurine is the most rare and is worth $40.00; the others are worth $20.00. Leslie Tannenbaum collection.

Shirley Temple chalk bust made in the 1930s by F. Coffin. This lovely bust of Shirley was made in France. $500.00. Loretta Beilstein collection.

Salt figurine made in Shirley's image and playing a drum. $30.00. Leslie Tannenbaum collection.

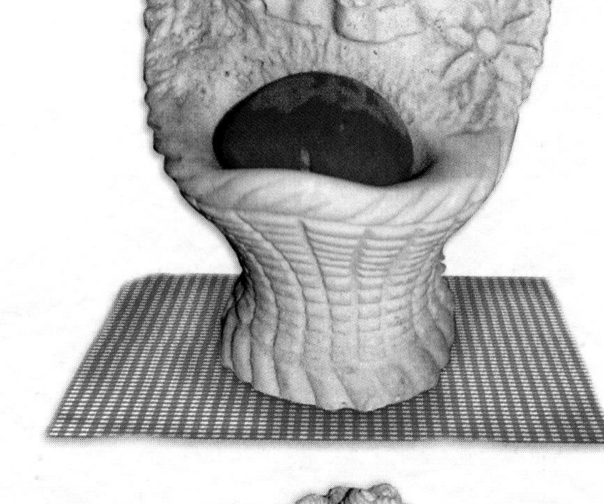

Salt figurine with pin cushion, 1930s, made in Shirley's *Baby Take a Bow* image. $30.00. Loretta Beilstein collection.

From left: 7" tall salt figurine resembling Shirley Temple in her *Baby Take a Bow* pose and gold-painted 4" tall figurine resembling Shirley with her hands on her hips. Both are believed to be from the 1930s. $20.00 each. Leslie Tannenbaum collection.

12" tall salt figurine resembling Shirley in her *Baby Take a Bow* pose, from the 1930s. $40.00. Janet Mitchell collection.

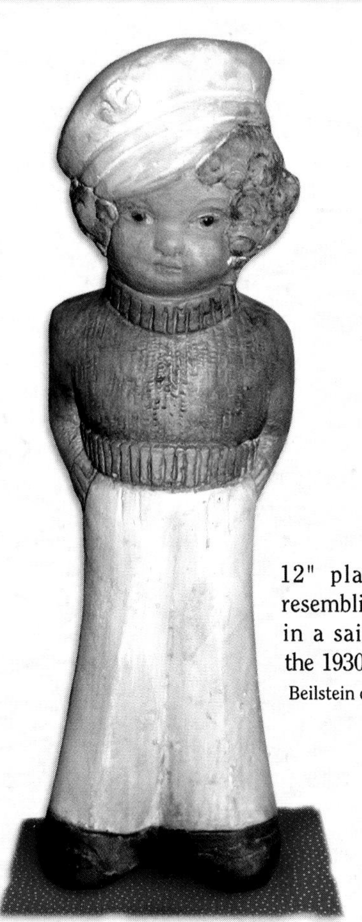

12" plaster figurine resembling Shirley and in a sailor pose, from the 1930s. $20.00. Loretta Beilstein collection.

Gold-painted plaster figurine that resembles Shirley in her *Baby Take a Bow* pose. About 7" tall and from the 1930s. $20.00. Leslie Tannenbaum collection.

Gold-painted 4" chalk figurine marked "Shirley" on the base. $10.00. Loretta Beilstein collection.

Advertisement for a Dolly Dancer chalk figurine that had a pose very similar to Shirley's in *Stand Up and Cheer*. Marge Meisinger collection.

Bronze-painted 4" chalk figurine marked "Shirley" on the base. $10.00. Leslie Tannenbaum collection.

Molded plastic figurine resembling Shirley in her *Baby Take a Bow* pose. Origin and date unknown. $20.00. Leslie Tannenbaum collection.

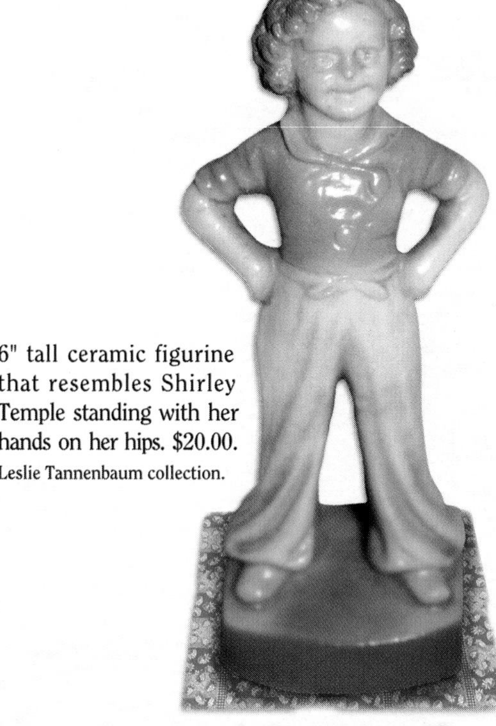

6" tall ceramic figurine that resembles Shirley Temple standing with her hands on her hips. $20.00. Leslie Tannenbaum collection.

Celluloid

Lightweight celluloid baby rattles from the 1930s. Very rare pieces. $50.00 each. Leslie Tannenbaum collection.

Shirley Temple penny bank from the 1930s, made of lightweight celluloid. $35.00. Loretta Beilstein collection.

Doll Carriages

Ideal blanket and pillow set that went in the doll carriage, very rare. The words "Shirley Temple" and a small lamb are embroidered on the blanket. The pillow is tagged "Ideal." $80.00 for both. Keith and Loretta McKenzie collection.

Wicker Shirley Temple doll carriage by Whitney, made in the 1930s. Came in three different sizes and two different colors (green or tan). Had Shirley Temple decals on each side of the carriage and had metal "Shirley Temple" wheel hubs and hood knobs. Price varies due to size and condition. $300.00 and up. Iva Mae Jones collection.

Wooden Shirley Temple doll carriage by Whitney, made in the 1930s. Came in either gray or blue. Also included leather hood, Shirley Temple decals on each side of the carriage, and metal "Shirley Temple" wheel hubs and hood knobs. $200.00 and up. Iva Mae Jones collection.

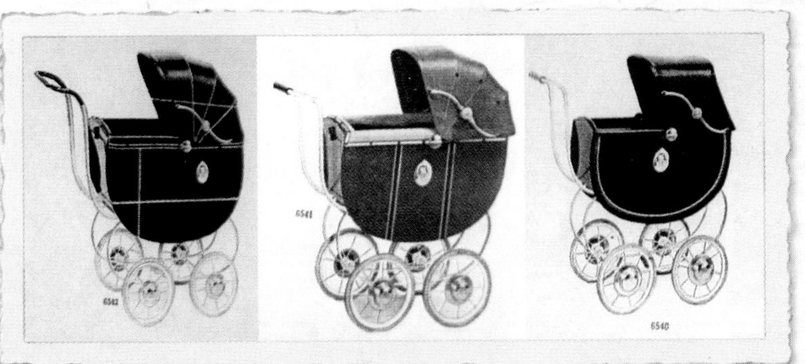

From the Whitney Carriage Company catalog, other types of Shirley Temple doll carriages made by Whitney in the 1930s. All were offered in either gray or blue. Janet Mitchell collection.

Film

Super 8 8mm films of Shirley Temple shorts, released in 1958. Clockwise from top left: *War Babies* (#233), *Pie-Covered Wagon* (#222), *Glad Rags to Riches* (#223), and *Kid 'N Africa* (#234). These came in both smaller and larger box versions. Shown are the smaller boxes. $15.00 each. Janet Mitchell collection.

Kiddie Komics released small boxes of film for the Kiddie Kamera. One box featured Shirley Temple. $10.00. Iva Mae Jones collection.

From left: Larger box version of *Glad Rags to Riches* from 1958, and a 16mm film of Shirley from the movie *The Red-Haired Alibi* (1932), by Safety Films and produced by Keystone Mfg. Co. in the 1930s; it included 100 feet of film. $15.00 – 30.00 each. Leslie Tannenbaum collection.

Metal Items

Silver bowls engraved "Merry Christmas from Shirley Temple." These are believed to be gifts given out to guests at a Christmas party hosted by Shirley Temple in the 1930s. Marked "Reed and Barton 101" on the bottom. $200.00 and up. Leslie Tannenbaum collection.

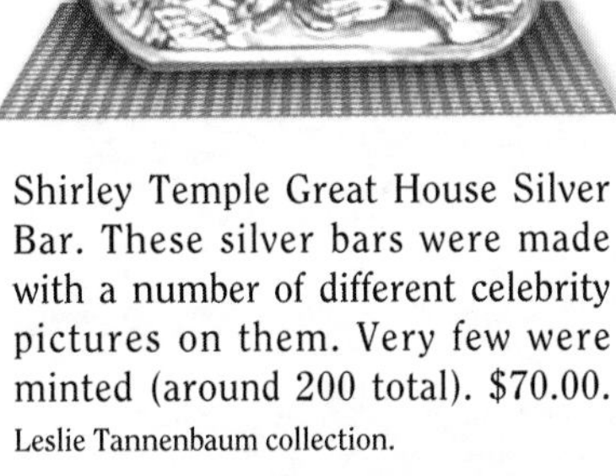

Shirley Temple Great House Silver Bar. These silver bars were made with a number of different celebrity pictures on them. Very few were minted (around 200 total). $70.00. Leslie Tannenbaum collection.

Some of the Shirley Temple Great House Silver Bars were marked "cancelled" across them. These are even rarer than the others; there were only 20 minted. $110.00. Leslie Tannenbaum collection.

Printing plate believed to be from the 1930s. Ink was applied to the plate, and the image was then stamped on to paper. $100.00. Leslie Tannenbaum collection.

Original Shirley Temple police badge. Probably one of the rarest pieces of Shirley memorabilia. Often the reproduction badge is sold as original. On the left is the original: gold in color, imprinted black lettering, space is filled in between the eagle head and the wing. On the right is the reproduction: bronze in color, letters are raised, there is space between the eagle head and the wing. Original, $1,000.00 and up; reproduction, $10.00. Leslie Tannenbaum collection.

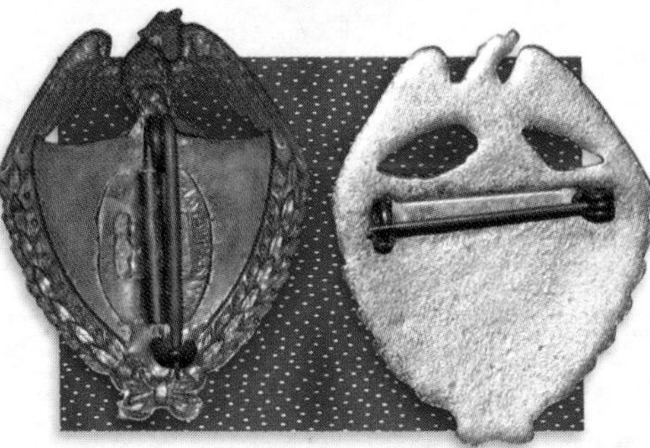

Backs of the police badges. Original is on the left, reproduction is on the right. Leslie Tannenbaum collection.

Small metal figurine that resembles Shirley Temple wearing the fancy dress from *The Littlest Rebel*. Made in the 1930s. $40.00. Leslie Tannenbaum collection.

Metal statue that resembles Shirley in her *Baby Take a Bow* pose. $30.00. Leslie Tannenbaum collection.

Shirley Temple metal candy mold from the 1930s. $50.00 and up. Leslie Tannenbaum collection.

Metal Shirley Temple cookie tin from Melbourne, Australia. A very rare piece from the 1930s. $200.00 and up. Leslie Tannenbaum collection.

Ceres medal honoring Shirley Temple Black, 1970s, released by the Food and Agriculture Organization of the United Nations. On the back is a quote from a speech that Ms. Black made at the UN in 1972: "We must acknowledge our kinship as human beings." $20.00. Janet Mitchell collection.

Little Miss sewing machine by Lindstrom, 1930s. Not officially Shirley Temple, but the picture on it certainly resembles her. $100.00. Loretta Beilstein collection.

Metal Shirley bank from the 1970s. $30.00. Janet Mitchell collection.

Small 3" tall metal bell from India that resembles Shirley in the movie *Wee Willie Winkie*. Believed to be from the 1930s. $50.00. Leslie Tannenbaum collection.

Records

Shirley Temple in The Littlest Rebel, a recording of a radio show that Shirley voiced on October 14, 1940. A 1980 Radio Import release. $20.00. Loretta Beilstein collection.

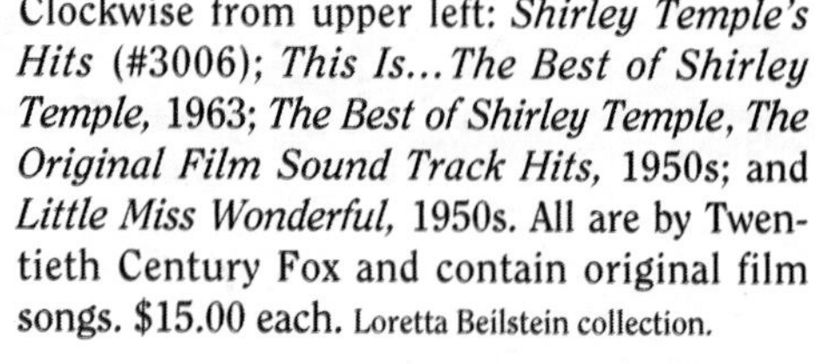

Clockwise from upper left: *Shirley Temple's Hits* (#3006); *This Is...The Best of Shirley Temple*, 1963; *The Best of Shirley Temple, The Original Film Sound Track Hits*, 1950s; and *Little Miss Wonderful*, 1950s. All are by Twentieth Century Fox and contain original film songs. $15.00 each. Loretta Beilstein collection.

Clockwise from upper left: *The Best of Shirley Temple, Volume II*, 1965, Twentieth Century Fox; *On the Good Ship Lollipop*, 1965, Movietone; *Curtain Call*, 1965, Movietone; and *Remember Shirley*, 1973. $15.00 each. Loretta Beilstein collection.

Clockwise from upper left: *Little Miss Shirley Temple,* 1970s, Pickwick; *On the Good Ship Lollipop,* 1979; *The Best of Shirley Temple,* 1978, HRB Music; *Golden Hour of Shirley Temple,* 1974, Golden Hour. $15.00 each. Loretta Beilstein collection.

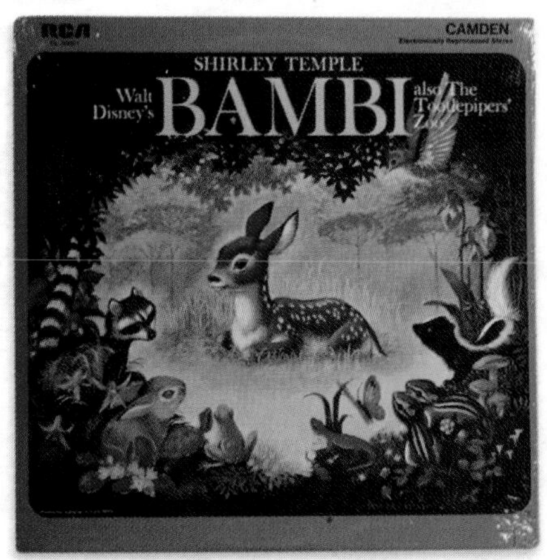

Shirley recorded the *Bambi* children's storybook. The records were released by RCA Victor in 1960, and used recordings that Shirley made of the Bambi story between 1945 and 1949. The catalog numbers were LBY1012, Y395, EP, and WY391. $15.00. Loretta Beilstein collection.

Rarer hardcover version of *Bambi* (Y-391). $20.00. Iva Mae Jones collection.

Another version of the Bambi recording. $20.00. Janet Mitchell collection.

Two records of Shirley narrating the children's book *Dumbo*, RCA, 1960, from recordings made in the 1940s. $20.00 each. Janet Mitchell collection.

Newer small Shirley Temple record. $10.00. Leslie Tannenbaum collection.

Two records of *Songs from Shirley Temple Movies*. The songs were sung by other people, and the records were produced by Golden Records. From left: #602 and #606. $10.00 each. Janet Mitchell collection.

From left: *The Best of Shirley Temple* (SPB-4672) and *More Little Miss Wonderful,* 1950s, Twentieth Century Fox. $10.00 each. Janet Mitchell collection.

Pins

Top row shows three original Ideal Shirley Temple doll pins; on the bottom is a Canadian Shirley Temple doll pin by the Reliable Doll Company. $80.00 each.

Close-up of the writing around the edge of a Shirley Temple pin from the 1930s. Most can be distinguished as originals in this way. Janet Mitchell collection.

Many of the 1930s pins were reproduced in the 1960s and 1970s. On the left is the reproduction, on the right is the original (notice the writing around the edge of the original pin). Reproduction, $5.00; original, $30.00. Janet Mitchell collection.

Other original pins from the 1930s. The top middle pin is from England; the others are all from America. $30.00 – 40.00 each. Janet Mitchell collection.

Shirley Temple Club postcard and pin, from America, 1930s. $50.00. Leslie Tannenbaum collection.

Original Shirley Temple mirror and pin, 1935. $30.00 each.

Large Shirley Temple pins from England, 1930s. $50.00 each. Leslie Tannenbaum collection.

Australian Shirley Temple doll pins. This type of pin came on the Australian version of the Shirley Temple doll. $40.00 each. Leslie Tannenbaum collection.

This is to Certify that
Miss Dorothy Kukla
is a member of the only official
SHIRLEY TEMPLE FAN CLUB
From January-46 To January-47
Jeanne Smitka
PRES.

A Shirley Temple Fan Club membership card. $20.00. Loretta Beilstein collection.

Shirley Temple Klub pin, may be from Czechoslovakia, 1930s. $30.00. Leslie Tannenbaum collection.

Shirley Temple Club pins from England, 1930s. $30.00 and up each. Leslie Tannenbaum collection.

Very intricate metal Shirley Temple Club pin from the 1930s, may be from England. $50.00 and up. Leslie Tannenbaum collection.

Recent (1960s through present) Shirley Temple pins and three Shirley Temple look-alike pins from the 1930s. $2.00 – 10.00 each. Look-alike pins, $30.00 each. Janet Mitchell collection.

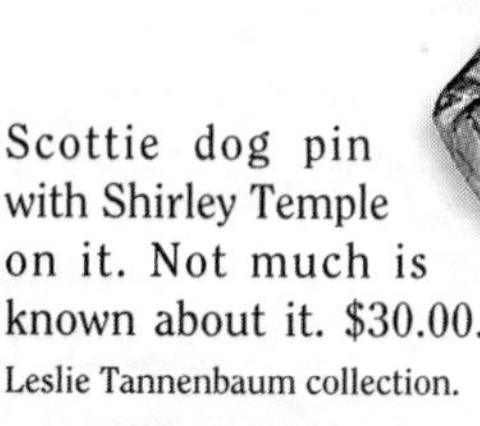

Scottie dog pin with Shirley Temple on it. Not much is known about it. $30.00. Leslie Tannenbaum collection.

Very unusual pin with Shirley Temple's picture in it; not much is known about it. Probably from the 1930s. $50.00 and up. Leslie Tannenbaum collection.

Other Items

Loblaws 5¢ Premium Certificates

I—79490—SHIRLEY TEMPLE IRONING SET. Includes all metal adjustable ironing board with tubular legs, enamel top. Length 30". Electric iron has all-chrome base and sole plate. Pad is Tufflex with aluminized silicone cover, both bagged. Usual retail price, $7.95.
89 5¢ Premium Certificates

An ad from the 1950s for the Shirley Temple ironing board was recently featured in *The Shirley Temple Collectors News*. Janet Mitchell collection.

Shirley Temple Ironing Set from the 1950s, a very rare find. $500.00 and up. Janet Mitchell collection.

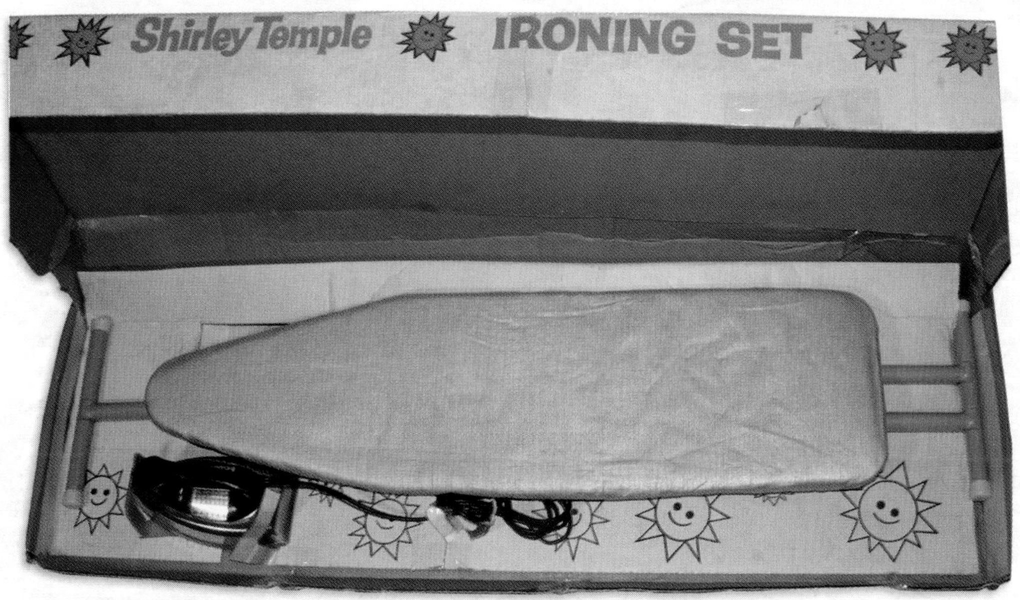

The ironing board and iron themselves were not marked "Shirley Temple."
Janet Mitchell collection.

Men's bathroom accessories set with leather case contains a shaving mirror with Shirley on it. It is believed to be from the 1930s; not much more information is known about this set. $100.00 and up. Leslie Tannenbaum collection.

Shirley Temple lunch box. Actual origin is unknown, but this is most likely from the 1930s. $100.00 and up. Leslie Tannenbaum collection.

Bongo-style rattle with Shirley's picture on it, marked "Made in Japan." It also has a whistle at the bottom. It is believed to be from the 1930s, perhaps from overseas, and is incredibly rare. $500.00. This is the price it went for on eBay; oftentimes many excited collectors bid each other up significantly on items that have never been seen before. Leslie Tannenbaum collection.

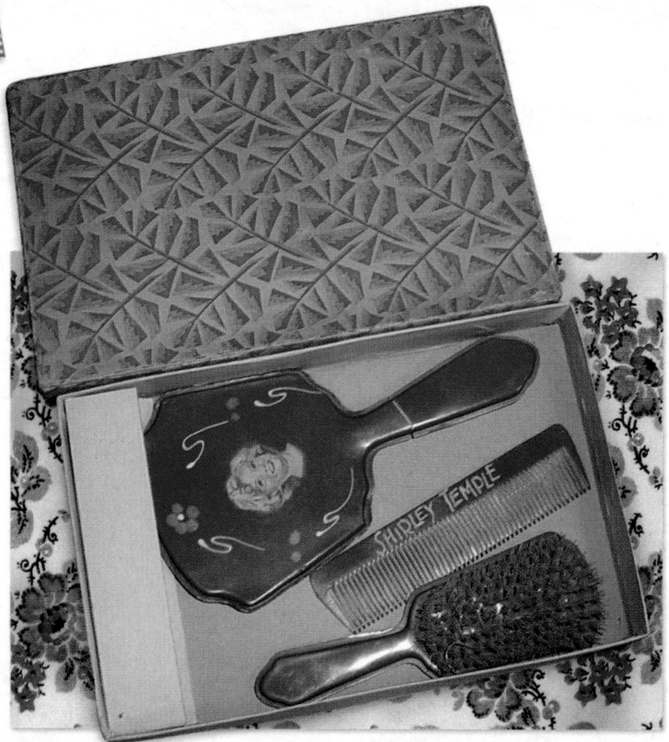

Shirley Temple hairbrush set, most likely made in Japan, from the 1930s. Not much is known about this set. $100.00 and up. Leslie Tannenbaum collection.

Japanese Shirley Temple fans from the 1930s. Very fragile and hard to find. $100.00 each. Janet Mitchell collection.

Walking stick with Shirley Temple picture underneath the glass knob. Not much is known about this item, which is believed to be from the 1930s. $100.00 and up. Leslie Tannenbaum collection.

Children's game marked "made in Japan," from the 1930s. The goal of the game is to get Shirley's eyes (which are loose) into the eye sockets. $40.00 and up. Leslie Tannenbaum collection.

Banners for Shirley Temple fan clubs, from the 1930s. $35.00 each. Leslie Tannenbaum collection.

Match boxes from the 1930s with Shirley Temple on the cover, from Cuba. $50.00 each. Leslie Tannenbaum collection.

Shirley Temple Sweet Peas were originally produced in 1936 and continued to be sold through the early 1970s. Other flowers were also named after Shirley. $40.00. Leslie Tannenbaum collection.

Another Shirley Temple Sweet Peas seed package sold in the 1930s. $40.00. Janet Mitchell collection.

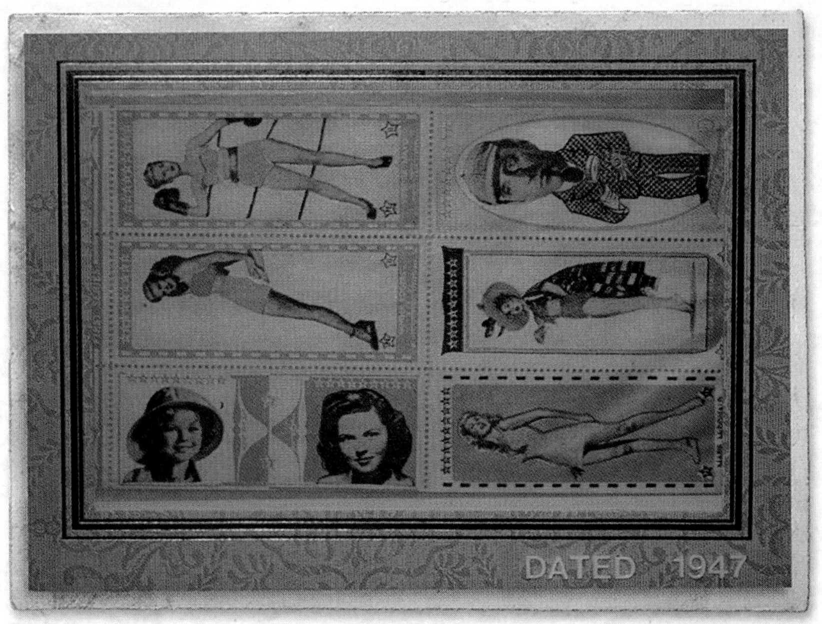

Stamps from 1947 featuring Shirley Temple. $20.00. Iva Mae Jones collection.

Recent Items

Ghana and Grenada stamp sheets featuring Shirley Temple along with other movie stars. $10.00 each. Janet Mitchell collection.

The Shirley Temple *drink* was created in the 1930s; it combines ginger ale, grenadine, and a maraschino cherry. Recently companies have marketed the drink to grocery stores. From left: caffeine free diet Shirley Temple, Saranac Shirley Temple, The All American Shirley Temple (still available — it has an actual maraschino cherry in it), and The Original Shirley Temple. In front is a Shirley Temple–flavored ring pop (still available at some Toys-R-Us stores). $1.00 (for those still available) to $15.00 each. Leslie Tannenbaum collection.

Shirley Temple Radko Christmas Ornament, very rare. From the year 2000. $50.00. Loretta Beilstein collection.

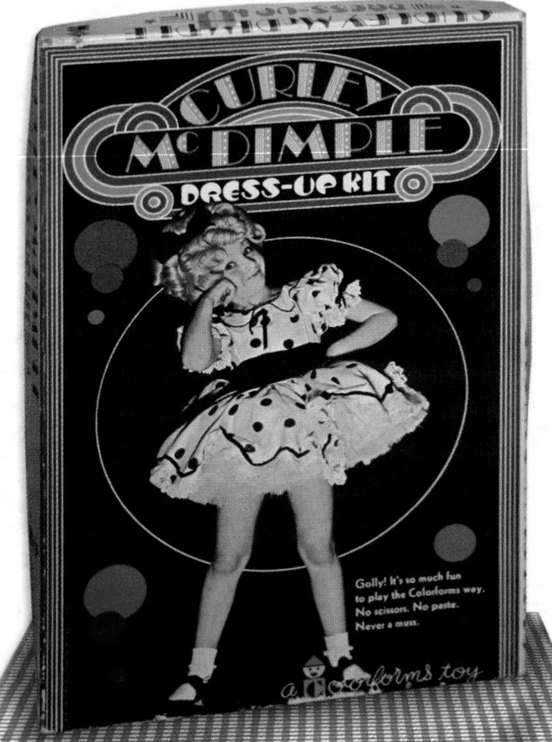

Recent Shirley Temple marbles came in an assortment of sizes. $5.00 each. Janet Mitchell collection.

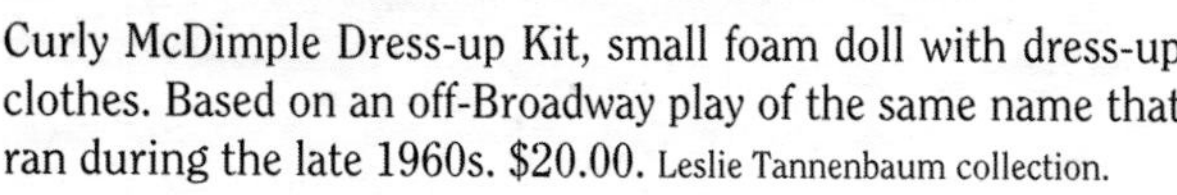

Curly McDimple Dress-up Kit, small foam doll with dress-up clothes. Based on an off-Broadway play of the same name that ran during the late 1960s. $20.00. Leslie Tannenbaum collection.

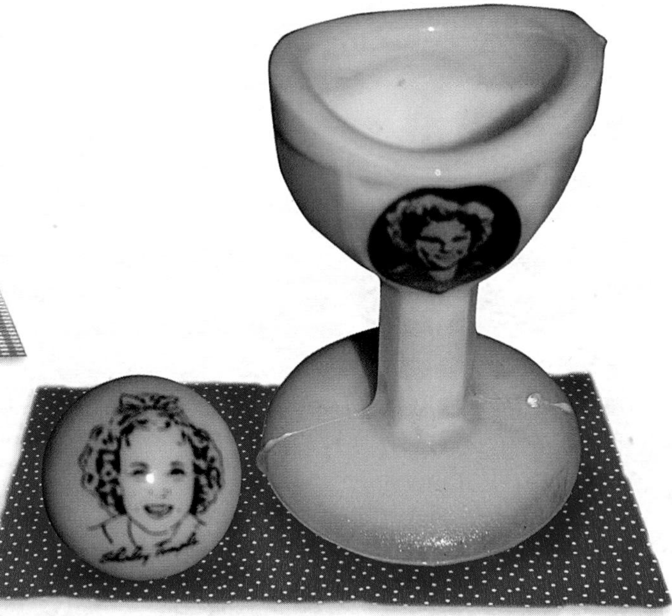

Recent Shirley Temple marble and eyecup. $5.00 each. Iva Mae Jones collection.

Shirley Temple for President, a paper headdress from 1984. $15.00. Leslie Tannenbaum collection.

Collector Items

In 1982, Nostalgia Collectibles released the Shirley Temple Collection. This series of three detailed Shirley Temple collectible plates include scenes from *Baby Take a Bow*, *Curly Top*, and *Stand Up and Cheer*. $40.00 each. Leslie Tannenbaum collection.

Matching Nostalgia figurines from the Shirley Temple Collection, 1982. A limited number of these came autographed by Shirley Temple herself on the bottom. $60.00 each unsigned, $100.00 each if signed. Leslie Tannenbaum collection.

The Danbury Mint released a series of six Shirley music boxes in the 1990s. Oddly enough, the music they played had nothing to do with Shirley. This is the *Little Miss Broadway* scene music box. Plays "That's Entertainment." $20.00. Iva Mae Jones collection.

The Shirley Temple "Talkies" figurine (actually sings in Shirley's own voice), very hard to find, by Nostalgia Collectibles, 1984. $150.00. Janet Mitchell collection.

The next series released by Nostalgia, eight plate and figurine sets known as Shirley Temple Classics, 1983, included scenes from *Captain January*, *Wee Willie Winkie*, *Heidi*, *Little Miss Marker*, *Rebecca of Sunnybrook Farm*, *Bright Eyes*, *Poor Little Rich Girl*, and *The Little Colonel*. Pictured is the *Heidi* plate and figurine. Set, $100.00; plate, $30.00; figurine, $60.00. Janet Mitchell collection.

In 1990, the Danbury Mint released a number of collector plates with Shirley Temple movie scenes. Top row, from left: *Rebecca of Sunnybrook Farm*, *Poor Little Rich Girl*, *The Littlest Rebel*, and *Captain January*. Middle row, from left: *Stowaway*, *Stand Up and Cheer*, *Little Miss Broadway*, and *Bright Eyes*. Bottom row, from left: *Wee Willie Winkie*, *Heidi*, *The Little Princess*, and *The Little Colonel*. $20.00 each.

The Shirley Temple Signature Plate Collection, by the Danbury Mint, 1995. Plates include Something Special, Ambassador of Smiles, Pride and Joy, Precious, Simply Irresistible, One in a Million, and America's Sweetheart. Not pictured: Little Angel. $20.00 each. Iva Mae Jones collection.

The Danbury Mint also released a number of figurines from Shirley Temple's movies during the 1990s. These don't have the quality of the Nostalgia Collectibles figurines. The Shirley Temple Silver Screen Collection had 18 figurines. Nine are pictured here. $20.00 each. Janet Mitchell collection.

The other nine Shirley Temple Silver Screen figurines. The complete set came with a display case as well (not pictured). $20.00 each. Janet Mitchell collection.

On the left and on the right are figurines from the Shirley Temple Singing Figurine Collection by the Danbury Mint, 1996. These figurines play songs that Shirley sang in her movies. In the middle is a *Stand Up and Cheer* figurine from 1994 also made by the Danbury Mint (it does not sing). $45.00 each. Leslie Tannenbaum collection.

Charm bracelet from the Danbury Mint, released in the late 1990s through the early 2000s. The same charms were also released on a longer necklace. $75.00. Iva Mae Jones collection.

Twelve gold-plated ornaments were released by the Danbury Mint in the early 2000s. The set came in a fitted box. This ornament is from *Rebecca of Sunnybrook Farm*. Set, $200.00. Loretta Beilstein collection.

Porcelain tea set by the Danbury Mint, 2000. $50.00.

Westland giftware music box and trinket boxes, from the year 2000. $20.00 each. Leslie Tannenbaum collection.

A set of 18 Shirley Temple collector mugs was released by the Danbury Mint in the early 2000s. These mugs could actually be used to drink out of. Pictured are six of them. $10.00 each. Janet Mitchell collection.

Large *Baby Take a Bow* plate from the Danbury Mint, 2002. Other plates representing some of her most famous movies were also released. $30.00.

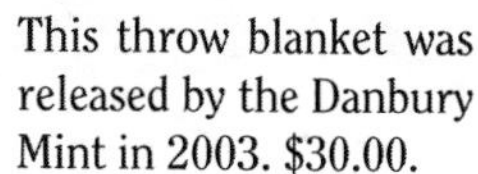

This throw blanket was released by the Danbury Mint in 2003. $30.00.

Shirley Temple stamp panels, from the Postal Commemorative Society, have scenes from many of her most famous movies and were released between 2000 and 2004. Complete set, $300.00.

This 2003 Danbury Mint Shirley Temple calendar set featured 12 Shirley Temple figurines, one for every month of the year. $200.00.

Convention Souvenirs

One souvenir from the 1990 Shirley Temple Convention was this Shirley Temple charm bracelet. $125.00. Iva Mae Jones collection.

Shirley Temple music box, *Littlest Rebel* pin, and *Littlest Rebel* charm, all souvenirs from the 2000 Shirley Temple convention (the theme was the movie *The Littlest Rebel*). $50.00.

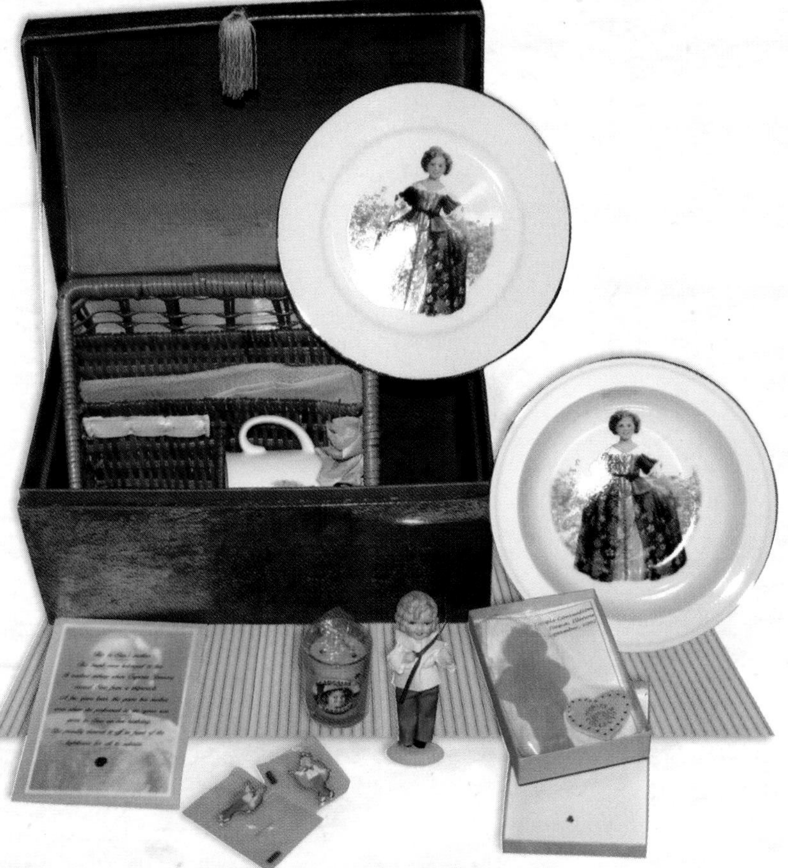

Shirley Temple picnic trunk, sailor doll, *Captain January* pin and charm, and soap. Souvenirs from the 2002 Shirley Temple Convention (the theme was the movie *Captain January*). $150.00.

Shirley Temple Black's slanted cursive autograph is very recognizable and is hard to duplicate. Her autograph from when she was a child is much more generic and is easier to forge. It is also much more valuable. There are two versions of Shirley's signature as a child: the print block letters from when she was six and under, and the awkward cursive signature from when she was seven to twelve years old. Shirley herself has said that the early block signature was, more often than not, signed for her by adults. Her early cursive writing is more distinctly hers. Nonetheless, always be cautious when paying a lot of money for an early Shirley Temple autograph. There is really no way to guarantee that it is authentic. Always get a signature from the most reputable place possible and try to learn the story behind the autograph, i.e., how it was obtained. This can help guarantee the autograph's authenticity.

Shirley's signature changed over the years. When Shirley became a teenager, her signature took on its characteristic slant. When she married John Agar, she signed as either "Shirley Agar" or "Shirley Temple Agar." These autographs are quite hard to find, since she was only married to John Agar for four years. After marrying Charles Black in 1950, she began signing as "Shirley Temple Black."

Shirley has always been a generous signer. During her adult life, she spent nearly every Saturday afternoon autographing all of the requests that came to her door. However, the Internet led to easy access to information, and many more people were able to get her address and write her requesting an autograph. Most unfortunately, autograph dealers began taking advantage of her generous signing policy and requesting autographs with the sole purpose of selling them for a profit. Because of this, she stopped signing autographs through the mail in late 1998, when she was 70 years old.

Autograph from 1934, on the back of a postcard. This is the earliest block-print Shirley Temple autograph; it is the hardest the find and the easiest to forge. Be very careful when you buy one of these early autographs, because you want to be sure to get what you pay for. Do not pay top dollar for one that may or may not be authentic. $300.00 and up for the postcard, $400.00 and up if the signature is on a picture of Shirley. Leslie Tannenbaum collection.

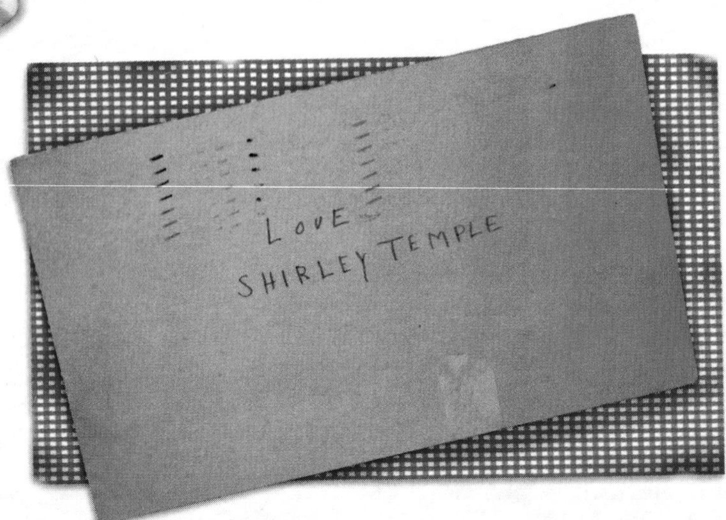

Autograph from mid-1935, on the back of a postcard. This is another example of an early block letter autograph. $250.00. Leslie Tannenbaum collection.

Shirley Temple original drawing from 1935. $500.00 and up. Leslie Tannenbaum collection.

CERTIFICATE OF AUTHENTICITY

The Autographs World Memorabilia guarantees the following item to be authentic:

Shirley Temple Sketch

Proud member in good standing of the UACC Society

Suciu T. Adrian, Owner

THE AUTOGRAPHS WORLD MEMORABILIA

Certificate of authenticity that came with the Shirley Temple drawing. Even with an authenticity certificate, there is no 100% guarantee that the autograph is authentic. The more reputable the source, the better. Leslie Tannenbaum collection.

Autograph from 1936, an early example of Shirley's cursive signature. This particular photo is addressed to "Uncle Stan" (Stan Chapman), who was a sound engineer on four of her films. Came with many other items from his estate, which helps verify that the items are authentic. $300.00. Leslie Tannenbaum collection.

Signed 8" x 10" photo from approximately 1937. $250.00. Leslie Tannenbaum collection.

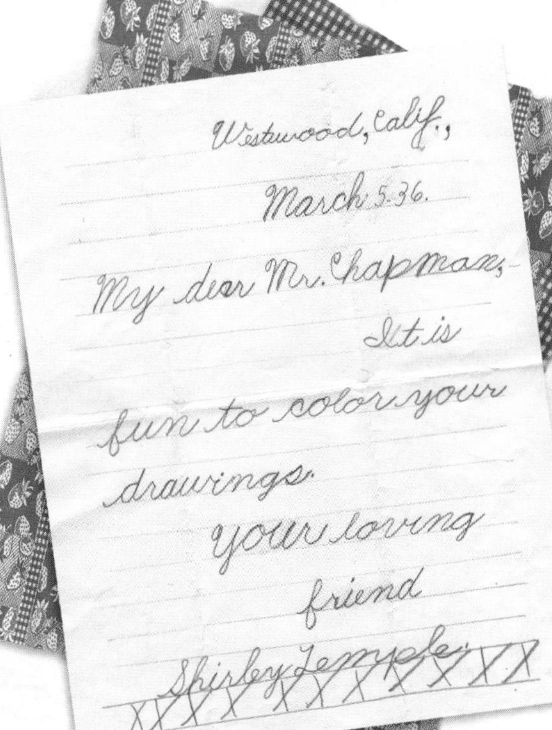

Westwood, Calif.,

March 5-36.

My dear Mr. Chapman,-

It is fun to color your drawings.

your loving friend

Shirley Temple.

XXXXXXXXXXXXX

Handwritten letter to "Mr. Chapman," from 1936, with cursive signature. $350.00. Leslie Tannenbaum collection.

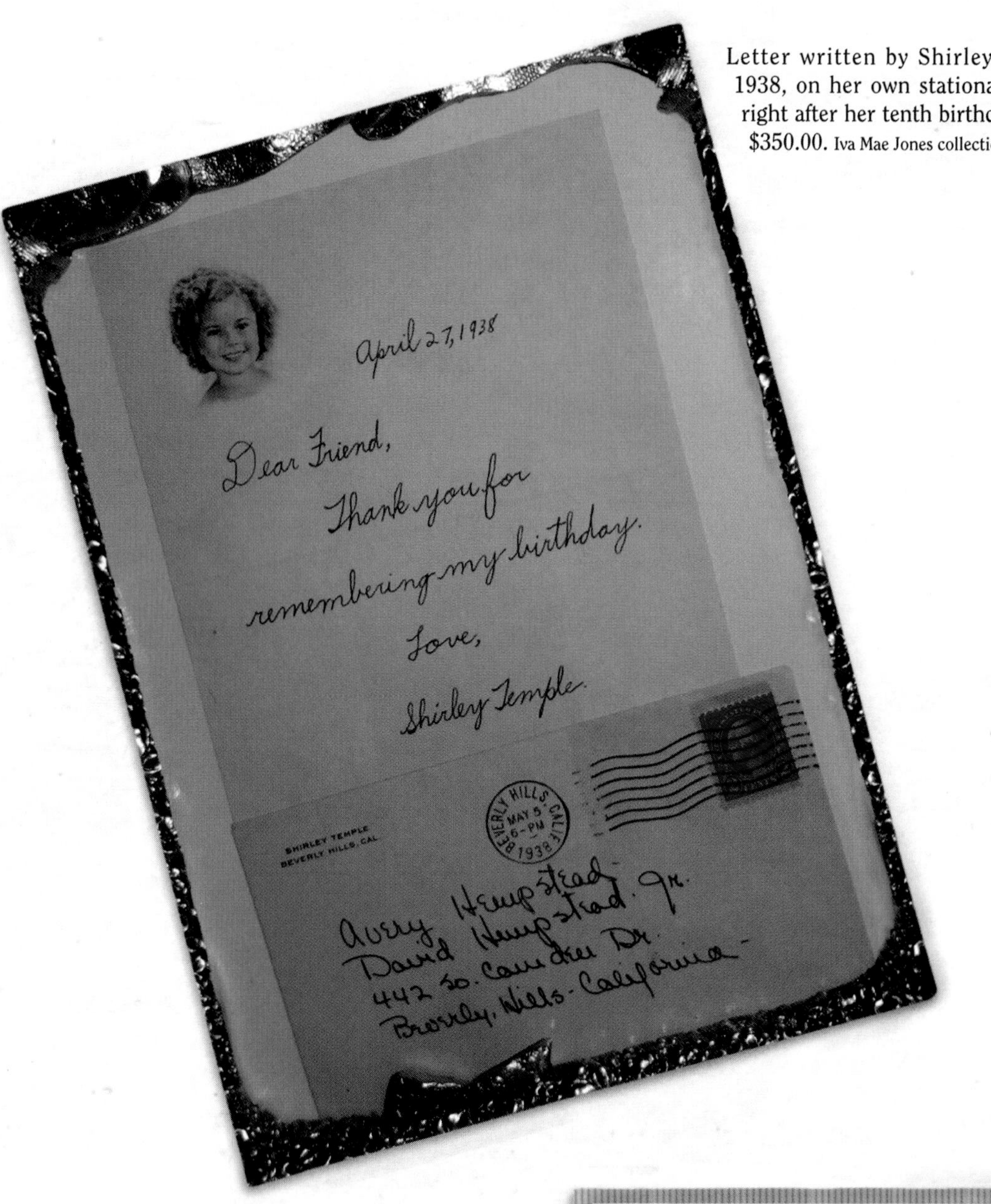

April 27, 1938

Dear Friend,
Thank you for
remembering my birthday.
Love,
Shirley Temple.

SHIRLEY TEMPLE
BEVERLY HILLS, CAL.

BEVERLY HILLS, CALIF.
MAY 5
6-PM
1938

Avery Hempstead
David Hempstead, Jr.
442 So. Camden Dr.
Beverly Hills - California

Letter written by Shirley in 1938, on her own stationary, right after her tenth birthday. $350.00. Iva Mae Jones collection.

Oftentimes, Shirley's signature was written on her very own signature card. This one is from around 1939. At this point, her signature really began to take on its characteristic slant. $100.00. Loretta McKenzie collection.

Photo from 1940 inscribed "To Patsy." $150.00. Leslie Tannenbaum collection.

The teenage Shirley Temple signature is very similar to the one she signs today. This one is from 1944. $60.00.

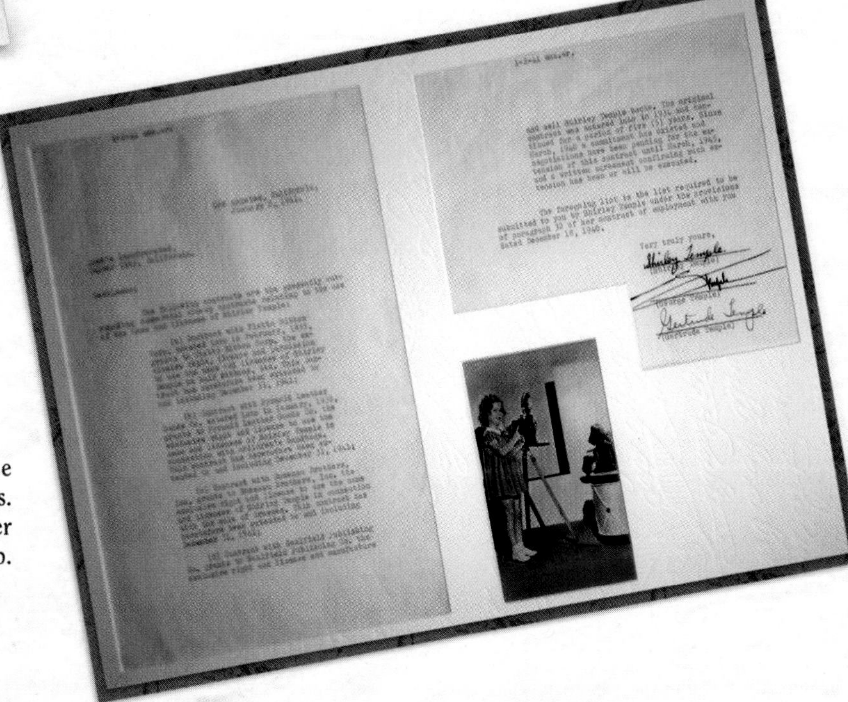

The foregoing list is the list required to be submitted to you by Shirley Temple under the provisions of paragraph 32 of her contract of employment with you dated December 16, 1940.

Very truly yours,

(Shirley Temple)

(George Temple)

(Gertrude Temple)

This contract allows companies to use Shirley's likeness to market their products. From 1941; signed by Shirley Temple, her father, and her mother. $500.00 and up. Leslie Tannenbaum collection.

Signed "Ambassador Shirley Temple Black," from when she was serving as the chief of protocol in the 1970s. $50.00. Leslie Tannenbaum collection.

Hard-to-find Shirley autograph, signed as "Shirley and Jack Agar." $125.00. Loretta McKenzie collection.

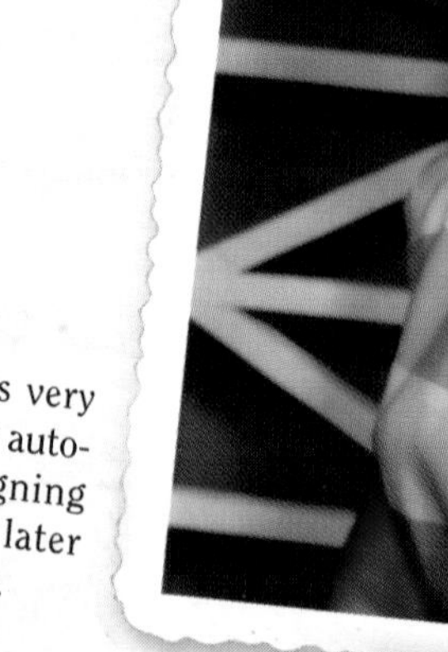

Shirley Temple Black was always very generous when fans requested her autograph. However, she stopped signing autographs through the mail in later 1998. This one is from 1998. $30.00.

Chapter 15
Shirley Stories Spanning the Generations

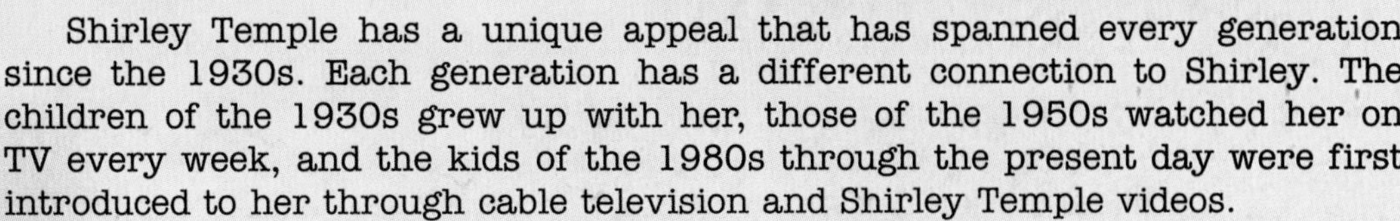

Shirley Temple has a unique appeal that has spanned every generation since the 1930s. Each generation has a different connection to Shirley. The children of the 1930s grew up with her, those of the 1950s watched her on TV every week, and the kids of the 1980s through the present day were first introduced to her through cable television and Shirley Temple videos.

My own enjoyment of little Shirley Temple began when I was a young child in the 1980s, watching her movies on cable television. I couldn't help but smile seeing the cute little girl sing and dance. I curled my hair like Shirley, took tap dancing lessons, tried to sing like her, and even copied her mannerisms. Her movies made me happy, which is what a little girl wants to be the most.

My admiration for Shirley Temple came when I was a teenager, after reading her autobiography, **Child Star**, and a biography by Anne Edwards, **Shirley Temple: American Princess**. I enjoyed watching her movies even more knowing that she grew up to become a happy and successful adult. At that time, I became a "fan", and began to collect Shirley Temple memorabilia. My mom and I would spend every weekend together going to antique shops and doll shows looking for any Shirley Temple item we could find. We would come home, excitedly showing my incredulous dad what we had found. I also joined the Shirley Temple Collectors Club, and began corresponding with Shirley Temple fans all over the country.

As I got older, I packed my Shirley Temple dolls away. I had more important things to think about, like boys. After all, boys were not exactly interested in Shirley Temple. Yet, I still watched my Shirley movies occasionally. No matter what my situation, I could always depend on little Shirley to put a smile on my face. Eventually, the dolls came back out, and the boys learned that they had to like the dolls if they were going to like me. What a litmus test that was!

Every Shirley Temple fan has a personal story, a reason why Shirley is so special to him or her. My own is the memory of pure happiness, the instant smile that comes to my face thinking of little Shirley, the bond that my mom and I share from years of collecting together, and the lifelong friendships that I have made corresponding with others who feel the same way. Most importantly, it is the admiration and inspiration that she provides even now to be something more, the importance of public service and helping others.

Exactly 60 years ago this month, I was a member of a US Navy unit headquartered in Manila, capital city of the Philippines. WWII was nearly over, and most of the Japanese troops had just retreated to Bataan, where they eventually surrendered in August. However, before and during the battle for the city, a brutal, systematic destruction of the once-beautiful Pearl of the Orient was carried out by the Japanese army. Thousands of civilians were killed, and almost all were homeless, hungry and destitute. American and Filipino troops, in addition to rooting out the remaining enemy forces, did everything possible to start rebuilding and caring for the people. I joined a crew of Navy volunteers who went to various parts of the city and passed out some of our own food, water, and clothing supplies. On one trip, we entered the grounds of Santo Tomas University, which had been a Japanese prison camp for American civilian captives. At that time, the men, women and children were being processed by Army medics and leaving on flights and ships to the United States. Compared to military prisoners, who suffered murderously brutal treatment by Japanese guards, the civilians had been on near-starvation rations, but in relatively good health. In their rush to get away from the prison camp, they left many of their possessions behind. We gathered them up, including clothing, kids' toys, and added them to the supplies we were taking to the Filipino civilians. One incident stands out in my mind as clearly today as it did in 1945. I found a Shirley Temple doll left behind in the prison by a freed American child. It was bit frayed, but the curly hair and dimples were intact. The next day, as we made our rounds of the refugee areas, we handed out all the items we had taken from the prison camp. The Filipino kids surrounded us, but one shy little girl of about eight lagged behind. Like many of the kids, she had lived through bombings and atrocities, and obviously was afraid to approach the strange big men in uniform. I offered some food, dresses, and shoes, but she seemed to shrink further away. Then I reached into a box of toys and picked up the Shirley Temple doll. As I turned back to the crowd, I heard a cry of "Shirley Temple." She smiled, probably for the first time since the war began, and ran over to me. When I gave her the doll, she took my hand, kissed it, and darted back into the crowd. I hope she still has the doll today, because I'll always have that sweet memory.

By: Ted S.
Age: 80

By: Dorothy C.
Age: 73

I admire Shirley Temple for all of her good qualities. She is a role model for her positive attitude. She really does "sparkle." She has given me many years of happiness through her films and following her subsequent careers and life. In all of her movies, which I have seen repeatedly, she prevails against all trials and tribulations. In real life she attains this, too.

When I was a child, to make me happy, my mother told me that Shirley and I were born on the same day in the same hospital. I told that story for many years, until I "wised up." I was born in April, too, but not on the 23rd. As a child, I had a composition Shirley Temple doll. Unfortunately, my sister and cousin were fighting over it and the doll didn't survive. Maybe that's why when I grew up I acquired more Shirleys. When my daughter was born, my mother and I bought her every size Shirley Temple from the 1959 and 60's versions. I even set my daughter's hair each night in pin curls so that her hair looked just like Shirley's. Luckily, when my granddaughter Liz was born, she had naturally curly hair. In fact she was even selected to play Shirley Temple in her kindergarten play. She has become the recipient of many current Shirley dolls and items.

When I finally met Shirley at Marshall Fields (downtown Chicago) at her book signing event in 1988, my expectations of her were realized. She was warm and friendly. She is truly a beautiful person. She even said, "Bye, Douglas" to my grandson, who was 10 months old at the time.

Shirley Temple is special to many others, too. Through the Shirley Temple clubs, I have met many lifelong friends, who share my interest. We have attended many Shirley conventions and parties.

Lifelong fan Dorothy Cassidy meets Shirley Temple for the first time at a book signing for *Child Star* in 1988.

I sat on a blanket with my grandmother at the tiny town's square watching Shirley dance on the stairs in *The Little Colonel*. Every Saturday night they had free movies in this little Illinois town that looked just like it came straight out of *The Music Man*. Usually they showed westerns, but that night they had a double feature of Shirley movies. I was only four years old, but Shirley captivated me. I couldn't believe that a little girl could sing and dance. I think I started my lifelong love of musicals that night too.

There was another little girl named Peggy there that night, too. She had a Shirley Temple doll, and Peggy's mother had curled her hair and she had a short red and white dress. I never went anywhere without my doll, and at intermission we started playing with our dolls together. My doll was pretty, but hers was Shirley and mine had on a dress my grandmother had made for my doll. How wonderful it was to feel those curls on that doll. When the second feature started, I made up my mind I wanted a Shirley doll too.

For months I tried to sing and dance and wanted my hair in curls. My wise mother pointed out to me that Shirley was great, but everyone has their own place to shine. I might never be in a movie, but I sure could dance and sing too. Now I know she just didn't say how well I could sing and dance. She then guided me toward thinking about other "talents" I could find, such as a love of reading and helping with my sister.

This was during the early forties and it was wartime. My parents always made sure that we had everything my sister and I needed, but there wasn't a lot of money. When Christmastime came, I saw a Shirley doll in a magazine and I knew that would be a lot of money for one Christmas present. I told my mother I had plenty of dolls and I really needed doll clothes for my doll. I didn't get a Shirley doll, but some beautiful handmade doll clothes. There was one red and white short dress that looked a lot like Shirley's dress!

Our small town had a theater and I went to all of Shirley's movies. When she was a teenager I thought she was the most beautiful girl in the world. My friends and I would pore over movie magazines when we could find them. She was always smiling and you never read any of the wild Hollywood stories about her. I started a scrapbook and Shirley continued to influence my life.

Well, now sixty years have passed and I still feel the same awe I did as a four-year-old. The difference is that I have even more admiration for her as an adult. Thank goodness we have classic movie channels, and I can still watch that bounce, smile, and her dimples. Now I notice her real ability to act, and find it even more amazing. When I find a Shirley movie, everything stops, and I sit down to enjoy it again. The old magic is still there and I can remember that first summer night. I am sure I have romanticized that night in my mind and surely everything around me didn't look as magical as I remember it.

Yes, I am still also a doll lover and have the doll I had with me that night. She is a treasure and has her own place of honor in my family room. I just have never found my Shirley doll. Thanks, Shirley, for being a part of my life and bringing such a positive influence on many of your fans!

By: Sandra B.
Age: 67

By: Dorothy C.
Age: 58

Shirley Temple represents a large piece of a very happy childhood. I spent many a day during my childhood watching her movies with my mom by my side. It's one of my favorite memories. We would laugh and cry together — it was always the same, whether it was the first time we watched *Heidi* or the tenth time. If a Shirley Temple movie was on we were in front of the television tissues in hand. I can't tell you how many times my dad would come home from work and ask us what was wrong, only to have us laugh and respond that we had just finished watching a movie.

Unfortunately, we share another link to Shirley in that my mother in 1974 was diagnosed with breast cancer. For eight years she fought the good fight, but finally lost her battle in June of 1982 at the age of fifty-eight.

Because I lost her so young we missed out on sharing a lot of mother/daughter milestones together. Twenty-three years have passed since her death, and Mother's Day is still the hardest holiday to get through. Yet, because I lost her so young, my childhood years and the subsequent memories of our time together are even more precious to me.

In March 2000 I was also diagnosed with breast cancer, and I recently celebrated my five-year survival anniversary. Shirley reminds me to look at everyday circumstances/problems through my Mother's eyes. She causes me to reflect and remember her words, which will pick me up when I'm down, give me a push forward when necessary, and remind me that courage is in all of us.

BUT MOST IMPORTANT TO ME, SHE REPRESENTS VICTORY AGAINST A COMMON ENEMY.

My Shirley Temple doll means the world to me for so many reasons. I wanted a Shirley Temple doll more than anything in the world when I was eight years old. I admit that it confused both my mother and father, as I am an African American woman and in those days, most of my friends wanted dolls of color. I had the nappiest head of hair you would ever see and also eyes of chocolate milk, yet the Shirley Temple doll was the only doll I wanted.

I knew that a lot of people back then thought it was because I secretly wanted golden hair that did not go in ten different directions, or maybe I secretly wanted the eyes of the sky, but it was not for any of those reasons. My dad sat down with me one night and asked me why I wanted that particular doll. I remember how he sat me down and with the most loving smile and brown eyes softly asked me what was so special about this doll. I told him that I liked the way she was so brave in Heidi *and also that since she was with Mr. Bojangles and danced with him in a movie then the dolls must be for "colored girls too!" My dad looked at me and just nodded.*

My dad worked two jobs back then, one for the railroad and another as a janitor for a local hospital. I had five brothers and sisters, so money was pretty tight, yet I knew that someday my dad would buy me that doll and maybe even for Christmas!

On Christmas Eve, all of us opened our gifts, which were mainly homemade items but included one store-bought gift as well. When I opened my store-bought gift, it was a brand new pair of Mary Janes, which I loved. In my heart, though, I knew I would not be getting a doll. I brushed my teeth, put on my pajamas, and went to get into bed. There beside my pillow was a Shirley Temple doll! I grabbed her and ran down the stairs, straight into my father's arms. Then I ran to my mother and hugged her just as hard. All my mom and dad said was that "this must be a special doll to be wanted so much" and that I "must take good care of her and her heart."

They understood that the doll was more than blond hair and blue eyes and instead was the outlook of a little girl that Shirley Temple represented all little girls regardless of color.

By: Laura R.
Age: 52

By: Rita L.
Age: 36

When I was a young girl, my grandmother and I would watch classic movies all of the time. I spent much of my time with my Abuela *("Grandmother" in Spanish). She would watch English ones with me, even if she didn't quite understand the language, and I would watch Spanish ones with her. She and I would particularly enjoy the "Cherli Temple" (as she would pronounce it) movies. I can still close my eyes and hear her sweet voice saying her name, as only my Abuela could.*

Knowing how much I wanted to be just like Shirley Temple, my Abuela ripped up 4" wide and about 10" long strips from paper bags to create rollers and give me Shirley's beautiful curls. My hair was wet and ready to go. There I was wearing my amazing look of several strips of paper bag rollers on my head. I still look back on it and smile.

This is something I would only do with my Abuela. My mother was a very refined and proper woman and would have probably fainted from seeing me that way. I must admit it was a little uncomfortable sleeping that night, but the excitement of seeing myself in the morning was worth it all. The incredible sight in the morning once my hair had dried overnight was really another story. We worked hard to tame those curls as much as we could. When it was done I believe I wore those tight curls proudly.

My Abuela loved to have me sing songs for her from all the classics, and I loved to dance and sing for everyone. However, I truly believe that no one could have appreciated it as much as she did.

We didn't have much money to buy things then. But there was one thing I wanted more than anything. Well, on my seventh birthday, I was blessed to receive a Shirley Temple doll. She was beautiful! I took her everywhere, and she was my very special friend.

I remember as I grew older my mother threatened to give her away for something I had done. I was so afraid that I ran into my room, locked the door, and took my Shirley Temple off my dresser, and with a pen I wrote "Rita" on the back of her pretty white bloomers, where I thought no one would find my name but me. Somehow that doll has always been a part of who I am. I can't quite remember what my mother did with her as I grew into my teens. But somewhere there is a very beautiful Shirley Temple doll with my name on her bloomers.

Well, many years have gone by and I have two boys and a precious little girl named Miranda. *She has big brown eyes and the curliest, short light brown hair you could imagine. She is a true delight and amazingly loves to sing and dance* EVERY DAY *and* EVERYWHERE! *She is anything but shy and that is just how I like it. She is my "Little Princess," and for her birthday I was able to find a Shirley Temple movie to begin the tradition all over again.*

I often tell her the story of my Shirley Temple doll and she just laughs. I try to remind her often that God blessed me with my very own Shirley Temple!

It was Christmas Eve, and we were at Grandma and Grandpa's house. Amid the magic and excitement of the season, we were filled with great anticipation at the sight of the huge, beautifully decorated tree. Around it were piles of attractively wrapped gifts of all sizes and shapes. Old-fashioned Christmas music was playing merrily in the background, and we had just been stuffed by means of a delicious turkey dinner with all the trimmings.

The grown-ups seemed to pretend nothing exciting was coming, and talked endlessly of past family times. For a while, all of us children entertained ourselves with biting off the heads, hands, and legs of fat gingerbread men and trying to follow the cheerful chatter of the parents.

Finally, though, we headed downstairs and cuddled all together in big fleece blankets in front of Grandma's huge 3' x 4' television screen. Then we watched good, old movies for hours while the grown-ups talked (after all, we never left before midnight!).

And as we had every Christmas so far, we turned on the black and white *Heidi* movie. There, surrounded with the peace and joy of the season, we watched a most delightful little girl. As the story unfolded, we felt with her through her Aunt Dete's coldness, her Grandfather's growing to love her, being taken away to Klara's rich house in Frankfurt, Fraulein Rottenmeier's harshness, being torn between her new friend and her Grandfather, and then being joyously reunited with him. We felt as she brought joy to everyone — Klara, Grandfather, Herr Sesemann, the many friends she had made, and us.

And after all the gifts were open, and we were piled into the car with full tummies and heavy eyes, we dreamt of curly-headed angels and Christmas joys.

So from such good memories came our first Shirley Temple experiences. For many years, "Heidi at Christmas" was all we knew of the world's darling baby. Then last year we checked out a biography movie from our library, and it contained clips from almost all her movies. We were instantly captivated, and Shirley Temple mania in our family had started!

In a flurry of a few months, we saw 24 Shirley Temple movies. We bought tap-dancing shoes and learned to tap dance. We looked at every website we could, downloaded hundreds of pictures, and learned every song she had sung. Since then, there has not been a single day when Shirley hasn't been mentioned, one of her songs hasn't been sung, one of her movies hasn't been watched, or one of her merry tap routines hasn't been performed.

The reason Shirley Temple appeals to me is not just that she was a very cute and talented little girl, but that she grew up in a time of strong character and morals in America. It was a time of old values and heroism, the greatest generation. Our country was going through a very hard period, but it never gave up. Because of their virtue and integrity, people pulled together, helped each other, and kept trusting God through seemingly insurmountable odds. And dear little Shirley helped put smiles on peoples' faces and happiness in their hearts!

By: Laura C.
Age: 19

By: Amanda H.
Age: 15

My first Shirley temple experience began on a trip, when I stayed at my grandmother's house. I was homesick and missed my parents and big brother terribly. I was five. I was lying in my grandmother's bed eating a bowl of soup and snuggling up with my ratty yellow blanket, which I took everywhere, and my favorite stuffed giraffe, named Jeremy, but I was still upset. My grandmother tried to make me feel better, and then offered a movie to me. She put in *Our Little Girl.* She said she wanted me to watch this movie, because I reminded her of Molly, and it was her favorite one.

Needless to say, I have been captivated by Shirley Temple ever since. She became a comfort for me. My grandmother said that the entire week I stayed with her, I insisted she play more Shirley Temple. It was almost a routine, she said. We would wake up, eat breakfast while watching Shirley Temple, go outside for a little while, eat lunch, have a nap, and when I awoke I would ask the question, "Time for more Shirley yet Grandma?" and she would cave. After all, she was the culprit who started my early childhood obsession. Now what would she tell my parents?

Shirley Temple means family to me, because a majority of my childhood memories involve a Shirley Temple movie, some popcorn, cuddling up on the couch with my family, and a whole lot of laughter. When I was lonely or home sick from school for the day, Shirley was on the TV screen for me. Christmas mornings, after we opened all of our presents and while my parents were making breakfast, a Shirley Temple movie was in our VCR. It didn't matter when, Shirley was there.

Even now that I'm a great deal older, I still love Shirley Temple. I love her smile and her laugh, and how she can always bring a smile to my face and even a good laugh, too. When I'm upset and feel alone and like I have no one to turn to, I know that I have Shirley, and as soon as I pop in that movie, a smile appears on my face, and I remember my life is okay and that I shouldn't be upset because I have so many people around me that care about me and want to be there for me. It may sound odd, but Shirley Temple reminds me of that, the amazing and wonderful life that I have.

Chapter 16
Shirley Temple Inventory

Listing of authorized Shirley Temple memorabilia; includes item number, year of release, name of product, and other pertinent information. A huge thank-you to Janet Mitchell for being so generous with this information.

SAALFIELD PAPER DOLLS

#280 (1935) Six Shirley Temple Paper dolls (dolls from #2112 and #1715)
#283 (1942) The New Shirley Temple (re-release of #2425)
#290 (1936) Shirley Temple (re-release of #1715)
#303 (1937) Shirley Temple (re-release of #1761)
#304 (1944) Kelly Sisters (has Shirley clothes from #2425)
#399 (1939) Shirley Temple (re-release of #1782)
#450 (1943) The New Shirley Temple Paper Doll (re-release of #2425)
#853 (1959) Shirley Temple (re-release of #4435)
#1053 (1959) Shirley Temple Dolls and Dresses (re-release of #4435)
#1320 (1959) Shirley Temple (re-release of #5110)
#1348 (1959) Shirley Temple An 18" Standing Doll (re-release of #5110)
#1420 (1959) Shirley Temple (re-release of #5110)
#1715 (1935) Shirley Temple Standing Dolls
#1719 (1935) Shirley Temple Standing Doll
#1725 (1960) Shirley Temple (re-release of #4435)
#1727 (1960) Shirley Temple (re-release of #4435)
#1727 (1935) Shirley Temple (boxed)
#1739 (1959) Shirley Temple (re-release of #4435)
#1739 (1935) Shirley Temple Playhouse (with costumes)
#1761 (1937) Shirley Temple Dolls and Dresses (personal and movie wardrobe)
#1765 (1936) Shirley Temple, a Life-like Paper Doll Cutout (34" tall)
#1773 (1938) Shirley Temple Dolls and Dresses, Her Movie Wardrobe
#1777 (1959) Shirley Temple (re-release of #4435)
#1780 (1935) Shirley Temple Playhouse (re-release of #1739)
#1782 (1939) Shirley Temple Paper Dolls
#1787 (1940) Shirley Temple in Masquerade Costumes
#1789 (1960) Shirley Temple Dolls and Dresses (Canadian, re-release of #4435)
#2112 (1934) Shirley Temple Dolls and Dresses (first Shirley Temple paper doll set)
#2425 (1942) The New Shirley Temple in Paper Dolls
#4420 (1959) Shirley Temple (re-release of #5110)
#4435 (1958) Shirley Temple Paper Dolls (in folder)
#4437 (1960) Shirley Temple (includes scissors, re-release of #4435)
#4440 (1959) Shirley Temple (re-release of #4435)
#4470 (1959) Shirley Temple (re-release of #5110)
#4485 (1959) Shirley Temple (re-release of #4435)
#4487 (1959) Shirley Temple (re-release of #4435)
#4490 (1959) Shirley Temple (re-release of #4435)
#5110 (1958) Shirley Temple (folder)
#5160 (1958) Shirley Temple Large Folding Doll with Easel (folder)

GABRIEL PAPER DOLLS

#299 (1959) Shirley Temple Snap-on Paper Doll (bagged)
#300 (1958) Shirley Temple Snap-on Paper Dolls (boxed)
#301 (1961) Shirley Temple Magnetic Dolls (boxed)
#303 (1961) Shirley Temple Magnetic Dolls and Jewelry (boxed)
#304 (1958) Shirley Temple Stand-Up Paper Doll with Authentic Life-like Hair (boxed)
#305 (1960) Shirley Temple Paper Doll Life Size (boxed)

WHITMAN PAPER DOLLS

#1986 (1976) Shirley Temple Paper Doll (boxed)
#1986 (1976) Shirley Temple Paper Doll Book

PAPER DOLL REISSUES

Original Shirley Temple Paper Dolls in Full Color by Dover (1988 – present)
Classic Shirley Temple Dolls in Full Color by Dover (1980s – present)
Authentic Shirley Temple Dolls and Dresses by Dover (1980s – present)
Shirley Temple Movie Wardrobe by H. Sharkman Company (2001)
Shirley Temple Masquerade Costumes by H. Sharkman Company (1999)
Other, unofficial Shirley Temple dolls included those by Emma Terry and Marilyn Henry.

SHEET MUSIC

Stand Up and Cheer (1934): "Baby Take a Bow," by Movietone Music Corp. (Shirley edition; had Shirley on the cover, other editions did not)
Little Miss Marker (1934): "Laugh You Son-of-a-Gun," "I'm a Black Sheep Who's Blue," by Famous Music Corp.
Now and Forever (1934): "Now and Forever," "The World Owes Me a Living," by Famous Music Corp.
Baby Take a Bow (1934): "On Account-a I Love You," by Movietone Music Corp.
Bright Eyes (1934): "On the Good Ship Lollipop" (two editions), by Movietone Music Corp.
The Little Colonel (1935): "Little Colonel" and "Love's Young Dream" (both), "Love's Young Dream," by Movietone Music Corp.
Our Little Girl (1935): "Our Little Girl," by Movietone Music Corp.
Curly Top (1935): "Animal Crackers in my Soup," "The Simple Things in Life," "Curly Top," "It's All So New to Me," and "When I Grow Up," by Sam Fox Publishing Company
The Littlest Rebel (1935): "Polly-Wolly Doodle," "Believe Me, If All Those Endearing Young Charms" by Movietone Music Corp.
Sing with Shirley Temple, Shirley Temple Song Album (1935): "Baby Take a Bow," "When I Grow Up," "On the Good Ship

Lollipop," "On Account-a I Love You," "Little Colonel," "Our Little Girl," "Curly Top," "Love's Young Dream," by Movietone Music Corp.

Captain January (1936): "At the Codfish Ball," "Early Bird," "The Right Somebody to Love"

Poor Little Rich Girl (1936): "When I'm with You," "You Gotta Eat Your Spinach, Baby," "But Definitely," "Oh, My Goodness," "Military Man," "Ride a Cock-Horse to Bambury Cross," by Robbins Music Corp.

Dimples (1936): "Hey! What Did the Blue Jay Say?" "Picture Me without You," "He Was a Dandy," by Leo Feist Inc.

Stowaway (1936): "Goodnight My Love," "One Never Knows, Does One?" "You Gotta S-M-I-L-E to be H-A-Double-P-Y," "That's What I Want for Christmas," by Robbins Music Corp.

Shirley Temple Song Album No. 2 (1936): "Animal Crackers in My Soup," "At the Codfish Ball," "Believe Me, If All Those Endearing Young Charms," "Early Bird," "Polly-Wolly-Doodle," "Ride a Cock-Horse to Banbury Cross," "The Right Somebody to Love," by Movietone Music Corp.

Heidi (1937): "In Our Little Wooden Shoes," by Sam Fox Publishing Co.

"Curly Top's Birthday" (1937), song dedicated to Shirley Temple by Movietone Music Corp.

Shirley Temple's Favorite Songs (1937): "Goodnight My Love," "One Never Knows, Does One?" "I Wanna Go to the Zoo," "When I'm With You," "But Definitely," "Oh, My Goodness," "Hey! What Did the Blue Jay Say?" "You've Gotta Eat Your Spinach, Baby," "You've Gotta S-M-I-L-E to be H-A-Double-P-Y," by Robbins Music Corp.

Rebecca of Sunnybrook Farm (1938): "The Toy Trumpet," "An Old Straw Hat," "Come and Get Your Happiness," "Alone with You," "Crackly Grain Flakes," "Happy Endings." Many different publishers: Circle Music Pub. Inc., Crawford Music Corp., Leo Feist Inc.

Little Miss Broadway (1938): "Be Optimistic," "How Can I Thank You," "If All the World Were Paper," "We Should Be Together," "Little Miss Broadway," "Thank You For the Use of the Hall," "Swing Me an Old Fashioned Song," "Hop Skip Jump & Slide," by Robbins Music Corp.

Just Around the Corner (1939): "This Is a Happy Little Ditty," "I Love to Walk in the Rain," "I'll Always Be Lucky with You," "Brass Buttons and Epaulets," "I'm Not Myself Today," "Just Around the Corner," by Robbins Music Corp.

The Blue Bird (1940): "Someday You'll Find Your Bluebird," by Robbins Music Corp.

Young People (1940): "I Wouldn't Take a Million," "Young People," "Tra-la-la-la," by Robbins Music Corp.

Kathleen (1941): "Around the Corner"

Since You Went Away (1944): "Together," "Since You Went Away," by Crawford Music Corp.

I'll Be Seeing You (1944): "I'll Be Seeing You," by Williamson Music Inc.

Honeymoon (1946): "I Love Geraniums," "Ven Aqui," by Edward H. Morris and Co. Inc.

The Bachelor and the Bobby-Soxer (1947): "The Bachelor and the Bobby-Soxer," by Paull-Pioneer Music Corp.

Shirley Temple Storybook (1950s): "Dreams Are Made for Children," "The Enchanted Melody," by Fullerton Music Inc.

Shirley Temple Song Album, (1957): "On the Good Ship Lollipop," "When I Grow Up," "Early Bird," "At the Codfish Ball," "Animal Crackers in My Soup," "On Account-a I Love You," "Baby Take a Bow," "Little Colonel," "The Right Somebody to Love," "Polly-Wolly-Doodle," Movietone Music Corp.

BOOKS (by Saalfield unless noted otherwise)

#337 (1937) *Shirley Temple in Heidi* (black and white softcover)

#945 (1935) *How I Raised Shirley Temple*, by her mother, Gertrude Shirley (softcover)

#1089 (1934) *The Story of Shirley Temple* (Big Little Book, hardcover)

#1095 (1935) *Shirley Temple in The Little Colonel* (Big Little Book, hardcover)

#1115 (1935) *Shirley Temple in The Littlest Rebel* (Big Little Book, hardcover)

#1116 (1936) *My Life and Times*, by Shirley Temple (Big Little Book, hardcover)

#1319 (1934) *The Story of Shirley Temple* (Big Little Book, softcover)

#1575 (1935) *Shirley Temple in The Little Colonel* (Big Little Book, softcover)

#1595 (1935) *Shirley Temple in The Littlest Rebel* (Big Little Book, softcover)

#1596 (1936) *My Life and Times*, by Shirley Temple (Big Little Book, softcover)

#1712 (1935) *Shirley Temple at Play* (softcover)

#1714 (1935) *Shirley Temple Scrapbook* (softcover)

#1716 (1936) *Shirley Temple Throughout the Day* (softcover)

#1720 (1936) *Shirley Temple Favorite Poems* (hardcover)

#1722 (1936) *Shirley Temple Scrapbook* (softcover)

#1723 (1936) *Shirley Temple in Poor Little Rich Girl* (softcover)

#1730 (1936) Shirley Temple: Five Books about Me (boxed set)

- #1730A *Shirley Temple: Little Playmate* (softcover)
- #1730B *Shirley Temple Starring Roles* (softcover)
- #1730C *Just a Little Girl* (softcover)
- #1730D *Shirley Temple on the Movie Lot* (softcover)
- #1730E *Shirley Temple Twinkle Toes* (softcover)

#1736 (1935) *Shirley Temple Story Book* (hardcover)

#1737 (1935) *Shirley Temple*, by Jerome Beatty (hardcover)

#1748 (1936) *Shirley Temple Book of Fairy Tales* (hardcover)

#1749 (1935) Shirley Temple: Her Books (boxed set)

- #1736 *Shirley Temple Story Book*
- #1737 *Shirley Temple*, by Jerome Beatty

#1760 (1936) *Shirley Temple in Dimples* (softcover)

#1762 (1936) *Shirley Temple: Little Star* (softcover)

#1763 (1937) *Shirley Temple Scrapbook* (softcover)

#1766 (1937) *Now I Am Eight* (softcover)

#1767 (1937) *Shirley Temple in Stowaway* (softcover)

#1769 (1937) *Shirley Temple in Wee Willie Winkie* (softcover)

#1771 (1937) *Shirley Temple in Heidi* (color softcover)

#1774 (1938) *Shirley Temple: Her Life in Pictures* (softcover)

#1775 (1938) *Shirley Temple: The Real Little Girl* (softcover)

#1778 (1938) *Shirley Temple in Little Miss Broadway* (softcover)

#1783 (1938) *Shirley Temple in The Little Princess* (softcover)

#1785 (1939) *Shirley Temple in Susannah of the Mounties* (softcover)

COLORING AND ACTIVITY SETS (all Saalfield)
#287 (1935) *This Is My Crayon Book, Shirley Temple* (white top)
#1711 (1936) *This Is My Crayon Book, Shirley Temple* (cut-out top)
#1717 (1936) *Shirley Temple: A Great Big Book to Color*
#1718 (1935) Shirley Temple Coloring Set (boxed set)
#1721 (1936) Shirley Temple Sewing Cards (boxed set)
#1724 (1936) *Shirley Temple Drawing and Coloring Book* (hardcover)
#1725 (1935) *Shirley Temple Drawing Book* (hardcover)
#1726 (1935) *Shirley Temple Pastime Book* (hardcover)
#1728 (1935) Shirley Temple Coloring Box (boxed set)
#1731 (1935) Shirley Temple Coloring Box (boxed set)
#1732 (1937) Shirley Temple Pastime Box (boxed set)
#1732A *Shirley Temple Favorite Games* (softcover)
#1732B *Shirley Temple Favorite Puzzles* (softcover)
#1732C Shirley Temple Favorite Sewing Cards (softcover)
#1732D *Shirley Temple Favorite Coloring Book* (softcover)
#1735 (1935) *Shirley Temple Coloring Book* (hardcover)
#1738 (1935) Shirley Temple Drawing Set (boxed set)
#1740 (1935) Shirley Temple: My Coloring Box (boxed set, same as #1735)
#1750 (1936) Shirley Temple Work with Yarn (boxed set)
#1768 (1937) *Shirley Temple: My Book to Color*
#1770 (1937) Shirley Temple Christmas Book (contains paper doll from #1739)
#1772 (1937) *Shirley Temple Color Book*
#1779 (1938) *Shirley Temple Crosses the Country: A Coloring Book*
#1784 (1939) *Shirley Temple* The Little Princess *Coloring Book*
#1788 (1940) *Shirley Temple* Bluebird *Coloring Book*
#1554 (1958) *Shirley Temple Coloring Book*
#1654 (1958) *The Favorite Pictures of Shirley Temple: A Book to Color*
#4513 (1959) *Shirley Temple Busy Book* (with paper doll, re-release of #5326)
#4584 (1958) *Shirley Temple Coloring Book* (w/paint palette)
#4589 (1958) *Shirley Temple Coloring Book* (red dress w/dog)
#4624 (1958) *Shirley Temple Coloring Book* (red dress w/dog)
#4648 (1959) *Shirley Temple Coloring Book* (red dress w/dog)
#4884 (1966) *Shirley Temple Coloring Book* (w/paint palette)
#5326 (1959) *Shirley Temple Busy Book* (with paper doll)
#5526 (1959) *Shirley Temple Busy Book* (with paper doll, re-release of #5326)
#5353 (1958) *Shirley Temple Coloring Book* (red dress w/dog)
#5653 (1958) *Shirley Temple Coloring Book* (red dress w/dog)
#6030 (1958) Shirley Temple Play Kit (re-release of #9859)
#6032 (1958) Shirley Temple Play Kit (re-release of #9859)
#8806 (1959) Shirley Temple Treasure Board
#9859 (1958) Shirley Temple Play Kit (in yellow dress)
Shirley and Her Dolly Paper Dolls (with laces)
Shirley Temple Favorite Pictures to Color and Playtime Crayons
#9869 (1961) Shirley Temple Play Kit
Push-out and Stand-up Paper Dolls (w/laces)
Shirley Temple Coloring Book and Cray-O-Tec Crayons
Shirley Temple Daisy Chain Necklace

\WHITMAN BOOKS
#2311 (1945) *Shirley Temple and the Spirit of Dragonwood*
#2330 (1945) *Shirley Temple and the Screaming Specter*

RANDOM HOUSE BOOKS
X-1 (1959) *Heidi*
X-2 (1959) *The Littlest Rebel*
X-3 (1959) *Rebecca of the Sunnybrook Farm*
X-4 (1959) *Susannah of the Mounties*
X-5 (1959) *Captain January* and *The Little Colonel*
The Shirley Temple Treasury (1959)
Shirley Temple's Fairyland (1958)
Shirley Temple Stories That Never Grow Old (1958)
Shirley Temple's Favorite Tales of Long Ago (1959).
Shirley Temple's Storybook (1958)
Shirley Temple's Storytime Favorites (1962)
Shirley Temple's Bedtime Book (1960s)
Shirley Temple's Nursery Tales (1961)

MISCELLANEOUS PRODUCTS
Shirley Temple Birthday Book (1935), by The Dell Publishing Company
My Young Life (1945), by the Garden City Publishing Company
#103 (1946) *Honeymoon,* by Bart House
Shirley Temple 21st Birthday Album (1949), by the Dell Publishing Company
Shirley Temple Magnetic TV Theater (1959), by Amsco
Shirley Temple (1962), by Lois Ely, by Monarch Books

OTHER GABRIEL PRODUCTS
#301 (1960) Shirley Temple Movie Favorites Embroidery Set
#302 (late 50s/early 60s) Shirley Temple Snap-On Jewelry Set
#310 (1959) Shirley Temple Movie Favorites Embroidery Set
#311 (1960) Shirley Temple Luncheon Embroidery Set
#325 (late 50s/early 60s) Shirley Temple Beauty Bath
#326 (late 50s/early 60s) Shirley Temple Fresh-up Kit
#327 (late 50s/early 60s) Shirley Temple Hair Care
#330 (late 50s/early 60s) Shirley Temple Lady Fair
#339 (late 50s/early 60s) Shirley Temple Hair Styler
#340 (late 50s/early 60s) Shirley Temple Pretty Play (came in either blue or orange box)
#341 (late 50s/early 60s) Shirley Temple Beauty Bar
#342 (late 50s/early 60s) Shirley Temple Glamour
#450 (late 50s/early 60s) Shirley Temple Glamour Bar

MAGAZINES
The number of Shirley Temple magazines released is beyond the scope of this book. However, a listing is available: "Shirley in the Magazines" — a detailed listing of (almost) every Shirley Temple magazine (article and/or cover), from the start of her career (early 1930s) through the present day — about 12,000 entries.

Gen Jones
294 Park St.
Medford, MA 02155
Email: genjones@earthlink.net
$25.00 for the entire listing printed out

I recommend it; it is a wonderful resource for your Shirley magazine collection.

I have been collecting Shirley Temple memorabilia for more than 15 years, and am very particular about what I buy. These are the places that I recommend highly for everything from doll repair to buying dolls and collectibles.

Wonderful World of Shirley Temple and Shirley Temple Dolls — my own website. Contains a lot of Shirley information.

Website: www.shirleytempledolls.com
Email: questions@shirleytempledolls.com

Dollspart Supply Catalog — has elastic for restringing, rayon socks, leather shoes, mohair Shirley Temple wigs (and some Pattikins Shirley outfits). Also has replacement parts for the 1973 vinyl Shirley doll. This company has both a website and a mail-order catalog.

Website: www.dollspart.com
Phone: 1-800-336-DOLL (3655)

Twin Pines of Maine — specializes in products for care of vinyl dolls, Formula 9-1-1 (recommended — great for dolls that have gotten "sticky").

Website: www.twinpines.com
Phone: 1-800-770-DOLL (3655)

Sandra Lee Products — Staintique Doll clothing cleaner (for cleaning doll clothes).

Website: www.sandralee.com
Phone: (425) 482-0570

Whitehorse Design Ltd. — if your composition doll is in bad shape, beyond the repair tips discussed in this book, this is the only place to send your Shirley. The proprietress does an excellent job restoring Shirley Temple composition dolls.

Website: www.whitehorsedesign.net

Old B Dolls — the best reproduction Shirley Temple dresses that I have ever seen. Specializes in compo Shirley Temple outfits by Pattikins, but does have a few vinyl-doll dresses, including a beautiful rose dress for the 36" vinyl doll. Also has double-faced silk ribbon for sale, which can be used for hair bows.

Website: www.oldbdolls.com

This Old Doll — the best reproduction Shirley Temple shoes that I have seen (not pictured in this book). Also, some good tips for fixing up the dolls.

Website: www.thisolddoll.com

eBay — the one-stop shop for Shirley Temple collectors. Shirley paper products are cheaper than you will find anywhere else. Good-condition vinyl dolls are a steal, and you can find cheaper compo dolls as well, though the rarer items can get very pricey.

Website: www.ebay.com

Theriaults — nice interactive doll auction house on the web; even allows you to bid online during a live doll auction. Doll auctions occasionally have rare Shirley Temple items, but they can get expensive.

Website: www.theriaults.com

All My Dolls — run by one of the foremost Shirley collectors, includes pictures of rare dolls and outfits and has very reasonably priced dolls for sale.

Website: www.allmydolls.com

Shirley Temple Collector Clubs:

Australian Shirley Temple Collectors News
PO box 4086
Mulgrave Victoria 3150
Australia
30 page newsletter — four times per year — cost US $40/year.

The Shirley Temple Collectors News
Contact: Rita Dubas
8811 Colonial Road, Brooklyn, NY 11209
$25 USA, $30 Canada/overseas
For info send stamped/addressed envelope.
Quarterly newsletters.

Shirley Temple Collectors by the Sea Club
PO Box 6203, Oxnard, CA 93031
$18 USA, $20 Canada, $30 overseas
Monthly **Lollipop News** newsletter.
Editor: Gloria Rodriguez

Black, Shirley Temple. **Child Star**. New York, NY: McGraw-Hill, 1988.

Burdick, Loraine. "Shirley Temple — The 12 Inch Doll." **Celebrity Doll Journal** 19, no.4, 1985.

____. **Shirley Temple Dolls and Related Delights**. Puyallup, WA: Quest Books, 1966.

____. **The Shirley Temple Scrapbook, Collector's Edition**. Norwalk, CT: The Easton Press, 2001.

Dubas, Rita. **The Shirley Temple Collectors News**, 1998 – 2004.

Horne, Graeme. Shirley Temple Fan Page, www.geocities.com/Hollywood/Hills/8038/ (accessed January – July 2005).

Horner, Kelly. "Doll Restoration, Doll Cleaning, and Doll Repair Tips." A Dolly's World, www.adollysworld.com/doll_cleaning_and_care_tips.html (accessed May – July 2005).

Izen, Judith. **Collector's Guide to Ideal Dolls**, 2nd ed. Paducah, KY: Collector Books, 1999.

Mitchell, Janet. "Shirley Temple and Saalfield Publishing Co." Dunedin, FL: 1995 (unpublished).

Neumann, May. **The World and Shirley Temple**. Billings, MO: McGrain Publications, 1978.

Smith, Patricia R. **Shirley Temple Dolls and Collectibles**. Paducah, KY: Collector Books, 1977.

____. **Shirley Temple Dolls and Collectibles**, 2nd ed. Paducah, KY: Collector Books, 1979.

A few final words...

Probably the most highly anticipated Shirley Temple book is the second half of Shirley Temple's autobiography (the first half being **Child Star**, 1988). A few years back, I wrote Ms. Black asking about it, and this was her response:

Tonya, It will be a few more years before the second book will be ready. (It took me eight years to write 'Child Star.' Thank you for your interest! S.